S0-AVA-216

PEOPLE'S
COMMENTARY
BIBLE

Kings

Arno J. Wolfgramm

CPH™

SAINT LOUIS

The interior illustrations were originally executed by James Tissot (1836–1902), except for the following: illustrations on pages 43, 156, and 312 are by Julius Schnorr von Carolsfeld. The map on page 176 was drawn by Dr. John C. Lawrenz and was originally used in *Bible History Commentary—Old Testament* by Werner H. Franzmann. The illustrations on pages 51 and 79 are from *Cyclopedia of Biblical, Theological, and Ecclesiastical Literature* by McClintock and Strong (Harper and Brothers, 1867–87, reprinted by Baker Book House, 1981).

Commentary and pictures are reprinted from KINGS (The People's Bible Series), Copyright © 1990 by Northwestern Publishing House. Used by permission.

Scripture is taken from The Holy Bible: NEW INTERNATIONAL VERSION®. Copyright © 1973, 1978, 1984 by the International Bible Society. Used by permission of Zondervan Publishing House. All rights reserved.

The "NIV" and "New International Version" trademarks are registered in the United States Patent and Trademark Office by International Bible Society. Use of either trademark requires the permission of International Bible Society.

1 2 3 4 5 6 7 8 9 10   03 02 01 00 99 98 97 96 95 94

CONTENTS

ILLUSTRATIONS

MAP

PREFACE

The People's Bible Commentary is just what the name implies—a Bible and commentary for the people. It includes the complete text of the Holy Scriptures in the popular New International Version. The commentary following the Scripture sections contains personal applications as well as historical background and explanations of the text.

The authors of *The People's Bible Commentary* are men of scholarship and practical insight, gained from years of experience in the teaching and preaching ministries. They have tried to avoid the technical jargon which limits so many commentary series to professional Bible scholars.

The most important feature of these books is that they are Christ-centered. Speaking of the Old Testament Scriptures, Jesus himself declared, "These are the Scriptures that testify about me" (John 5:39). Each volume of *The People's Bible Commentary* directs our attention to Jesus Christ. He is the center of the entire Bible. He is our only Savior.

We dedicate these volumes to the glory of God and to the good of his people.

The Publishers

INTRODUCTION

The two books of Kings show us the disgusting nature of man's sin and the surpassing greatness of God's grace.

They show us the kings of Judah—polygamists like Solomon, backsliders like Joash, idolaters like Ahaz, and wicked men like Manasseh—each of whom was an ancestor of our Savior. They show us the kings of Israel—one man worse than the other—kings who worshiped golden calves, a bloodthirsty god named Baal, and a filthy, disgusting fertility goddess named Asherah.

As we look closely at these men, we see a reflection of our own times, perhaps even a reflection of our own sins and weaknesses.

The two books also show us the patient love of God toward his elect—individuals like King Joash, Naaman the Aramean, and the widow of Zarephath. The marvelous grace of God is the only reason these individuals were chosen by God for eternal life. In these books we see God's patient love as he tries again and again to turn his wayward people from idolatry.

The two books of Kings contain stories of heroic faith and devilish unbelief, accounts of Gentiles coming to faith while God's chosen people spurn their Lord. The books show us God's merciful deliverance of the poor and his merciless judgments on the impenitent.

These books fill the hearts of God's people with exuberant confidence as we see the almighty God standing at the side of his children, protecting them by means of unseen angelic hosts and chariots of fire.

They contain the fast-paced narrative of Jehu, who carried out God's will with a vengeance; and the cowardice of a king like Jehoash, who was afraid to seize God's blessings.

These books contain a message for everyone. They are books for parents, showing us that, if we fail to instruct our children, Satan will do the job for us; if we neglect to guide our children to a God-fearing spouse, we jeopardize the faith of our grandchildren, for we are constantly one generation away from heathenism.

These are books for children, showing us how Solomon heeded the advice of his father and gave honor to his mother, and how Joash heeded the advice of his uncle, the high priest.

They are books for any church body that wants to be orthodox, reminding us to separate ourselves from every form of idolatry, to mark and avoid every false teacher. They warn us not to rely one bit on the power and methods of the unbelieving world but to rest ourselves completely on the mercy of God in every situation.

Author

The author of 1 and 2 Kings does not identify himself. Other books of the Bible do not name him either.

For the following reasons this writer is convinced that 1 and 2 Kings were written by the Prophet Jeremiah:

1. There is no reason why Jeremiah could not have written these books. The author apparently witnessed the destruction of Jerusalem but was not carried into captivity in Babylon. Nor, it seems, was the author living to see the return of the Jews from Babylon seventy years later.

2. The author does not mention Jeremiah by name. If someone other than Jeremiah had written these books, he almost certainly would have mentioned that prophet who

played such an important role in the later history of Judah. Jeremiah would not have to mention himself, because he has reported personal information and anecdotes in the book which bears his name.

3. Some portions of Kings and of Jeremiah are almost identical, notably 2 Kings 24:18—25:30 and Jeremiah 52. Because these portions are so much alike and because each contains unique information, it appears that they were written by the same author.

Purpose and Scope

The two books of Kings were originally counted as one book in the Hebrew Bible. The Septuagint (the Greek translation of the Old Testament) counted them as two books and entitled them 3 and 4 Kings. (1 and 2 Samuel are called 1 and 2 Kings in the Septuagint.)

These books contain the history of God's people from the death of David through the glorious reign of Solomon and the days of the divided kingdom (Israel and Judah). But the author is not interested simply in recording historical facts. He is giving us a religious history of God's people. He emphasizes the building of the temple, devotes many chapters to the reign of Ahab (Israel's worst king), and records numerous incidents from the lives of God's prophets Elijah and Elisha. He evaluates the morals and the faithfulness of each king, frequently comparing them to the standard of great King David, the man after God's own heart.

The average reader will be impressed by the multitude of names in 1 and 2 Kings. Let no one become discouraged! These names will become more familiar in subsequent readings. To simplify things we have attached a list of the kings at the end of this volume.

In Matthew 1:17 we read, "Thus there were fourteen generations in all from Abraham to David, fourteen from David to the exile to Babylon, and fourteen from the exile to the Christ." St. Matthew might describe 1 and 2 Kings as the history of the middle "fourteen generations." It is the story of THE KING (God) and the kings of Israel and Judah.

Outline

THE **KING** AND THE KINGS

1 KINGS

THE KINGS REJECT THE **KING**

I. King Solomon Rejects The King Who Has Blessed Him (1:1- 11:43)

   A. The Blessings (1:1-10:29)

   B. The Rejection (11:1-43)

II. The Kings of Israel Reject The King Who Desired To Bless Them (12:1-22:53)

   A. Jeroboam (12:1-14:31)

   B. Jeroboam's Unworthy Successors (15:1-16:34)

   C. Ahab, the Worst King over Israel (17:1-22:53)

2 KINGS

THE **KING** REJECTS THE KINGS

I. The King Rejects Israel (1:1- 17:41)
  A. The Ministry of Elijah and Elisha (1:1-8:29)

  B. Jehu's Reforms in Israel (9:1-10:36)

  C. Reforms in Judah (11:1-12:21)

  D. Other Weak Kings (13:1-16:20)

  E. Israel Falls to Assyria (17:1-41)

II. The King Rejects Judah (18:1-25:30)

  A. The Good Rule of Hezekiah (18:1-20:21)

  B. Wicked Reigns of Manasseh and Amon (21:1-26)

  C. Josiah's Reforms in Judah (22:1-23:35)

  D. Judah Falls to Babylon (23:36-25:30)

THE **KING** AND THE KINGS
1 KINGS

THE KINGS REJECT THE **KING**
1:1- 11:43

In the name of the Father and of the Son and of the Holy Spirit. Amen.

The President of the United States is elected by the people according to certain constitutional requirements and restrictions. His term of office is four years, and he may serve no more than two four-year terms. If he dies in office, he is automatically succeeded by the Vice-President.

Ancient Israel did not operate under such a constitution. In 1 and 2 Samuel we heard how King Saul and then King David ruled over Israel. In each case God himself, through the prophet Samuel, chose the man he wanted to rule as king. 1 and 2 Kings tell us about the kings who succeeded David. Some of these men gained power only after bloody conflict. The First Book of Kings begins with the account of such a struggle.

It is important, however, that we view this account as more than merely an interesting story. History is really HIS story, the account of God's plan to send a Savior into the world. That Savior would be a descendant of King David. The men who succeeded David would become part of the Savior's family tree.

PART I

KING SOLOMON REJECTS THE KING WHO HAS BLESSED HIM
1 KINGS 1:1-11:43

The Blessing

1 When King David was old and well advanced in years, he could not keep warm even when they put covers over him. ²So his servants said to him, "Let us look for a young virgin to attend the king and take care of him. She can lie beside him so that our lord the king may keep warm."

³Then they searched throughout Israel for a beautiful girl and found Abishag, a Shunammite, and brought her to the king. ⁴The girl was very beautiful; she took care of the king and waited on him, but the king had no intimate relations with her.

⁵Now Adonijah, whose mother was Haggith, put himself forward and said, "I will be king." So he got chariots and horses ready, with fifty men to run ahead of him. ⁶(His father had never interfered with him by asking, "Why do you behave as you do?" He was also very handsome and was born next after Absalom.)

⁷Adonijah conferred with Joab son of Zeruiah and with Abiathar the priest, and they gave him their support. ⁸But Zadok the priest, Benaiah son of Jehoiada, Nathan the prophet, Shimei and Rei and David's special guard did not join Adonijah.

⁹Adonijah then sacrificed sheep, cattle and fattened calves at the Stone of Zoheleth near En Rogel. He invited all his brothers, the king's sons, and all the men of Judah who were royal officials, ¹⁰but he did not invite Nathan the prophet or Benaiah or the special guard or his brother Solomon.

King David was now an old man confined to his room and to his bed. Although his servants covered him with blankets, he could not keep warm.

It is contrary to God's will for a man to have more than one wife. We know this from Genesis 2:24, where God instituted marriage by saying, "For this reason a man [singular] will leave his father and mother and be united to his wife [singular]." In Deuteronomy 17:17 God declared that the king in particular "must not take many wives, or his heart will be led astray." Nevertheless the servants selected yet another woman to serve David and keep him warm in bed. Abishag is not referred to as David's wife in this section; she may have been a concubine. Later, however, both Solomon and Adonijah regarded her as a wife (1 Kings 2:22).

We cannot applaud the sins of David and the people, just as we cannot condone the sins God's people commit today. At the same time, we trust that David died as a penitent sinner.

David's failing health revealed to everyone that his forty-year reign over Israel would soon come to an end. Soon one of his sons would take his place.

Which son would it be?

Of the sons born to David while he ruled only over Judah, Adonijah apparently was the oldest survivor (2 Samuel 3:2-5). Since Adonijah was used to having his own way and since his father was old and weak, this handsome but spoiled young man decided that he would seize power and become the next ruler.

First he prepared a retinue of chariots and horsemen to make him look important. Then he conferred with Joab, David's commander-in-chief. Although Joab had not supported Absalom's rebellion, he now gave support to Adonijah. Next Adonijah talked to Abiathar, one of the high priests. Abiathar had been at David's side in the war against Saul (1 Samuel 22:20-23), he had helped David move the ark of the covenant up to Jerusalem (1 Chronicles 15:11), and he had remained faithful to David during Absalom's rebellion (2 Samuel 15:35). But Abiathar also took the side of the young rebel.

Now that he had the support of the military and religious leaders, Adonijah invited his brothers and other dignitaries to the spring of En Rogel, just south of Jerusalem. There the priest offered many sheep, oxen, and cattle, and Adonijah declared himself king.

Although Adonijah appeared to have the support of the leading people, there is evidence that his ambitions were not pleasing to God. Adonijah neglected to invite Nathan the prophet and his brother Solomon. He also failed to tell his father about his plans. Secrecy often indicates that someone's conscience is not at ease.

¹¹Then Nathan asked Bathsheba, Solomon's mother, "Have you not heard that Adonijah, the son of Haggith, has become king without our lord David's knowing it? ¹²Now then, let me advise you how you can save your own life and the life of your son Solomon. ¹³Go in to King David and say to him, 'My lord the king, did you not swear to me your servant: "Surely Solomon your son shall be king after me, and he will sit on my throne"? Why then has Adonijah become king?' ¹⁴While you are still there talking to the king, I will come in and confirm what you have said."

¹⁵So Bathsheba went to see the aged king in his room, where Abishag the Shunammite was attending him. ¹⁶Bathsheba bowed low and knelt before the king.

"What is it you want?" the king asked.

¹⁷She said to him, "My lord, you yourself swore to me your servant by the LORD your God: 'Solomon your son shall be king after me, and he will sit on my throne.' ¹⁸But now Adonijah has become king, and you, my lord the king, do not know about it. ¹⁹He has sacrificed great numbers of cattle, fattened calves, and

sheep, and has invited all the king's sons, Abiathar the priest and Joab the commander of the army, but he has not invited Solomon your servant. [20]My lord the king, the eyes of all Israel are on you, to learn from you who will sit on the throne of my lord the king after him. [21]Otherwise, as soon as my lord the king is laid to rest with his fathers, I and my son Solomon will be treated as criminals."

[22]While she was still speaking with the king, Nathan the prophet arrived. [23]And they told the king, "Nathan the prophet is here." So he went before the king and bowed with his face to the ground.

[24]Nathan said, "Have you, my lord the king, declared that Adonijah shall be king after you, and that he will sit on your throne? [25]Today he has gone down and sacrificed great numbers of cattle, fattened calves, and sheep. He has invited all the king's sons, the commanders of the army and Abiathar the priest. Right now they are eating and drinking with him and saying, 'Long live King Adonijah!' [26]But me your servant, and Zadok the priest, and Benaiah son of Jehoiada, and your servant Solomon he did not invite. [27]Is this something my lord the king has done without letting his servants know who should sit on the throne of my lord the king after him?"

God had already told David that Solomon would become his successor and would build the temple in Jerusalem (1 Chronicles 22:8,9). Apparently God's spokesman, Nathan, also knew of God's plan. Nathan also realized that his life, the life of Solomon, and the life of Solomon's mother would be in danger if Adonijah succeeded in establishing his power. Therefore the prophet decided to act immediately.

Many years earlier Nathan had rebuked David for his adultery with Bathsheba. Now he continued to be at the king's side to offer his counsel. Proverbs 27:6 tells us, "Wounds from a friend can be trusted." A faithful friend offers counsel when we need to be rebuked for a fault and offers support in time of trouble. Nathan was such a friend to David. May all pastors learn to imitate his example.

Joab did not prove to be such a faithful friend. Although he had carried out David's plan to kill Uriah (2 Samuel 11:14-17), Joab now turned his back on the king.

Bathsheba was the first to speak to King David about Adonijah's secret coronation. The writer does not tell us what thoughts and memories came to the mind of Bathsheba as she entered the king's bedroom and saw him there with Abishag. Years earlier, while she was still Uriah's wife, Bathsheba also had had a love affair with the king.

Nathan's plan, however, worked perfectly. Although David was old and weak in body, his mind was clear. He remembered his oath, and he gave orders that Solomon be made king immediately.

David Makes Solomon King

28Then King David said, "Call in Bathsheba." So she came into the king's presence and stood before him.

29The king then took an oath: "As surely as the LORD lives, who has delivered me out of every trouble, 30I will surely carry out today what I swore to you by the LORD, the God of Israel: Solomon your son shall be king after me, and he will sit on my throne in my place."

31Then Bathsheba bowed low with her face to the ground and, kneeling before the king, said, "May my lord King David live forever!"

32King David said, "Call in Zadok the priest, Nathan the prophet and Benaiah son of Jehoiada." When they came before the king, 33he said to them: "Take your lord's servants with you and set Solomon my son on my own mule and take him down to Gihon. 34There have Zadok the priest and Nathan the prophet anoint him king over Israel. Blow the trumpet and shout, 'Long live King Solomon!' 35Then you are to go up with him, and he is to come and sit on my throne and reign in my place. I have appointed him ruler over Israel and Judah."

³⁶Benaiah son of Jehoiada answered the king, "Amen! May the LORD, the God of my lord the king, so declare it. ³⁷As the LORD was with my lord the king, so may he be with Solomon to make his throne even greater than the throne of my lord King David!"

³⁸So Zadok the priest, Nathan the prophet, Benaiah son of Jehoiada, the Kerethites and the Pelethites went down and put Solomon on King David's mule and escorted him to Gihon. ³⁹Zadok the priest took the horn of oil from the sacred tent and anointed Solomon. Then they sounded the trumpet and all the people shouted, "Long live King Solomon!" ⁴⁰And all the people went up after him, playing flutes and rejoicing greatly, so that the ground shook with the sound.

David asked three of his trusted leaders to arrange Solomon's coronation: Nathan the prophet; Benaiah, the captain over David's personal bodyguard; and Zadok, the other high priest. It appears that the Kerethites and Pelethites were mercenary soldiers from Crete and from Philistia respectively. Zadok, it seems, had been appointed to his office by King Saul and was the co-high priest with Abiathar during David's reign.

These three men carried out David's instructions exactly. They put Solomon on the king's mule, an act which already showed that he was to be David's successor. They escorted him to Gihon, a fountain just outside Jerusalem. There Zadok anointed Solomon as king. They blew the trumpets while the people shouted, "Long live King Solomon!" Others joined the celebration by playing wooden flutes. It was a time of rejoicing for God's people.

Adonijah was *a* son of King David, but he was not *the* son of David. Nevertheless, many were fooled into giving him their allegiance. The great Son of David, the Lord Jesus, has warned us not to be fooled by pretenders. He said, "I am the gate for the sheep. All who ever came before me were thieves and robbers" (John 10:7,8). The thieves and robbers are usurpers and pretenders. They are false prophets who do not enter the sheep pen through the door but must climb up over the walls. We must beware of them.

At the same time we join God's faithful people of all ages in giving honor to that Son of David who comes riding on a donkey bringing salvation to his people. To his name we also joyfully sing, "Hosanna to the Son of David! Blessed is he who comes in the name of the Lord!" (Matthew 21:9).

⁴¹Adonijah and all the guests who were with him heard it as they were finishing their feast. On hearing the sound of the trumpet, Joab asked, "What's the meaning of all the noise in the city?"

⁴²Even as he was speaking, Jonathan son of Abiathar the priest arrived. Adonijah said, "Come in. A worthy man like you must be bringing good news."

⁴³"Not at all!" Jonathan answered. "Our lord King David has made Solomon king. ⁴⁴The king has sent with him Zadok the priest, Nathan the prophet, Benaiah son of Jehoiada, the Kerethites and the Pelethites, and they have put him on the king's mule, ⁴⁵and Zadok the priest and Nathan the prophet have anointed him king at Gihon. From there they have gone up cheering, and the city resounds with it. That's the noise you hear. ⁴⁶Moreover, Solomon has taken his seat on the royal throne. ⁴⁷Also, the royal officials have come to congratulate our lord King David, saying, 'May your God make Solomon's name more famous than yours and his throne greater than yours!" And the king bowed in worship on his bed, ⁴⁸and said, 'Praise be to the LORD, the God of Israel, who has allowed my eyes to see a successor on my throne today.' "

⁴⁹At this, all Adonijah's guests rose in alarm and dispersed. ⁵⁰But Adonijah, in fear of Solomon, went and took hold of the horns of the altar. ⁵¹Then Solomon was told, "Adonijah is afraid of King Solomon and is clinging to the horns of the altar. He says, 'Let King Solomon swear to me today that he will not put his servant to death with the sword.' "

⁵²Solomon replied, "If he shows himself to be a worthy man, not a hair of his head will fall to the ground; but if evil is found in him, he will die." ⁵³Then King Solomon sent men, and they brought him down from the altar. And Adonijah came and bowed down to King Solomon, and Solomon said, "Go to your home."

When Adonijah and his friends learned what was going on, they went to their homes. That was a wise decision. Their rebellion could justly be punished with death. Adonijah himself sought refuge at the Lord's altar. The criminal who took hold of the projecting point at the corner of the altar of burnt offerings found asylum and safety. According to Exodus 21:13, however, this refuge was intended only when the crime was accidental. In the next chapter we will hear how Adonijah tried again to seize power and was put to death.

There are some significant differences between Adonijah and Solomon. Adonijah was a pretender; Solomon was the man to whom the kingdom was promised. Adonijah tried to exalt himself; God exalted Solomon. Adonijah tried to seize power and authority for himself; Solomon waited quietly, even passively, until he received power and authority from God. Our Lord continues to resist the proud while he gives grace to the humble. May we also learn to wait humbly and patiently for God to raise us up to eternal glory.

David had been in great danger on many occasions. But in each case God spared his life. Now, however, according to God's plan, David also was to "go the way of all the earth." Because he was a sinful descendant of our first parents, David would suffer the same earthly death which claims all human flesh.

It was time for David to speak final words to the son who had already been anointed king. Parents today also have only a limited time to train their children before they (and their children) "go the way of all the earth." Christian parents will want to make good use of that time.

The words that follow are more than advice. They are commands.

David's Charge to Solomon

2 **When the time drew near for David to die, he gave a charge to Solomon his son.**

²"I am about to go the way of all the earth," he said. "So be strong, show yourself a man, ³and observe what the LORD your God requires: Walk in his ways, and keep his decrees and commands, his laws and requirements, as written in the Law of Moses, so that you may prosper in all you do and wherever you go, ⁴and that the LORD may keep his promise to me: 'If your descendants watch how they live, and if they walk faithfully before me with all their heart and soul, you will never fail to have a man on the throne of Israel.'**

In Deuteronomy 17:18-20 Moses gave instructions to the kings who would rule Israel in the future. The king was to make a handwritten copy of the law of Moses and to study it daily. Apparently David had those directions in mind when he charged Solomon to observe all that Moses had written.

By observing those commands Solomon would show himself to be a real "man." "His delight is in the law of the LORD, and on his law he meditates day and night. He is like a tree planted by streams of water, which yields its fruit in season and whose leaf does not wither. Whatever he does prospers" (Psalm 1:2,3).

In those five books of Moses Solomon would learn how everything came into existence, why our world is so full of sin and trouble, and how God repeatedly promised to send a Savior from sin. The sacrifices prescribed in that law were constant reminders of sin and were shadows of the sacrifice

17

which the Lamb of God would someday offer. "Walking in God's ways" would be a proper response from one who has come to appreciate God's love and forgiveness.

God will bless all who observe what he has written. In Solomon's case the blessing would be a long line of descendants who would rule God's people. The greatest of those descendants would be the Messiah, who would establish an eternal kingdom (2 Samuel 7:13).

God continues to bless all who hear his word and keep it. The greatest blessing for the believer is eternal life in God's presence eternally.

⁵"Now you yourself know what Joab son of Zeruiah did to me—what he did to the two commanders of Israel's armies, Abner son of Ner and Amasa son of Jether. He killed them, shedding their blood in peacetime as if in battle, and with that blood stained the belt around his waist and the sandals on his feet. ⁶Deal with him according to your wisdom, but do not let his gray head go down to the grave in peace.

⁷"But show kindness to the sons of Barzillai of Gilead and let them be among those who eat at your table. They stood by me when I fled from your brother Absalom.

⁸"And remember, you have with you Shimei son of Gera, the Benjamite from Bahurim, who called down bitter curses on me the day I went to Mahanaim. When he came down to meet me at the Jordan, I swore to him by the LORD: 'I will not put you to death by the sword.' ⁹But now, do not consider him innocent. You are a man of wisdom; you will know what to do to him. Bring his gray head down to the grave in blood."

David had some specific requests to make of Solomon concerning some people who had been involved with David during his years as king. Joab had been David's commander-in-chief. He was a valiant soldier who had led Israel's armies against their ancient heathen enemies. But there were two blots on his record. He had killed two innocent men, Abner and Amasa, in a fit of anger and jealousy. David apparently thought it improper that he punish Joab, because he had benefited from Joab's military leadership.

Abner had been King Saul's field commander. Amasa had been the commander-in-chief of Absalom's army at the time of the rebellion. Both of these men, it is true, had fought against Joab on the battlefield. But Joab had considered them his rivals, lured each of them into a friendly meeting and had killed them when they were not prepared to defend themselves (2 Samuel 3:26-28; 20:9,10). In so doing Joab had gone beyond the orders of his king, had taken the law into his own hands, and was guilty of murder (1 Kings 2:32). Because of that deception and murder Joab deserved punishment.

Shimei had cursed David when he left Jerusalem and fled across the Jordan at the time of Absalom's rebellion. Although Shimei later apologized to David and although David accepted his apology (2 Samuel 19:18-23), there was still the matter of public disloyalty to the king whom God had appointed over Israel.

Since the blood of a human being is sacred, Joab had deserved the death penalty (Genesis 9:6). "An eye for an eye and a tooth for a tooth" is the principle which is to guide a government in executing justice. Rebellion against the government is tantamount to rebellion against God. That crime also deserves a severe sentence.

Why did David himself not execute Joab and Shimei? Perhaps David did not care to act as judge and jury in cases which affected him personally.

On the other hand, when David and his men were camped at Mahanaim at the time of Absalom's rebellion, a man named Barzillai brought food and other provisions to the king. Solomon was to remember that act of kindness by permitting the family of Barzillai to eat at the king's expense.

Since these words were spoken by one king to another king, it is not likely that any father today will give his son similar advice. Kings are responsible for taking revenge; private citizens are not. But a wise father today will advise his children regarding the friends they choose. He will warn his son about murderers like Joab and about rebels and blasphemers like Shimei. He will encourage his son to build friendships with God-fearing men like Barzillai. He will give special guidance for choosing that friend who will become the spouse of his son or daughter. The wise advice of concerned Christian parents will help children avoid problems and heartaches and will guide them on the narrow path to eternal life.

¹⁰Then David rested with his fathers and was buried in the City of David. ¹¹He had reigned forty years over Israel—seven years in Hebron and thirty-three in Jerusalem. ¹²So Solomon sat on the throne of his father David, and his rule was firmly established.

David's tomb was still in Jerusalem at the time of Jesus and the apostles. As a matter of fact, Peter used that tomb as an object lesson on the day of Pentecost. Although David's tomb still contained his decaying bones, the tomb of David's greater Son was empty on the third day (Acts 2:29).

Because of the Savior's resurrection, death has lost its sting. "David *slept* with his fathers" (KJV). The risen prince of life will some day awaken every Christian (and every unbeliever!) from that sleep.

Solomon's Throne Established

¹³Now Adonijah, the son of Haggith, went to Bathsheba, Solomon's mother. Bathsheba asked him, "Do you come peacefully?"

He answered, "Yes, peacefully." [14]Then he added, "I have something to say to you."

"You may say it," she replied.

[15]"As you know," he said, "the kingdom was mine. All Israel looked to me as their king. But things changed, and the kingdom has gone to my brother; for it has come to him from the LORD. [16]Now I have one request to make of you. Do not refuse me."

"You may make it," she said.

[17]So he continued, "Please ask King Solomon—he will not refuse you—to give me Abishag the Shunammite as my wife."

[18]"Very well," Bathsheba replied, "I will speak to the king for you."

King David was right. Even though Solomon had become king, he would have to deal with several pockets of resistance.

Solomon's half brother, Adonijah, had failed in his first attempt to become David's successor. Now he devised a more subtle plan.

Asking for Abishag as his wife may appear to us as an innocent request. In the eyes of ancient people, however, the man who married the king's wife (or wives) could lay claim to the throne. When Absalom rebelled against his father, he was advised to establish his power by taking David's concubines for himself (2 Samuel 16:21,22). Since Abishag was the last of several women whom David had taken, Adonijah would have another opportunity to seize the power he wanted.

Bathsheba perhaps thought that this marriage would satisfy all of Adonijah's desires and would establish Solomon's authority. But Solomon was not fooled.

[19]When Bathsheba went to King Solomon to speak to him for Adonijah, the king stood up to meet her, bowed down to her and sat down on his throne. He had a throne brought for the king's mother, and she sat down at his right hand.

²⁰"I have one small request to make of you," she said. "Do not refuse me."

The king replied, "Make it, my mother; I will not refuse you."

²¹So she said, "Let Abishag the Shunammite be given in marriage to your brother Adonijah."

²²King Solomon answered his mother, "Why do you request Abishag the Shunammite for Adonijah? You might as well request the kingdom for him—after all, he is my older brother—yes, for him and for Abiathar the priest and Joab son of Zeruiah!"

²³Then King Solomon swore by the LORD: "May God deal with me, be it ever so severely, if Adonijah does not pay with his life for this request! ²⁴And now, as surely as the LORD lives—he who has established me securely on the throne of my father David and has founded a dynasty for me as he promised—Adonijah shall be put to death today!" ²⁵So King Solomon gave orders to Benaiah son of Jehoiada, and he struck down Adonijah and he died.

²⁶"To Abiathar the priest the king said, "Go back to your fields in Anathoth. You deserve to die, but I will not put you to death now, because you carried the ark of the Sovereign LORD before my father David and shared all my father's hardships." ²⁷So Solomon removed Abiathar from the priesthood of the LORD, fulfilling the word the LORD had spoken at Shiloh about the house of Eli.

Although Bathsheba appears to have acted innocently, Solomon recognized Adonijah's wicked intentions immediately. For Solomon to grant his mother's request would have meant death for both of them. Solomon swore instead that the traitor would be put to death that very day.

Throughout the Scripture God views rebellion against the government as a serious offense. "The authorities that exist have been established by God. Consequently, he who rebels against the authority is rebelling against what God has instituted, and those who do so will bring judgment on themselves" (Romans 13:1,2).

Abiathar the high priest and his son Jonathan were also part of the conspiracy (1 Kings 1:42). Therefore Solomon deposed Abiathar and asked him to return to his home in Anathoth, one of the cities assigned to the Levites. A man of God who is not faithful to the word of God forfeits his office.

In this way the last members of Eli's family were removed from the priesthood, just as God had threatened earlier (1 Samuel 3:12-14).

Every son or daughter ought to note the honor Solomon accorded his mother. The king bowed before her and insisted that she sit on another throne. The fourth commandment demands that we give the highest honor to the man and woman God has placed over us as father and mother.

28When the news reached Joab, who had conspired with Adonijah though not with Absalom, he fled to the tent of the LORD and took hold of the horns of the altar. 29King Solomon was told that Joab had fled to the tent of the LORD and was beside the altar. Then Solomon ordered Benaiah son of Jehoiada, "Go, strike him down!"

30So Benaiah entered the tent of the LORD and said to Joab, "The king says, 'Come out!' "

But he answered, "No, I will die here."

Benaiah reported to the king, "This is how Joab answered me."

31Then the king commanded Benaiah, "Do as he says. Strike him down and bury him, and so clear me and my father's house of the guilt of the innocent blood that Joab shed. 32The LORD will repay him for the blood he shed, because without the knowledge of my father David he attacked two men and killed them with the sword. Both of them—Abner son of Ner, commander of Israel's army, and Amasa son of Jether, commander of Judah's army—were better men and more upright than he. 33May the guilt of their blood rest on the head of Joab and his descendants forever. But on David and his descendants, his house and his throne, may there be the LORD's peace forever."

³⁴So Benaiah son of Jehoiada went up and struck down Joab and killed him, and he was buried on his own land in the desert. ³⁵The king put Benaiah son of Jehoiada over the army in Joab's position and replaced Abiathar with Zadok the priest.

Joab, like Adonijah, looked for refuge at the Lord's altar. It was not God's intention that the altar should serve as a place of safety for every murderer, only for those who took a life unintentionally. Therefore Solomon, in accord with Exodus 21:14, ordered Joab's execution there at the altar.

The death of Joab serves as a warning for every Christian. If someone is a faithful servant of God for many years but then forsakes the will of God, that person's good deeds will all be forgotten.

God will replace those who do not serve faithfully. Just as Matthias replaced Judas as an apostle (Acts 1:15-26), so Benaiah replaced Joab as Solomon's commander-in-chief and Zadok replaced Abiathar as the priest.

It appears that Solomon considered Joab to be an unbeliever. If that is the case, Joab lost not only his earthly position but eternal life as well.

³⁶Then the king sent for Shimei and said to him, "Build yourself a house in Jerusalem and live there, but do not go anywhere else. ³⁷The day you leave and cross the Kidron Valley, you can be sure you will die; your blood will be on your own head."

³⁸Shimei answered the king, "What you say is good. Your servant will do as my lord the king has said." And Shimei stayed in Jerusalem for a long time.

³⁹But three years later, two of Shimei's slaves ran off to Achish son of Maacah, king of Gath, and Shimei was told, "Your slaves are in Gath." ⁴⁰At this, he saddled his donkey and went to Achish at Gath in search of his slaves. So Shimei went away and brought the slaves back from Gath.

⁴¹When Solomon was told that Shimei had gone from Jerusalem to Gath and returned, ⁴²the king summoned Shimei and said to him, "Did I not make you swear by the LORD and warn you, 'On the day you leave to go anywhere else, you can be sure you will die'? At that time you said to me, 'What you say is good. I will obey.' ⁴³Why then did you not keep your oath to the LORD and obey the command I gave you?"

⁴⁴The king also said to Shimei, "You know in your heart all the wrong you did to my father David. Now the LORD will repay you for your wrongdoing. ⁴⁵But King Solomon will be blessed, and David's throne will remain secure before the LORD forever."

⁴⁶Then the king gave the order to Benaiah son of Jehoiada, and he went out and struck Shimei down and killed him.

The kingdom was now firmly established in Solomon's hands.

According to the agreement Solomon made with Shimei, even crossing the Brook Kidron to go to his home in Bahurim east of Jerusalem would be punishable by death. Because of his crass disobedience, Shimei also was put to death.

Now the opposition to King Solomon had been eliminated, and Solomon was ready to begin his long, peaceful reign over God's people. It was clear to all that a strong hand was holding the reins of government in Jerusalem.

In this way Solomon also is a reminder of Christ. On the last day the Savior will expose and reject all who have been disloyal to him. But our Savior's true and faithful followers will live under him forever in perfect peace.

The new king now turned his attention to personal and spiritual matters.

Solomon Asks for Wisdom

3 Solomon made an alliance with Pharaoh king of Egypt and married his daughter. He brought her to the City of David until he finished building his palace and the temple of the LORD, and the wall around Jerusalem. ²The people, however, were still sacrificing at the high places, because a temple had not yet been built for the Name of the LORD. ³Solomon showed his love for the LORD by walking according to the statutes of his father David, except that he offered sacrifices and burned incense on the high places.

⁴The king went to Gibeon to offer sacrifices, for that was the most important high place, and Solomon offered a thousand burnt offerings on that altar. ⁵At Gibeon the LORD appeared to Solomon during the night in a dream, and God said, "Ask for whatever you want me to give you."

King David was a friend of the Egyptian pharaoh Thutmose I. This pharaoh gave one of his daughters to Solomon as his wife, and his wedding present to the couple was the city of Gezer, which he had captured from the Canaanites (1 Kings 9:16).

God's writer leads us to believe that this woman, like Ruth, left behind not only her family but also her gods at the time of her marriage. In chapter 11:1 the pharaoh's daughter is deliberately separated from the heathen women whom Solomon married later. It is possible that the Queen of Sheba, whom we will meet in chapter 10, was a half sister of Solomon's wife. It is also possible that King Solomon, when he wrote the Song of Songs, used his love for the Egyptian princess as a model to portray God's love for his church.

According to 2 Samuel 12:24 God loved Solomon from the time of his birth. Solomon loved the Lord in return. He showed his love for God by holding God's word in high regard and by bringing offerings to God.

Shortly after he became king, Solomon invited all Israel, especially the leaders of Israel, to come to Gibeon, five miles northwest of Jerusalem. Several years earlier David had moved the ark of the covenant to Jerusalem and had moved the altar and the tabernacle from Nob to Gibeon. There on a hilltop at Gibeon Solomon offered a thousand animals as sacrifices to God.

What a sight that must have been, to see God's people, led by their king, assembled for worship, to see the smoke of those many sacrifices rising into the sky!

It was on that very night that God appeared to Solomon in a dream and invited his faithful servant to ask for whatever he wanted.

Christians today need not envy Solomon. God has spoken to us also—not in a dream but through the Scriptures—and has invited us also to ask for what we desire. In John 16:23 Jesus says to his disciples, "I tell you the truth, my Father will give you whatever you ask in my name." That invitation is addressed to God-fearing people like Solomon. Those who love and serve the true God are able to pray in the name of Jesus. Believers in the Messiah have the privilege of calling God "Father."

⁶Solomon answered, "You have shown great kindness to your servant, my father David, because he was faithful to you and righteous and upright in heart. You have continued this great kindness to him and have given him a son to sit on his throne this very day.

⁷"Now, O LORD my God, you have made your servant king in place of my father David. But I am only a little child and do not know how to carry out my duties. ⁸Your servant is here among the people you have chosen, a great people, too numerous to count or number. ⁹So give your servant a discerning heart to govern your people and to distinguish between right and wrong. For who is able to govern this great people of yours?"

As Solomon considered God's invitation, he thought about the ways God had already blessed him. God had chosen David the shepherd boy to be the king over his people. God had permitted David's son to become the next king. (This is remarkable, for it is the first time in Israel's history that a ruler was succeeded by his son.) God had promised to show his greatest kindness to David's family by sending the Savior into the world through his family.

When Solomon thought about the heavy responsibility resting on his shoulders, he saw his own weakness and inability. He therefore prayed that God would give him a wise and understanding heart that he might rule well the people God had chosen.

Since God's people today often find themselves inadequate for the work God has assigned to them, they do well to imitate Solomon's prayer for wisdom. Children might pray, "God, give me wisdom so that I know how to honor my parents and other superiors." Parents might pray, "God, give me wisdom to understand my children and to discipline them in love." Church leaders might pray, "God, give me wisdom so that I properly rebuke all sin and unbelief and so that I speak words of real comfort to all who need them." All Christians might pray, "God, give me wisdom to understand correctly the situations that confront me, wisdom to speak fitting words so that others might come to glorify you as their Savior."

When we have finished praying for ourselves, then we might ask God to give that same blessing to others.

[10]The Lord was pleased that Solomon had asked for this. [11]So God said to him, "Since you have asked for this and not for long life or wealth for yourself, nor have asked for the death of your enemies but for discernment in administering justice, [12]I will do what you have asked. I will give you a wise and discerning heart, so that there will never have been anyone like you, nor will there ever be. [13]Moreover, I will give you what you have not asked for—both riches and honor—so that in your lifetime you will

have no equal among kings. ¹⁴And if you walk in my ways and obey my statutes and commands as David your father did, I will give you a long life." ¹⁵Then Solomon awoke—and he realized it had been a dream.

He returned to Jerusalem, stood before the ark of the Lord's covenant and sacrificed burnt offerings and fellowship offerings. Then he gave a feast for all his court.

Jesus once said, "Seek first his [God's] kingdom and his righteousness, and all these things [food, drink, clothing] will be given to you as well" (Matthew 6:33). That is what happened here. Solomon's prayer was not a selfish request. He prayed for practical gifts that could be used in God's kingdom. Therefore God gave him not only what he asked for but much more. God gave Solomon wisdom the likes of which this world had never seen and would never see again. God also gave him riches and power. And, if Solomon would continue to walk in God's ways, God promised to prolong his life on earth.

To show his gratitude for those blessings, Solomon offered more sacrifices to God when he returned to Jerusalem.

St. James assures us (James 1:5) that God will also hear and answer our prayers for wisdom. God chose Solomon to write the books called Proverbs, Song of Songs, and Ecclesiastes. As we read those books, God imparts to us some of the very same wisdom he once gave Solomon.

A Wise Ruling

¹⁶Now two prostitutes came to the king and stood before him. ¹⁷One of them said, "My lord, this woman and I live in the same house. I had a baby while she was there with me. ¹⁸The third day after my child was born, this woman also had a baby. We were alone; there was no one in the house but the two of us.

¹⁹"During the night this woman's son died because she lay on him. ²⁰So she got up in the middle of the night and took my son

from my side while I your servant was asleep. She put him by her breast and put her dead son by my breast. [21]The next morning, I got up to nurse my son—and he was dead! But when I looked at him closely in the morning light, I saw that it wasn't the son I had borne."

[22]The other woman said, "No! The living one is my son; the dead one is yours."

But the first one insisted, "No! The dead one is yours; the living one is mine." And so they argued before the king.

[23]The king said, "This one says, 'My son is alive and your son is dead,' while that one says, 'No! Your son is dead and mine is alive.'"

[24]Then the king said, "Bring me a sword." So they brought a sword for the king. [25]He then gave an order: "Cut the living child in two and give half to one and half to the other."

[26]The woman whose son was alive was filled with compassion for her son and said to the king, "Please, my lord, give her the living baby! Don't kill him!"

But the other, "Neither I nor you shall have him. Cut him in two!"

[27]Then the king gave his ruling: "Give the living baby to the first woman. Do not kill him; she is his mother."

[28]When all Israel heard the verdict the king had given, they held the king in awe, because they saw that he had wisdom from God to administer justice.

Who could decide which woman was telling the truth? There were no witnesses. The babies could not speak for themselves. But Solomon made use of the wisdom God had given him. No wonder Solomon's wise judgments soon became known in Israel and (as we learn in chapter 10) throughout the world.

Most of us will never be called upon to decide a case between two prostitutes—except to condemn the sin of fornication. But dealing with other situations in life often

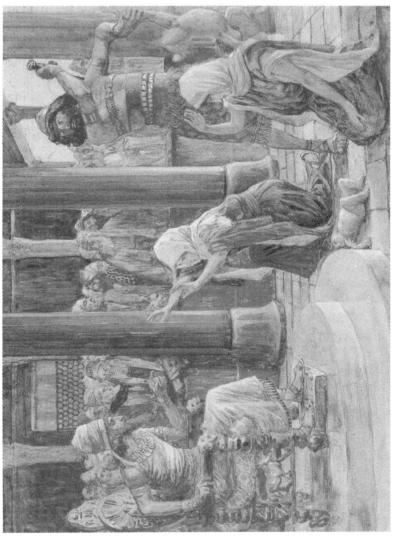

The Wisdom of Solomon (1 Kings 3:27)

requires "the wisdom of Solomon." Today's parents need God-given wisdom to rear their young children and to deal with the problems modern teenagers face. Spouses need God-given wisdom to deal with the sins and the selfishness of their mates. Christian young people need that wisdom to give an answer to their unbelieving friends and teachers and to cope with the world's temptations. Our pastors need that wisdom to deal with complex problems.

The God who caused multitudes to stand in awe at the wisdom of Solomon continues to instruct his people through his word. May the Holy Spirit bless our learning so that others marvel at our faith and wisdom.

Solomon's Officals and Governors

4 **So King Solomon ruled over all Israel. ²And these were his chief officials:**

 Azariah son of Zadok—the priest;
 ³Elihoreph and Ahijah, sons of Shisha—secretaries;
 Jehoshaphat son of Ahilud—recorder;
 ⁴Benaiah son of Jehoiada—commander in chief;
 Zadok and Abiathar—priests;
 ⁵Azariah son of Nathan—in charge of the district officers;
 Zabud son of Nathan—a priest and personal adviser to the king;
 ⁶Ahishar—in charge of the palace;
 Adoniram son of Abda—in charge of forced labor.

The list of names at the beginning of this chapter is an indication that Solomon's reign would be well organized religiously, politically, and personally. It would be much grander (and much more expensive) than that of David or Saul.

Even though Abiathar had been put out of office, verse 4 still mentions him as a priest, perhaps out of respect for his office.

The Nathan mentioned in verse 5 is either Nathan the prophet or one of the sons of David, who had the same name (2 Samuel 5:14). We will hear more about Adoniram and the "forced labor" when we read about the building of the temple in chapter 5.

7Solomon also had twelve district governors over all Israel, who supplied provisions for the king and the royal household. Each one had to provide supplies for one month in the year. 8These are their names:

> Ben-Hur—in the hill country of Ephraim;
> 9Ben-Deker—in Makaz, Shaalbim, Beth Shemesh and Elon Bethhanan;
> 10Ben-Hesed—in Arubboth (Socoh and all the land of Hepher were his);
> 11Ben-Abinadab—in Naphoth Dor (he was married to Taphath daughter of Solomon);
> 12Baana son of Ahilud—in Taanach and Megiddo, and in all of Beth Shan next to Zarethan below Jezreel, from Beth Shan to Abel Meholah across to Jokmeam;
> 13Ben-Geber—in Ramoth Gilead (the settlements of Jair son of Manasseh in Gilead were his, as well as the district of Argob in Bashan and its sixty large walled cities with bronze gate bars);
> 14Ahinadab son of Iddo—in Mahanaim;
> 15Ahimaaz—in Naphtali (he had married Basemath daughter of Solomon);
> 16Baana son of Hushai—in Asher and in Aloth;
> 17Jehoshaphat son of Paruah—in Issachar;
> 18Shimei son of Ela—in Benjamin;
> 19Geber son of Uri—in Gilead (the country of Sihon king of the Amorites and the country of Og king of Bashan). He was the only governor over the district.

Centuries earlier the land of Israel had been divided among the twelve tribes of Israel. Solomon's twelve governors ruled over areas that in some cases roughly resembled the old tribal boundaries.

Providing food for the many religious and political officials in Solomon's bureaucracy was no small task for these governors.

Solomon's Daily Provisions

[20]The people of Judah and Israel were as numerous as the sand on the seashore; they ate, they drank and they were happy. [21]And Solomon ruled over all the kingdoms from the River to the land of the Philistines, as far as the border of Egypt. These countries brought tribute and were Solomon's subjects all his life.

[22]Solomon's daily provisions were thirty cors of fine flour and sixty cors of meal, [23]ten head of stall-fed cattle, twenty of pasture-fed cattle and a hundred sheep and goats, as well as deer, gazelles, roe-bucks and choice fowl. [24]For he ruled over all the kingdoms west of the River, from Tiphsah to Gaza, and had peace on all sides. [25]During Solomon's lifetime Judah and Israel, from Dan to Beer-sheba, lived in safety, each man under his own vine and fig tree.

[26]Solomon had four thousand stalls for chariot horses, and twelve thousand horses.

[27]The district officers, each in his month, supplied provisions for King Solomon and all who came to the king's table. They saw to it that nothing was lacking. [28]They also brought to the proper place their quotas of barley and straw for the chariot horses and the other horses.

God had made three great promises to Abraham: he would become the ancestor of a great nation; his descendants would possess the land of Canaan; and the Savior would be born from his family.

Solomon lived midway between the time of Abraham and the time of the Savior. At this time God had fulfilled two of those three promises. The people of Judah and Israel had become "as numerous as the sand on the seashore," just as God had foretold in Genesis 13:16. God's people firmly possessed their promised land, an area much bigger than the present State of Israel. It extended from the borders of Egypt and the city of Gaza on the south up to the city of Tiphsah on the Euphrates River, some 400 miles north of Gaza. This also is what God had promised to Abraham a thousand years earlier in Genesis 13:15.

Ruling this area effectively required the help of many individuals. Feeding these employees, the members of Solomon's family (especially when Solomon took many wives), and his many personal servants required huge amounts of food. The footnote in the NIV indicates that 185 bushels of fine flour and 375 bushels of meal were required daily. Each of the twelve governors mentioned earlier was in charge of supplying provisions for one month of the year.

But Solomon was not the only one living like a king. The people in general had been blessed by God. Several phrases from this section have become proverbial: The people "ate, they drank and they were happy." "From Dan to Beersheba" (from one end of the country to the other) they lived in peace and safety, "each under his own vine and fig tree."

Christians in America and in many other nations have been similarly blessed by God. The huge amounts of food displayed in our local supermarkets are evidence of God's earthly blessing. The peace the people enjoyed under Solomon's rule reminds us of the peace we enjoy in the Savior's kingdom. Isaiah describes that heavenly peace this way: "Before they call I will answer; while they are still speaking I will hear. The wolf and the lamb will feed together, and the lion will eat straw like the ox" (Isaiah 65:24,25).

There is a minor problem in verse 26. Did Solomon have 40,000 stalls for horses (KJV and NASB) or only 4,000

(NIV)? The parallel account in 2 Chronicles 9:25 lists the smaller number. Here is an example of where an ancient copyist, before the invention of the printing press, may have accidentally added or dropped a zero. Perhaps we will never know for sure exactly what the inspired number was, but the specific problem here is not a doctrinal problem and surely has nothing to do with our eternal salvation. We can be thankful to God that he has preserved his word so that we may know with certainty everything we need to know about the way to eternal life.

This author prefers the translation of the NASB: "And Solomon had 40,000 stalls of horses for his chariots, and 12,000 horsemen."

Solomon's Wisdom

²⁹**God gave Solomon wisdom and very great insight, and a breadth of understanding as measureless as the sand on the seashore. ³⁰Solomon's wisdom was greater than the wisdom of all the men of the East, and greater than all the wisdom of Egypt. ³¹He was wiser than any other man, including Ethan the Ezrahite—wiser than Heman, Calcol and Darda, the sons of Mahol. And his fame spread to all the surrounding nations. ³²He spoke three thousand proverbs and his songs numbered a thousand and five. ³³He described plant life, from the cedar of Lebanon to the hyssop that grows out of walls. He also taught about animals and birds, reptiles and fish. ³⁴Men of all nations came to listen to Solomon's wisdom, sent by all the kings of the world, who had heard of his wisdom.**

The depth of Solomon's wisdom distinguished him from all other men in the world. He was wiser than the best men of Egypt and of the East. He was wiser than Judah's finest, wisest men, including Ethan and Heman, who, according to 1 Chronicles 2:6, were among the temple singers.

At the end of chapter 3, where the king determined who the living infant's real mother was, we saw an example of how Solomon understood the human mind. But his wisdom included much more. Solomon was a biologist, a science teacher, and a botanist.

Some of Solomon's three thousand proverbs have been recorded for us in the Book of Proverbs. At least one of Solomon's thousand and five songs has been recorded in the Bible. That is the Song of Songs.

No wonder people from all over the world, including the Queen of Sheba (whom we will read about in chapter 10), came to visit Solomon.

The wisdom that filled Solomon's heart came from God in answer to Solomon's prayer. It was a wisdom which had "the fear of the Lord" as its very beginning and foundation. Those who seem to be the wisest men in the world today often do not share Solomon's attitude. Many scientists today deny that a mighty God made all things in six days and that God's foremost visible creatures, we human beings, are in need of a Savior. That sort of "wisdom" is not from God.

In Matthew 12:42 Jesus compared himself to King Solomon. Pointing to himself Jesus told the people, "One greater than Solomon is here." Several phrases from this chapter remind us of our Savior. Solomon ruled over a kingdom that had limited borders; the Savior's rule extends throughout the world and over the whole universe. Solomon was a man of peace (1 Chronicles 22:9); our Savior is the Prince of Peace. Solomon's rule provided earthly peace for his subjects; the Savior's kingdom offers perfect peace between a holy God and a sinful world.

Solomon ate the best food every day, food richer than the bread and fish Jesus provided for the multitudes; the Savior has given us living water to drink (John 4:10) and has also led us to eat his flesh and to drink his blood (John 6:53), that is, to believe that by his suffering and death he has won for us eternal life. Solomon lived in a splendid home which is described in chapter 7; Jesus is preparing a mansion for us in heaven, a permanent home in God's presence. Solomon had great wisdom; Jesus has greater wisdom—he is at the Father's side and declares to us the nature and love of God the Father. Solomon was a mighty king; the Savior's kingdom is mightier, stronger than death, and even the gates of hell shall not prevail against it.

If Solomon's subjects could rejoice, our joy and contentment can be greater.

Many a young man in Solomon's position has given his heart to power and riches. But Solomon was concerned with spiritual matters. We saw earlier how he had asked God for wisdom. Now his top priority was to build a house for God's name in Jerusalem.

Preparations for Building the Temple

5 **When Hiram king of Tyre heard that Solomon had been anointed king to succeed his father David, he sent his envoys to Solomon, because he had always been on friendly terms with David. ²Solomon sent back this message to Hiram:**

³**"You know that because of the wars waged against my father David from all sides, he could not build a temple for the Name of the LORD his God until the LORD put his enemies under his feet. ⁴But now the LORD my God has given me rest on every side, and there is no adversary or disaster. ⁵I intend, therefore, to build a temple for the Name of the LORD my God, as the LORD told my father David, when he said, 'Your son whom I will put on the throne in your place will build the temple for my Name.'**

⁶**"So give orders that cedars of Lebanon be cut for me. My men will work with yours, and I will pay you for your men whatever wages you set. You know that we have no one so skilled in felling timber as the Sidonians."**

⁷When Hiram heard Solomon's message, he was greatly pleased and said, "Praise be to the LORD today, for he has given David a wise son to rule over this great nation."

⁸So Hiram sent word to Solomon:

"I have received the message you sent me and will do all you want in providing the cedar and pine logs. ⁹My men will haul them down from Lebanon to the sea, and I will float them in rafts by sea to the place you specify. There I will separate them and you can take them away. And you are to grant my wish by providing food for my royal household."

¹⁰In this way Hiram kept Solomon supplied with all the cedar and pine logs he wanted, ¹¹and Solomon gave Hiram twenty thousand cors of wheat as food for his household, in addition to twenty thousand baths of pressed olive oil. Solomon continued to do this for Hiram year after year. ¹²The LORD gave Solomon wisdom, just as he had promised him. There were peaceful relations between Hiram and Solomon, and the two of them made a treaty.

Solomon's father, King David, had wanted to build the temple. As a matter of fact, David had already made building plans and had begun to gather materials (1 Chronicles 22 and 28). But David had been a man of war. Therefore the privilege of building the temple would not be given to David but to Solomon, "the peaceful one," who would rule during a time of peace.

It is here that we meet King Hiram, a Gentile king who ruled over Phoenicia at Tyre. This was north of Palestine on the Mediterranean Sea. Hiram had been a friend of David. By sending congratulations to the new king, he showed that he wanted to be friends with Solomon also. Hiram's words in verse 7 indicate that he may have been a true believer in the Lord God.

At an earlier time Hiram had sent trees from the forests of Lebanon to build a house for David. Those forests were famous throughout the world. The cedar and cypress trees that grew there were almost indestructible. Since quality wood was not readily available in Palestine, Solomon would buy timber from Lebanon for the temple. The Phoenicians were skilled woodworkers and shipbuilders. Therefore Solomon asked that Hiram's servants work with the Israelites in cutting trees from the forests, hauling them down to the Mediteranean Sea, and then floating them nearly 100 miles south to Joppa. From that seaport other men would haul the logs the forty miles or so up to Jerusalem.

Solomon in turn agreed to give Hiram a handsome payment for his services. Phoenicia had surplus timber but a shortage of food. According to the NIV footnote the annual stipend amounted to 125,000 bushels of wheat and 115,000 gallons of olive oil.

It is also noteworthy that the temple here is repeatedly called "a house for the name of the LORD." God's name is not only a word like "Jesus," "Lord," or "Redeemer." It is also God's "good name," that is, everything we know about our loving, merciful God from the Bible. In Exodus 20:24 God had said, "Wherever I cause my name to be honored, I will come to you and bless you." Although God fills heaven and earth, the temple was the place where he would come to his people and proclaim his love and forgiveness. The sacrifices offered there reminded the people that God would someday send his Lamb to be the final sacrifice for sin. The showbread in the temple reminded the people that someday the Bread of Life would come into the world. The Sabbath days observed there reminded the people that *the* Rest-Bringer would come into the world. The incense burned there reminded the people that God hears the prayers of his people.

Our churches also may rightly be called "houses for God's name." There God's saving name is proclaimed. There God comes to us through his word and sacraments to bless us.

13King Solomon conscripted laborers from all Israel—thirty thousand men. 14He sent them off to Lebanon in shifts of ten thousand a month, so that they spent one month in Lebanon and two months at home. Adoniram was in charge of the forced labor. 15Solomon had seventy thousand carriers and eighty thousand stonecutters in the hills, 16as well as thirty-three hundred foremen who supervised the project and directed the workmen. 17At the king's command they removed from the quarry large blocks of quality stone to provide a foundation of dressed stone for the temple. 18The craftsmen of Solomon and Hiram and the men of Gebal cut and prepared the timber and stone for the building of the temple.

It was a tremendous task to cut down huge trees and haul them over land and sea to Jerusalem and to quarry immense blocks of stone and haul them up to Jerusalem without the use of modern machinery. This work required the time and muscle of thousands of men. Solomon chose full-blooded Israelites to assist Hiram with cutting the trees in the forest. The other 153,000 carriers, stonecutters, and supervisors were not Israelites but aliens (that is, Canaanites) who were still living in the land of Palestine (2 Chronicles 2:17,18).

The city of Gebal, or Byblos, is another Phoenician seaport north of Tyre.

The word "temple" may suggest a huge auditorium that can seat thousands. The temple built by Solomon was not that kind of building. It was ninety feet long, thirty feet wide, and forty-five feet high. Although the temple was considerably larger than the tabernacle used in the wilderness, the temple was not intended for crowds. Only the priests were allowed to enter it to perform certain prescribed duties.

When we read in the New Testament that Jesus taught in the temple, the temple courtyards (or campus) are meant.

This magnificent, ornate building would become the center of Israel's worship, the place where God dwelt in the midst of his people, the place where he heard their prayers, received their offerings, and assured them of forgiveness.

Solomon Builds the Temple

6 In the four hundred and eightieth year after the Israelites had come out of Egypt, in the fourth year of Solomon's reign over Israel, in the month of Ziv, the second month, he began to build the temple of the LORD.

²The temple that King Solomon built for the LORD was sixty cubits long, twenty wide and thirty high. ³The portico at the front of the main hall of the temple extended the width of the temple, that is twenty cubits, and projected ten cubits from the front of the temple. ⁴He made narrow clerestory windows in the temple. ⁵Against the wall of the main hall and inner sanctuary he built a structure around the building, in which there were side rooms. ⁶The lowest floor was five cubits wide, the middle floor six cubits and the third floor seven. He made offset ledges around the outside of the temple so that nothing would be inserted into the temple walls.

⁷In building the temple, only blocks dressed at the quarry were used, and no hammer, chisel or any other iron tool was heard at the temple site while it was being built.

⁸The entrance to the lowest floor was on the south side of the temple; a stairway led up to the middle level and from there to the third. ⁹So he built the temple and completed it, roofing it with beams and cedar planks. ¹⁰And he built the side rooms all along the temple. The height of each was five cubits, and they were attached to the temple by beams of cedar.

¹¹The word of the LORD came to Solomon: ¹²"As for this temple you are building, if you follow my decrees, carry out my regulations and keep all my commands and obey them, I will fulfill through you the promise I gave to David your father. ¹³And I will live among the Israelites and will not abandon my people Israel."

The Building of the Temple (1 Kings 6:1)

The building of the temple in Jerusalem was the most significant event in the history of Israel since the exodus from Egypt. It may very well be the most important event recorded in the books of Kings. For that reason the writer gives us an exact date and a detailed description.

The site of the temple was Mount Moriah, the very place where Abraham had offered his son Isaac many years earlier (2 Chronicles 3:1).

Clerestory lighting refers to windows well above the first floor level. This would provide indirect lighting for the priests to do their work.

Just as Solomon built the Old Testament temple, so the Lord Jesus, whom Solomon foreshadowed, continues to build the New Testament temple, his holy Christian church (Zechariah 6:12; Ephesians 2:21,22). Just as the precut stones of Solomon's temple were assembled without the sound of hammer or chisel, so the church of Christ grows silently like a mustard seed or like yeast in a loaf of bread. Wherever God's word is proclaimed, there the Holy Spirit is quietly at work creating and strengthening faith in Christ.

Even before the temple was completed, the Lord came to Solomon and assured him that he would make this temple his home. As long as Solomon and the people served God faithfully, God would not forsake them. In the same way God continues to live in the midst of his faithful people today.

Just as each Christian is precious in God's sight, so the temple was a costly building; its wood panelings were overlaid with pure gold.

14So Solomon built the temple and completed it. 15He lined its interior walls with cedar boards, paneling them from the floor of the temple to the ceiling, and covered the floor of the temple with

planks of pine. ¹⁶He partitioned off twenty cubits at the rear of the temple with cedar boards from floor to ceiling to form within the temple an inner sanctuary, the Most Holy Place. ¹⁷The main hall in front of this room was forty cubits long. ¹⁸The inside of the temple was cedar, carved with gourds and open flowers. Everything was cedar; no stone was to be seen.

¹⁹He prepared the inner sanctuary within the temple to set the ark of the covenant of the LORD there. ²⁰The inner sanctuary was twenty cubits long, twenty wide and twenty high. He overlaid the inside with pure gold, and he also overlaid the altar of cedar. ²¹Solomon covered the inside of the temple with pure gold, and he extended gold chains across the front of the inner sanctuary, which was overlaid with gold. ²²So he overlaid the whole interior with gold. He also overlaid with gold the altar that belonged to the inner sanctuary.

²³In the inner sanctuary he made a pair of cherubim of olive wood, each ten cubits high. ²⁴One wing of the first cherub was five cubits long, and the other wing five cubits—ten cubits from wing tip to wing tip. ²⁵The second cherub also measured ten cubits, for the two cherubim were identical in size and shape. ²⁶The height of each cherub was ten cubits. ²⁷He placed the cherubim inside the innermost room of the temple, with their wings spread out. The wing of one cherub touched one wall, while the wing of the other touched the other wall, and their wings touched each other in the middle of the room. ²⁸He overlaid the cherubim with gold.

²⁹On the walls all around the temple, in both the inner and outer rooms, he carved cherubim, palm trees and open flowers. ³⁰He also covered the floors of both the inner and outer rooms of the temple with gold.

³¹For the entrance of the inner sanctuary he made doors of olive wood with five-sided jambs. ³²And on the two olive wood doors he carved cherubim, palm trees and open flowers, and overlaid the cherubim and palms trees with beaten gold. ³³In the same way he made four-sided jambs of olive wood for the entrance to the main hall. ³⁴He also made two pine doors, each having two leaves that turned in sockets. ³⁵He carved cherubim, palm trees and open

flowers on them and overlaid them with gold hammered evenly over the carvings.

³⁶And he built the inner courtyard of three courses of dressed stone and one course of trimmed cedar beams.

³⁷The foundation of the temple of the LORD was laid in the fourth year, in the month of Ziv. ³⁸In the eleventh year in the month of Bul, the eighth month, the temple was finished in all its details according to its specifications. He had spent seven years building it.

The inner sanctuary, like the Holy of Holies in the earlier tabernacle, was a perfect cube. It was a visible reminder of the equality among the three persons of the Triune God. Here is where that sacred chest, the ark of the covenant with its atonement cover, would be kept.

Once a year, on the great Day of Atonement, the high priest would go behind the heavy curtain which separated the inner sanctuary from the rest of the temple, and sprinkle blood on that atonement cover. The Old Testament priest used the blood of a goat to make his atonement (Leviticus 16). Jesus, our great high priest, offered his own blood to God as a real atoning sacrifice.

That heavy curtain which separated the people from God was torn apart when the Savior died.

Two huge cherubim, each fifteen feet high and each having a wingspan of fifteen feet, joined the two original cherubim which formed part of the mercy seat. Just as those two angelic beings kept silent vigil over the mercy seat, so God's angels continue to watch invisibly and silently over God's children.

The books of Kings relate the history of Israel from the building of this grand temple to its destruction. These books are, then, the story of people who had God's fullest earthly and spiritual blessings but failed to appreciate them and suffered the consequences.

When the temple of the Lord was completed, Solomon began to construct his own residence.

Solomon Builds His Palace

7 **It took Solomon thirteen years, however, to complete the construction of his palace. ²He built the Palace of the Forest of Lebanon a hundred cubits long, fifty wide and thirty high, with four rows of cedar columns supporting trimmed cedar beams. ³It was roofed with cedar above the beams that rested on the columns—forty-five beams, fifteen to a row. ⁴Its windows were placed high in sets of three, facing each other. ⁵All the doorways had rectangular frames; they were in the front part in sets of three, facing each other.**

⁶He made a colonnade fifty cubits long and thirty wide. In front of it was a portico, and in front of that were pillars and an overhanging roof.

⁷He built the throne hall, the Hall of Justice, where he was to judge, and he covered it with cedar from floor to ceiling. ⁸And the palace in which he was to live, set farther back, was similar in design. Solomon also made a palace like this hall for Pharaoh's daughter, whom he had married.

⁹All these structures, from the outside to the great courtyard and from foundation to eaves, were made of blocks of high-grade stone cut to size and trimmed with a saw on their inner and outer faces. ¹⁰The foundations were laid with large stones of good quality, some measuring ten cubits and some eight. ¹¹Above were high-grade stones, cut to size, and cedar beams. ¹²The great courtyard was surrounded by a wall of three courses of dressed stone and one course of trimmed cedar beams, as was the inner courtyard of the temple of the LORD with its portico.

The writer here describes a complex of several buildings. The first was the so-called Palace of the Forest of Lebanon, a building larger than the temple, which served as Solomon's treasure house. In it Solomon later placed 300 shields of beaten gold and his golden drinking vessels (1 Kings 10:17,21). If this palace smelled anything like a cedar chest of today, it must have had a distinct and pleasing scent.

The second was the colonnade, or "hall of pillars," as the other translations call it. It resembled the inner court of the temple and probably connected the first and third buildings.

The third building was the hall of judgment, a throne room, enclosed on three sides with walls of cedar.

The fourth building was Solomon's personal residence and was probably located behind the throne room.

Solomon prepared a similar building for his wife, the daughter of Pharaoh.

The whole complex was enclosed within a court and a wall of hewn stones and cedar timbers.

Although we will probably never know exactly what these buildings looked like, it is significant that Solomon built his residence on Mount Zion, just south of the temple. It seems that Solomon's desire at this time was to conduct his personal life and his political life in the shadow of God's temple.

The Temple's Furnishings

[13]King Solomon sent to Tyre and brought Huram, [14]whose mother was a widow from the tribe of Naphtali and whose father was a man of Tyre and a craftsman in bronze. Huram was highly skilled and experienced in all kinds of bronze work. He came to King Solomon and did all the work assigned to him. [15]He cast two bronze pillars, each eighteen cubits high and twelve cubits around, by line. [16]He also made two capitals of cast bronze to set on the tops of the pillars; each capital was five cubits high. [17]A network of interwoven chains festooned the capitals on top of the pillars, seven for each capital. [18]He made pomegranates in two rows encircling each network to decorate the capitals on top of the pillars. He did the same for each capital. [19]The capitals

on top of the pillars in the portico were in the shape of lilies, four cubits high. ²⁰On the capitals of both pillars, above the bowl-shaped part next to the network, were the two hundred pomegranates in rows all around. ²¹He erected the pillars at the portico of the temple. The pillar to the south he named Jakin and the one to the north Boaz. ²²The capitals on top were in the shape of lilies. And so the work on the pillars was completed.

²³He made the Sea of cast metal, circular in shape, measuring ten cubits from rim to rim and five cubits high. It took a line of thirty cubits to measure around it. ²⁴Below the rim, gourds encircled it—ten to a cubit. The gourds were cast in two rows in one piece with the Sea.

²⁵The Sea stood on twelve bulls, three facing north, three facing west, three facing south and three facing east. The Sea rested on top of them, and their hindquarters were toward the center. ²⁶It was a handbreadth in thickness, and its rim was like the rim of a cup, like a lily blossom. It held two thousand baths.

²⁷He also made ten movable stands of bronze; each was four cubits long, four wide and three high. ²⁸This is how the stands were made: They had side panels attached to uprights. ²⁹On the panels between the uprights were lions, bulls and cherubim—and on the uprights as well. Above and below the lions and bulls were wreaths of hammered work. ³⁰Each stand had four bronze wheels with bronze axles, and each had a basin resting on four supports, cast with wreaths on each side. ³¹On the inside of the stand there was an opening that had a circular frame one cubit deep. This opening was round, and with its basework it measured a cubit and a half. Around its opening there was engraving. The panels of the stands were square, not round. ³²The four wheels were under the panels, and the axles of the wheels were attached to the stand. The diameter of each wheel was a cubit and a half. ³³The wheels were made like chariot wheels; the axles, rims, spokes and hubs were all of cast metal.

³⁴Each stand had four handles, one on each corner, projecting from the stand. ³⁵At the top of the stand there was a circular band half a cubit deep. The supports and panels were attached to the

top of the stand. [36]He engraved cherubim, lions and palm trees on the surfaces of the supports and on the panels, in every available space, with wreaths all around. [37]This is the way he made the ten stands. They were all cast in the same molds and were identical in size and shape.

[38]He then made ten bronze basins, each holding forty baths and measuring four cubits across, one basin to go on each of the ten stands. [39]He placed five of the stands on the south side of the temple and five on the north. He placed the Sea on the south side, at the southeast corner of the temple. [40]He also made the basins and shovels and sprinkling bowls.

So Huram finished all the work he had undertaken for King Solomon in the temple of the LORD:

[41]the two pillars;

the two bowl-shaped capitals on top of the pillars;

the two sets of network decorating the two bowl-shaped capitals on top of the pillars;

[42]the four hundred pomegranates for the two sets of network (two rows of pomegranates for each network, decorating the bowl-shaped capitals on top of the pillars);

[43]the ten stands with their ten basins;

[44]the Sea and the twelve bulls under it;

[45]the pots, shovels and sprinkling bowls.

All these objects that Huram made for King Solomon for the temple of the LORD were of burnished bronze. [46]The king had them cast in clay molds in the plain of the Jordan between Succoth and Zarethan. [47]Solomon left all these things unweighed, because there were so many; the weight of the bronze was not determined.

A man named Huram (also known as Hiram) was a highly skilled worker in bronze. He prepared several items for the temple and for the priests. They included:

1. The two huge, free-standing pillars in front of the temple. They were named Jakin and Boaz, that is, "he shall establish" and "in it is strength." Those names reminded the

Israelites that God's gracious rule is so firmly established that no power of earth or hell can shake it.

2. The Sea was a huge container for water. According to the NIV footnote two thousand baths is the equivalent of 11,500 gallons of water. If its diameter was exactly ten cubits, its circumference would be more than thirty cubits. The writer evidently intends to give us approximate measurements. (The Greek translation of the Old Testament lists a circumference of thirty-three cubits.) According to 2 Chronicles 4:6 the Sea held the water the priests used to wash their hands and feet before approaching the altar or entering the Holy Place. It was placed between the front gate of the temple and the altar of burnt sacrifice.

3. The ten movable stands held basins with water for washing the pieces of meat to be sacrificed on the big bronze altar. The wheels under the stands and basins made them easily movable. Each of the basins held approximately 230 gallons of water.

4. The shovels mentioned in verse 40 were used for removing the ashes; the basins were used to catch the blood of the sacrificial animals.

These washings, which were carried on in the sight of the people, were all only external. They could never wash away sin. They pointed to the Savior who would cleanse people from sin and guilt.

The Laver (1 Kings 7:33)

The plants and flowers that are frequently mentioned are reminders of the peace and life the Savior offers his people.

The casting was carried on in an area west of the Jordan River. The bronze had been obtained earlier by King David through his conquests (1 Chronicles 18:8).

⁴⁸Solomon also made all the furnishings that were in the LORD's temple:

> **the golden altar;**
> **the golden table on which was the bread of the Presence;**
> **⁴⁹the lampstands of pure gold (five on the right and five on the left, in front of the inner sanctuary);**
> **the gold floral work and lamps and tongs;**
> **⁵⁰the pure gold basins, wick trimmers, sprinkling bowls, dishes and censers;**
> **and the gold sockets for the doors of the innermost room, the Most Holy Place, and also for the doors of the main hall of the temple.**

⁵¹When all the work King Solomon had done for the temple of the LORD was finished, he brought in the things his father David had dedicated—the silver and gold and the furnishings—and he placed them in the treasuries of the LORD's temple.

Many of the other furnishings and utensils in the temple were made of pure gold. The chief items were:

1. The altar of incense in the Holy Place. This is where Zechariah was burning incense when Gabriel appeared to him.

2. The table on which the bread of the Presence or the showbread was placed. Twelve fresh loaves of bread were placed there each Sabbath day. The old loaves were then eaten by the priests.

3. Whereas there had been only one lampstand in the tabernacle, there would be ten golden lampstands in the Holy Place of the temple.

David had acquired so much material that there was metal left over after the temple's furnishings had all been made.

Finally the great day had come. The leaders of the tribes and clans gathered to dedicate the temple to the glory of the Lord.

The Ark Brought to the Temple

8 Then King Solomon summoned into his presence at Jerusalem the elders of Israel, all the heads of the tribes and the chiefs of the Israelite families, to bring up the ark of the LORD's covenant from Zion, the City of David. ²All the men of Israel came together to King Solomon at the time of the festival in the month of Ethanim, the seventh month.

³When all the elders of Israel had arrived, the priests took up the ark, ⁴and they brought up the ark of the LORD and the Tent of Meeting and all the sacred furnishings in it. The priests and Levites carried them up, ⁵and King Solomon and the entire assembly of Israel that had gathered about him were before the ark, sacrificing so many sheep and cattle that they could not be recorded or counted.

⁶The priests then brought the ark of the LORD's covenant to its place in the inner sanctuary of the temple, the Most Holy Place, and put it beneath the wings of the cherubim. ⁷The cherubim spread their wings over the place of the ark and overshadowed the ark and its carrying poles. ⁸These poles were so long that their ends could be seen from the Holy Place in front of the inner sanctuary, but not from outside the Holy Place; and they are still there today. ⁹There was nothing in the ark except the two stone tablets that Moses had placed in it at Horeb, where the LORD made a covenant with the Israelites after they came out of Egypt.

¹⁰When the priests withdrew from the Holy Place, the cloud filled the temple of the LORD. ¹¹And the priests could not perform their service because of the cloud, for the glory of the LORD filled his temple.

The dedication of the temple took place in the month Ethanim, which corresponds approximately to our October. When the people were celebrating the Feast of Tabernacles (Leviticus 23:34), the tabernacle of the Lord and the sacred vessels would be brought from Gibeon, five miles north of Jerusalem, to the temple.

The ark of the covenant, however, was already in Jerusalem. When David brought it from the house of Obed-Edom to Mount Zion, he offered sacrifices to the Lord every time those carrying the ark took six steps (2 Samuel 6:13). King Solomon was equally generous. He showed his love for God by offering oxen and cattle without number.

At this moment, however, Solomon's magnificent temple was still like a lifeless body. God had not yet made it his home. But now the priests, accompanied by a choir of Levites and a band of 120 priests blowing on trumpets (2 Chronicles 5:12), carried the ark to its permanent resting place. When they set the ark in the Holy Place under the outstretched wings of the two cherubim, God showed his presence in a visible way. That ark was the throne of God. Now a cloud like the one at Sinai (Exodus 19:9) filled the temple so that the priests were no longer able to minister there.

According to Hebrews 9:4 a golden jar of manna and Aaron's budding rod had also been placed into the ark. At this time, however, only the two tables of the law were in it.

¹²Then Solomon said, "The LORD has said that he would dwell in a dark cloud; ¹³I have indeed built a magnificent temple for you, a place for you to dwell forever."

¹⁴While the whole assembly of Israel was standing there, the king turned around and blessed them. ¹⁵Then he said:

"Praise be to the LORD, the God of Israel, who with his own hand has fulfilled what he promised with his own

Solomon Dedicates the Temple at Jerusalem (1 Kings 8:13)

mouth to my father David. For he said, [16]"Since the day I brought my people Israel out of Egypt, I have not chosen a city in any tribe of Israel to have a temple built for my Name to be there, but I have chosen David to rule my people Israel.'

[17]"My father David had it in his heart to build a temple for the Name of the LORD, the God of Israel. [18]But the LORD said to my father David, 'Because it was in your heart to build a temple for my Name, you did well to have this in your heart. [19]Nevertheless, you are not the one to build the temple, but your son, who is your own flesh and blood—he is the one who will build the temple for my Name.'

[20]"The LORD has kept the promise he made: I have succeeded David my father and now I sit on the throne of Israel, just as the LORD promised, and I have built the temple for the Name of the LORD, the God of Israel. [21]I have provided a place there for the ark, in which is the covenant of the LORD that he made with our fathers when he brought them out of Egypt."

King Solomon blessed the people by reminding them of how God had kept his promises. God had chosen David to be king. God had chosen Solomon to succeed his father. God had now chosen a particular place to record his name. Intimately bound up with those promises is the promise to send the Messiah, the great Son of King David (2 Samuel 7:12,13). It is that Messiah who would literally dwell within his temple of believers "forever".

In Ephesians 2:21 Paul tells us that Solomon's temple was a shadow prefiguring God's holy temple of believers, the holy Christian church. There are several obvious similarities:

1. They both are the home of the triune God. God dwelt in the temple in Jerusalem; the Father, the Son, and the Holy Spirit dwell among the believers.

2. They both are the place where God accepts sacrifice. From now on sacrifices were to be offered to God only at Jerusalem. In the New Testament God's temple of believers are called a "royal priesthood" (1 Peter 2:9). They alone can rightly offer sacrifices of praise to God.
3. They both are the place where God blesses his people. The ark of the covenant was (among other things) a reminder that God had delivered his people from bondage in Egypt (note verses 9,16,21). The people who make up God's temple of believers are a blessing to others when they proclaim the gospel of deliverance from sin.

Solomon's Prayer of Dedication

²²Then Solomon stood before the altar of the LORD in front of the whole assembly of Israel, spread out his hands toward heaven ²³and said:

"O LORD, God of Israel, there is no God like you in heaven above or on earth below—you who keep your covenant of love with your servants who continue wholeheartedly in your way. ²⁴You have kept your promise to your servant David my father; with your mouth you have promised and with your hand you have fulfilled it—as it is today.

²⁵"Now LORD, God of Israel, keep for your servant David my father the promises you made to him when you said, 'You shall never fail to have a man to sit before me on the throne of Israel, if only your sons are careful in all they do to walk before me as you have done.' ²⁶And now, O God of Israel, let your word that you promised your servant David my father come true.

Solomon took his place before the people on a raised platform (2 Chronicles 6:13). With his arms stretched out toward the heavens, he knelt down and spoke a solemn prayer of dedication.

Earlier, when God had appeared to him at Gibeon, Solomon had asked God for a wise and understanding heart so that he could rule God's people. In the prayer of dedication we see that Solomon is still concerned with the welfare of God's people. God had promised to build a "house" for King David. One descendant from David's family would be the King of kings, the Messiah, who would rule over God's people eternally (2 Samuel 7:13-16). Solomon is praying, "May I and all of my descendants who rule as king be men like King David who 'continue wholeheartedly in your way.' May they be men who openly confess their sins, men who trust your forgiveness with their whole hearts, men who heartily desire to serve you. May they be true Israelites like Nathanael in whom there is no guile" (John 1:47).

²⁷"But will God really dwell on earth? The heavens, even the highest heaven, cannot contain you. How much less this temple I have built! ²⁸Yet give attention to your servant's prayer and his plea for mercy, O LORD my God. Hear the cry and the prayer that your servant is praying in your presence this day. ²⁹May your eyes be open toward this temple night and day, this place of which you said, 'My Name shall be there,' so that you will hear the prayer your servant prays toward this place. ³⁰Hear the supplication of your servant and of your people Israel when they pray toward this place. Hear from heaven, your dwelling place, and when you hear, forgive.

The heathen people thought there were many gods and that each god ruled a limited corner of the world. When the Arameans lost a battle to the Israelites, they were certain that it was because Israel's gods controlled the mountains where the battle had been fought and that the outcome might be different if the battle were fought in another place

(1 Kings 20:23). The God whom Solomon worshiped, however, cannot be limited to one area of the world, nor can he be contained in a building. All creation cannot contain him! Today it is the evolutionist who seeks to limit God's power and God's presence. The evolutionist talks as though God was not yet present when dinosaurs walked on the earth. He talks as though God is not present beyond the reaches of his telescope, and he thinks that human life may still be evolving on some distant planet. God answers those foolish thoughts by saying, "Of course I am present at all places! My hand made all these things!" (Cf. Isaiah 66:1,2.)

Note that Paul describes Jesus just as King Solomon describes God. In Ephesians 4:10 Paul tells us that Jesus "ascended higher than all the heavens, in order to fill the whole universe." Because Jesus has God's qualities, we know that he is God.

The sovereignty and omnipresence of God do not mean that he is an impersonal force or that he is unconcerned about individual persons. On the contrary, this Lord has observed our personal actions for many years. He has witnessed our "secret" sins. This Lord is also an "ever-present help in trouble" (Psalm 46:1). In Solomon's time the Lord had chosen the temple in Jerusalem as the special place to record his Name. Here God would meet with his people; here he would accept their sacrifices; here the Guardian of Israel who never sleeps or slumbers would hear and answer the prayers of his people.

This general introduction to Solomon's prayer is now followed by seven petitions.

31"When a man wrongs his neighbor and is required to take an oath and he comes and swears the oath before your altar in this temple, 32then hear from heaven and act. Judge between your servants, condemning the guilty and

bringing down on his own head what he has done. Declare the innocent not guilty, and so establish his innocence.

In certain legal cases an oath was required of the parties involved (cf. Exodus 22:6-12). Solomon's petition is that God would judge righteously between the two.

Verse 32 helps us understand the word "justify." ("Justifying the righteous, to give him according to his righteousness." KJV) "Justify" is a word used by a judge in a courtroom. The judge does not make the defendant a better man. He simply examines the evidence and on that basis declares the innocent man "not guilty." In Romans 3:24 Paul announces that God has "justified" all people. In doing so, God, the Judge, did not make sinners better people. But God did look at the evidence and, on the basis of Jesus' payment on the cross, he has declared us "not guilty."

33"When your people Israel have been defeated by an enemy because they have sinned against you, and when they turn back to you and confess your name, praying and making supplication to you in this temple, 34then hear from heaven and forgive the sin of your people Israel and bring them back to the land you gave to their fathers.

35"When the heavens are shut up and there is no rain because your people have sinned against you, and when they pray toward this place and confess your name and turn from their sin because you have afflicted them, 36then hear from heaven and forgive the sin of your servants, your people Israel. Teach them the right way to live, and send rain on the land you gave your people for an inheritance.

37"When famine or plague comes to the land, or blight or mildew, locusts or grasshoppers, or when an enemy besieges them in any of their cities, whatever disaster or disease may come, 38and when a prayer or plea is made by any of your people Israel—each one aware of the afflictions of his own heart, and spreading out his hands to-

ward this temple—³⁹then hear from heaven, your dwelling place. **Forgive and act; deal with each man according to all he does, since you know his heart (for you alone know the hearts of all men), ⁴⁰so that they will fear you all the time they live in the land you gave our fathers.**

Petitions 2, 3, and 4 deal with our daily bread. God had warned the Israelites already through Moses that if they would turn their backs on him and would worship false gods, then he would deliver them to their enemies, he would hold back rain from the heavens, and he would devastate their crops (Deuteronomy 28:25,38-40). Solomon evidently had this warning in mind when he asked God to deliver his penitent people from these troubles.

The heathen can do a rain dance. The weatherman can explain why it is raining or not raining. But, as we learn from 1 Kings 18:41-45, only God almighty can send rain and can cause the crops to grow.

When the land produces a harvest, God is preaching a sermon. He is telling Christians and heathen alike not only that there is a God but that he is a good and kind God.

According to verse 39 God alone knows the hearts of men. Since Jesus also "knew what was in a man" (John 2:25), we have further evidence that Jesus is indeed true God.

⁴¹"As for the foreigner who does not belong to your people Israel but has come from a distant land because of your name— ⁴²for men will hear of your great name and your mighty hand and your outstretched arm—when he comes and prays toward this temple, ⁴³then hear from heaven, your dwelling place, and do whatever the foreigner asks of you, so that all the peoples of the earth may know your name and fear you, as do your own people Israel, and may know that this house I have built bears your Name.

61

The temple Solomon had built was "a house of prayer for all nations" (Isaiah 56:7). Solomon prayed that God would also answer the pleas of Gentile believers who would visit the temple.

[44]"When your people go to war against their enemies, wherever you send them, and when they pray to the LORD toward the city you have chosen and the temple I have built for your Name, [45]then hear from heaven their prayer and their plea, and uphold their cause.

[46]"When they sin against you—for there is no one who does not sin—and you become angry with them and give them over to the enemy, who takes them captive to his own land, far away or near; [47]and if they have a change of heart in the land where they are held captive, and repent and plead with you in the land of their conquerors and say, 'We have sinned, we have done wrong, we have acted wickedly'; [48]and if they turn back to you with all their heart and soul in the land of their enemies who took them captive, and pray to you toward the land you gave their fathers, toward the city you have chosen and the temple I have built for your Name; [49]then from heaven, your dwelling place, hear their prayer and their plea, and uphold their cause. [50]And forgive your people, who have sinned against you; forgive all the offenses they have committed against you, and cause their conquerors to show them mercy; [51]for they are your people and your inheritance, whom you brought out of Egypt, out of that iron-smelting furnace.

[52]"May your eyes be open to your servant's plea and to the plea of your people Israel, and may you listen to them whenever they cry out to you. [53]For you singled them out from all the nations of the world to be your own inheritance, just as you declared through your servant Moses when you, O Sovereign LORD, brought our fathers out of Egypt."

Petitions 6 and 7 deal with a time of war, a time when God's people might be carried off as prisoners of war because of their sin.

The verses offer us a beautiful insight into the nature of God's forgiving love. Ever since the fall into sin, "there is no one who does not sin." But the omnipresent Creator also "forgives." The Hebrew word "forgive," which occurs in verse 50 and several other times in this prayer, is a word which the Bible uses only to describe the actions of God. The reason God forgives sin is not because of the animal blood shed there at the temple (Hebrews 10:4) or because of the behavior of the people. God forgives sin because he keeps his "covenant of love" (verse 23). He forgives because the Savior, whose legal lineage would be traced through the family of Solomon (Matthew 1:6), would shed his blood at Jerusalem on the altar of the cross. Those who confess their sins in humble repentance receive God's forgiveness (verse 47). The impenitent reject it by their unbelief.

This is the way God dealt with Daniel, who was living in Babylon a thousand miles from the temple. Daniel prayed facing Jerusalem (Daniel 6:10). He confessed his own sins and the sins of the people (Daniel 9:4-19). And Daniel received a favorable reply from a gracious Lord. God permitted the Jews, who were held captive in Babylon, to return to their homeland.

Solomon's dedicatory prayer was pleasing to God. The Lord appeared to him later (chapter 9) and told Solomon that all of these petitions would surely be granted (2 Chronicles 7:13-16).

The temple built by Solomon is no longer standing. But the Savior still wants us to pray to "our Father in heaven." Paul wants "men everywhere to lift up holy hands in prayer" (1 Timothy 2:8) to the God who fills the universe.

Then Solomon arose and faced the people to speak the final blessing.

54When Solomon had finished all these prayers and supplications to the LORD, he rose from before the altar of the LORD, where he had been kneeling with his hands spread out toward heaven. 55He stood and blessed the whole assembly of Israel in a loud voice, saying:

56"Praise be to the LORD, who has given rest to his people Israel just as he promised. Not one word has failed of all the good promises he gave through his servant Moses. 57May the LORD our God be with us as he was with our fathers; may he never leave us nor forsake us. 58May he turn our hearts to him, to walk in all his ways and to keep the commands, decrees and regulations he gave our fathers. 59And may these words of mine, which I have prayed before the LORD, be near to the LORD our God day and night, that he may uphold the cause of his servant and the cause of his people Israel according to each day's need, 60so that all the peoples of the earth may know that the LORD is God and that there is no other. 61But your hearts must be fully committed to the LORD our God, to live by his decrees and obey his commands, as at this time."

The completion of the temple was the culmination of God's Old Testament plans. Israel had become a great nation; Israel had received rest in their promised land. The land in which they lived and the temple in which God had his dwelling were constant reminders that the promised Messiah would also appear.

As we look over our shoulders, we also see a past studded with God's earthly and spiritual blessings. Our prayer for future blessing might well be the words spoken by Solomon, the words that are still printed as a motto on the masthead of the Northwestern Lutheran, the official publication of the Wisconsin Ev. Lutheran Synod: "May the Lord our God be with us as he was with our fathers." May he give us hearts that fear him and bodies that serve him!

The word "rest" in verse 56 deserves careful attention. The rest which God promised to his Old Testament people implied a victory over all of their enemies, enemies that were much stronger than the Israelites. It also implied a fulfillment of all that God had promised. In Joshua 21:44,45, for example, we read, "The LORD gave them rest on every side, . . . Not one of all the LORD's good promises to the house of Israel failed; every one was fulfilled."

That very same word "rest" is used to describe the heavenly rest which God has promised to us in Jesus (Psalm 95:11; Hebrews 3:7—4:11). Our eternal rest in heaven will mean a complete fulfillment of all God's most gracious promises and a complete victory over all enemies, even death.

The Dedication of the Temple

62Then the king and all Israel with him offered sacrifices before the LORD. 63Solomon offered a sacrifice of fellowship offerings to the LORD: twenty-two thousand cattle and a hundred and twenty thousand sheep and goats. So the king and all the Israelites dedicated the temple of the LORD.

64On that same day the king consecrated the middle part of the courtyard in front of the temple of the LORD, and there he offered burnt offerings, grain offerings and the fat of the fellowship offerings, because the bronze altar before the LORD was too small to hold the burnt offerings, the grain offerings and the fat of the fellowship offerings.

65So Solomon observed the festival at that time, and all Israel with him—a vast assembly, people from Lebo Hamath to the Wadi of Egypt. They celebrated it before the LORD our God for seven days and seven days more, fourteen days in all. 66On the following day he sent the people away. They blessed the king and then went home, joyful and glad in heart for all the good things the LORD had done for his servant David and his people Israel.

The day the temple was dedicated was a great day in the history of Israel. People had come from the farthest borders of Solomon's empire: from Hamath in the extreme north, and from the Wadi (the dry riverbed) of Egypt in the extreme southwest. Because there were so many animals to be sacrificed, temporary altars had to be set up in the temple courtyard.

The feast mentioned here and in verse 2 is the Feast of Tabernacles. Seven days were devoted to dedicating the temple, followed by another seven to celebrate the Feast of Tabernacles.

Oh, that the Lord God would so move the hearts of his people today to worship him in his house and bring their best sacrifices to him!

Solomon was privileged to see a vision of God not once but twice. At the beginning of his reign God had appeared to him and invited him to ask for whatever he wanted. Now twenty years have passed and Solomon is at the midpoint of his reign. Here God responds to the prayer Solomon spoke at the temple dedication, a prayer he probably repeated many times over the years.

The Lord Appears to Solomon

9 **When Solomon had finished building the temple of the LORD and the royal palace, and had achieved all he had desired to do, ²the LORD appeared to him a second time, as he had appeared to him at Gibeon. ³The LORD said to him:**

"I have heard the prayer and plea you have made before me; I have consecrated this temple, which you have built, by putting my Name there forever. My eyes and my heart will always be there.

⁴"As for you, if you walk before me in integrity of heart and uprightness, as David your father did, and do all I command and observe my decrees and laws, ⁵I will estab-

lish your royal throne over Israel forever, as I promised David your father when I said, 'You shall never fail to have a man on the throne of Israel.'

⁶"But if you or your sons turn away from me and do not observe the commands and decrees I have given you and go off to serve other gods and worship them, ⁷then I will cut off Israel from the land I have given them and will reject this temple I have consecrated for my Name. Israel will then become a byword and an object of ridicule among all peoples. ⁸And though this temple is now imposing, all who pass by will be appalled and will scoff and say, 'Why has the LORD done such a thing to this land and to this temple?' ⁹People will answer, 'Because they have forsaken the LORD their God, who brought their fathers out of Egypt, and have embraced other gods, worshiping and serving them—that is why the LORD brought all this disaster on them.' "

God fills heaven and earth. Yet out of all the cities of the world God had chosen Jerusalem as the place where he would record his saving name. Here, by accepting the sacrifices of his people, God would remind them continually of *the* Lamb who would one day take away the sin of the world. That temple was and would be a special blessing for Solomon and all the people.

In this vision God spoke a conditional promise to Solomon. If Solomon would heartily confess his sins and sincerely trust in God as David did, then one of Solomon's descendants would rule over Israel forever.

In this vision God also spoke a warning. If Solomon and his sons would give their hearts to idols, then God would utterly destroy Jerusalem and the temple. The temple was built on a hill and could be seen for miles. If the temple should be destroyed, that heap of ruins would also be seen for many miles. It would silently but solemnly testify to all people that Israel had rejected her God.

Perhaps it is significant that God appeared to Solomon at the midpoint of his reign, when he had finished his building programs. There are times in our lives when we also face special dangers and need a special warning from God. Perhaps that time is when we have "finished building"—when we have finished building our church and school; when we think we have finished building our faith so that further Bible study is not necessary; when we think we have finished expanding our gospel outreach and imagine that further mission efforts are not needed; when we think that now we can sit back and relax.

At such a time God might also remind us of his blessing, how he has recorded his name also in our churches. There God came to us and put his name on us in baptism. There we hear God's saving name, the gospel of free forgiveness in the blood of the Lamb. There God offers us salvation, for "everyone who calls on the name of the LORD will be saved" (Joel 2:32). If the time comes when God's people are no longer interested in hearing or believing that word, then that word will be taken away from them and given to others. Those who have God's word must be on guard constantly lest they lose it through ingratitude.

As a matter of fact, Solomon did not fulfill the condition God proposed. But some forty years earlier God spoke a similar promise without any conditions. In 2 Samuel 7:12,13 God told David, "I will raise up your offspring to succeed you, . . . and I will establish the throne of his kingdom forever." God forgives us unconditionally for the sake of that Savior.

Solomon's Other Activities

[10]At the end of twenty years, during which Solomon built these two buildings—the temple of the LORD and the royal palace—[11]King Solomon gave twenty towns in Galilee to Hiram king of

Tyre, because Hiram had supplied him with all the cedar and pine and gold he wanted. ¹²But when Hiram went from Tyre to see the towns that Solomon had given him, he was not pleased with them. ¹³"What kind of towns are these you have given me, my brother?" he asked. And he called them the Land of Cabul, a name they have to this day. ¹⁴Now Hiram had sent to the king 120 talents of gold.

From the beginning of Solomon's reign "there were peaceful relations between Hiram and Solomon, and the two of them made a treaty" (1 Kings 5:12). King Hiram, however, did not regard Solomon's gift, a kind of readjustment of the boundary line between Israel and Phoenicia, as befitting a man of Solomon's wealth. The cities of Cabul were, it seems, later returned to Israel (2 Chronicles 8:2).

We can only wonder how God regards the size of the gifts that we present to him.

The 120 talents of gold (the NIV footnote suggests it was four and a half tons of gold) was probably a loan from Hiram to Solomon.

¹⁵Here is the account of the forced labor King Solomon conscripted to build the LORD's temple, his own palace, the supporting terraces, the wall of Jerusalem, and Hazor, Megiddo and Gezer. ¹⁶(Pharaoh king of Egypt had attacked and captured Gezer. He had set it on fire. He killed its Canaanite inhabitants and then gave it as a wedding gift to his daughter, Solomon's wife. ¹⁷And Solomon rebuilt Gezer.) He built up Lower Beth Horon, ¹⁸Baalath, and Tadmor in the desert, within his land, ¹⁹as well as all his store cities and the towns for his chariots and for his horses—whatever he desired to build in Jerusalem, in Lebanon and throughout all the territory he ruled.

²⁰All the people left from the Amorites, Hittites, Perizzites, Hivites and Jebusites (these people were not Israelites), ²¹that is, their descendants remaining in the land, whom the Israelites could not exterminate—these Solomon conscripted for his slave labor force, as it is to this day. ²²But Solomon did not make slaves

of any of the Israelites; they were his fighting men, his government officials, his officers, his captains, and the commanders of his chariots and charioteers. 23They were also the chief officials in charge of Solomon's projects—550 officials supervising the men who did the work.

In order to defend his land against foreign attacks, Solomon fortified strategic towns. They included Hazor in northern Galilee, which controlled the invasion corridor from the north; Megiddo, which controlled the invasion route from the northwest along the plain of Jezreel; Gezer and Beth Horon, which controlled the most direct approaches to Jerusalem from the west; Baalath, in the neighborhood of the Philistine country; and Tadmor, an oasis north of Damascus. (We will hear more about Megiddo later.)

Other cities were used to store food supplies and as military outposts.

God's original command to Israel was to destroy all the heathen in the land of Palestine. But even in the time of Solomon that order had not been fully carried out. On the basis of Joshua's precedent (Joshua 9:21) these heathen were forced to perform menial labor.

24After Pharaoh's daughter had come up from the City of David to the palace Solomon had built for her, he constructed the supporting terraces.

25Three times a year Solomon sacrificed burnt offerings and fellowship offerings on the altar he had built for the LORD, burning incense before the LORD along with them, and so fulfilled the temple obligations.

26King Solomon also built ships at Ezion Geber, which is near Elath in Edom, on the shore of the Red Sea. 27And Hiram sent his men—sailors who knew the sea—to serve in the fleet with Solomon's men. 28They sailed to Ophir and brought back 240 talents of gold, which they delivered to King Solomon.

The three festivals referred to in verse 25 apparently are Passover, Pentecost, and the Feast of Tabernacles (Deuteronomy 16:16).

We are not able to identify Ophir with absolute certainty. It may have been in southern Arabia, eastern Africa, or even India. We do know, however, that the amount of gold Solomon's sailors brought to him from that area was enormous. The NIV footnote suggests that 420 talents is the equivalent of sixteen tons.

The spiritual riches we Christians enjoy in Jesus Christ are likewise beyond description.

Solomon's great wealth and wisdom did not remain a secret. Soon "the whole world sought audience with Solomon to hear the wisdom God had put in his heart"(verse 24). Among the dignitaries who traveled to Jerusalem was the queen of Sheba.

The Queen of Sheba Visits Solomon

10 **When the queen of Sheba heard about the fame of Solomon and his relation to the name of the LORD, she came to test him with hard questions. ²Arriving at Jerusalem with a very great caravan—with camels carrying spices, large quantities of gold, and precious stones—she came to Solomon and talked with him about all that she had on her mind. ³Solomon answered all her questions; nothing was too hard for the king to explain to her. ⁴When the queen of Sheba saw all the wisdom of Solomon and the palace he had built, ⁵the food on his table, the seating of his officials, the attending servants in their robes, his cupbearers, and the burnt offerings he made at the temple of the LORD, she was overwhelmed.**

⁶She said to the king, "The report I heard in my own country about your achievements and your wisdom is true. ⁷But I did not believe these things until I came and saw with my own eyes. Indeed, not even half was told me; in wisdom and wealth you have far exceeded the report I heard. ⁸How happy your men must be! How happy your officials, who continually stand before you and

Solomon and the Queen of Sheba (1 Kings 10:1)

hear your wisdom! ⁹Praise be to the LORD your God, who has delighted in you and placed you on the throne of Israel. Because of the LORD's eternal love for Israel, he has made you king, to maintain justice and righteousness."
¹⁰And she gave the king 120 talents of gold, large quantities of spices, and precious stones. Never again were so many spices brought in as those the queen of Sheba gave to King Solomon.

"Sheba" is sometimes used as a name for southern Egypt. For several reasons some historians are convinced that the queen of Sheba is none other than Hatshepsut, the famous Egyptian female pharaoh. This would make her a half-sister of Solomon's wife and might explain why she received such a cordial reception in Jerusalem. When she returned to Egypt, Hatshepsut described in detail her journey to "Punt" (Palestine). Her temple at Deir al Bahari was as close a copy of Solomon's temple in dimensions and in detail as circumstances permitted.

The queen brought along some "hard questions," literally, some "riddles," to see whether the stories about Solomon's wisdom were really true. Apparently she wanted to match wits with the king.

We can be certain that Solomon and the queen discussed more than politics. They surely also discussed spiritual matters. On the one hand, the queen opened her heart to Solomon and told him "all that she had on her mind." On the other hand, when Solomon talked about wisdom, he had in mind first of all spiritual matters. For Solomon "the fear of the LORD is the beginning of wisdom" (Proverbs 9:10).

The footnote at verse 5 in the NIV informs us that it is difficult to determine whether the Hebrew word used here, which literally means "a going up," refers to a stairway by which Solomon went up to the temple (KJV) or to the sacrifices which Solomon offered up to God. In either case it was Solomon's worship of the Lord in the temple that impressed the queen.

Before she returned home, the queen gave Solomon a token of her appreciation. The 120 talents of gold, the precious stones, and the huge amount of spices were worth millions of dollars. Obviously the giver ruled over a rich country.

More important, however, is the queen's attitude toward Israel's Savior-God and his word. Before leaving Jerusalem, she acclaimed the good fortune of Solomon's servants who daily had the privilege of hearing his words of divine wisdom. A thousand years later the greatest descendant of King David would echo those words by saying, "Blessed are they that hear the word of God and keep it" (Luke 11:28 KJV).

The words of the queen and the words of our Savior lead us to conclude that the queen of Sheba left Jerusalem as a believer in the Lord. In Matthew 12:42 the Savior says, "The Queen of the South will rise at the judgment with this generation and condemn it; for she came from the ends of the earth to listen to Solomon's wisdom, and now one greater than Solomon is here." The queen of Sheba traveled over a thousand miles to hear God's wisdom from the lips of Solomon. The Pharisees on the other hand were privileged to see the Son of God face to face but rejected the words which came from his lips. When God rejects those unbelievers on the last day, the queen of Sheba will be there to testify that God's sentence of condemnation is just.

As Christians we also possess divine wisdom. We have learned the Holy Scriptures, which are able to make us "wise for salvation through faith in Christ Jesus" (2 Timothy 3:15). Just as Solomon shared that wisdom with the Gentile queen from Sheba, so God wants us to share our divine wisdom with Gentiles throughout the world. Through Isaiah God foretold that many will come from Sheba and from other Gentile lands (Isaiah 60:6). They will hear the gospel.

They will bring gold and incense as gifts. They will return home praising the name of the Lord. The queen of Sheba and the wise men from the East are fulfillments of that prophecy. Christian mission fields throughout the world are a continuing fulfillment.

The remainder of the chapter describes Solomon's great wealth.

[11] (Hiram's ships brought gold from Ophir; and from there they brought great cargoes of almugwood and precious stones. [12] The king used the almugwood to make supports for the temple of the LORD and for the royal palace, and to make harps and lyres for the musicians. So much almugwood has never been imported or seen since that day.)

[13] King Solomon gave the queen of Sheba all she desired and asked for, besides what he had given her out of his royal bounty. Then she left and returned with her retinue to her own country.

Wood was not so common in Palestine as it is where most of us live today. Wood for building had to be imported. Cedar wood came from Lebanon to the north (verse 27). The almug tree may be the red sandalwood from India and Sri Lanka. Solomon used it not only as a building material but also to make instruments for the temple musicians.

Solomon's Splendor

[14] The weight of the gold that Solomon received yearly was 666 talents, [15] not including the revenues from merchants and traders and from all the Arabian kings and the governors of the land.

[16] King Solomon made two hundred large shields of hammered gold; six hundred bekas of gold went into each shield. [17] He also made three hundred small shields of hammered gold, with three minas of gold in each shield. The king put them in the Palace of the Forest of Lebanon.

¹⁸Then the king made a great throne inlaid with ivory and overlaid with fine gold. ¹⁹The throne had six steps, and its back had a rounded top. On both sides of the seat were armrests, with a lion standing beside each of them. ²⁰Twelve lions stood on the six steps, one at either end of each step. Nothing like it had ever been made for any other kingdom. ²¹All King Solomon's goblets were gold, and all the household articles in the Palace of the Forest of Lebanon were pure gold. Nothing was considered of little value in Solomon's days. ²²The king had a fleet of trading ships at sea along with the ships of Hiram. Once every three years it returned, carrying gold, silver and ivory, and apes and baboons.

²³King Solomon was greater in riches and wisdom than all the other kings of the earth. ²⁴The whole world sought audience with Solomon to hear the wisdom God had put in his heart. ²⁵Year after year, everyone who came brought a gift—articles of silver and gold, robes, weapons and spices, and horses and mules.

The amount of gold that came to Jerusalem each year from Ophir (cf. 1 Kings 9:28), from tariffs, as tribute from conquered kings, and from Solomon's governors staggers our imagination. The footnote in the NIV suggests that 666 talents are about twenty-five tons. Israel became one of the wealthiest states in the world. No wonder silver was accounted as being of little value! No wonder the queen of Sheba was impressed!

As we marvel at Solomon's splendor, we dare not forget that all of this came from God. When Solomon asked for wisdom, God answered by promising him not only wisdom but riches and power as well. God kept his promise.

We can only wonder what the queen of Sheba might think of the wealth that we enjoy. Even the oldest car on our streets would look impressive when compared to the camel caravan that brought her to Jerusalem. The crowded restaurants, the heaps of food on the salad bars and serving tables, the truckloads of fresh fruits and vegetables, the canned and frozen food that we see every day would again leave her speechless. Our wealth also has come from God as a fulfillment of his promise. Jesus said that when God's people seek his kingdom and his righteousness, our heavenly Father will give us food, clothing, and shelter. May we also, like the one thankful leper, acknowledge God as the giver of every good gift!

Even great earthly riches, however, are nothing when compared to the heavenly treasure, the forgiveness of sins, that is ours in Christ.

Tragically much of the gold that Solomon brought to Jerusalem was later paid to heathen kings who threatened to destroy Judah.

26 Solomon accumulated chariots and horses; he had fourteen hundred chariots and twelve thousand horses, which he kept in the chariot cities and also with him in Jerusalem. 27 The king made silver as common in Jerusalem as stones, and cedar as plentiful as sycamore-fig trees in the foothills. 28 Solomon's horses were imported from Egypt and from Kue—the royal merchants purchased them from Kue. 29 They imported a chariot from Egypt for six hundred shekels of silver, and a horse for a hundred and fifty. They also exported them to all the kings of the Hittites and of the Arameans.

Solomon was also concerned about strengthening his military power. Egypt was the great exporter of horses and chariots at the time. Solomon seems to have been their best customer.

We have a problem in verse 28. According to the modern translations "Kue" is the name of a place, probably a border town between Egypt and Palestine where the trading took place. The older versions, however, translate this Hebrew word either "linen yarn" (KJV) or "troop," referring to a troop of horses.

In Deuteronomy 17:16 God strictly forbade the kings of Israel to acquire large numbers of horses lest they begin to trust in their own might rather than in the Lord. Thus the impressive description of Solomon's wealth here in chapter 10 ends on a dissonant note and serves as a prelude to the sins and troubles described in chapter 11.

Up until this time we have read only good things about King Solomon. God appeared to him and blessed him with wisdom. God permitted him to build the temple and chose Solomon to write several portions of the Scripture. Against this background the actions recorded in this chapter are surprising and shocking, for Solomon despised God's blessings and actually began to behave worse than a heathen.

The Rejection (11:1-43)

Solomon's Wives

11 King Solomon, however, loved many foreign women besides Pharaoh's daughter—Moabites, Ammonites, Edomites, Sidonians and Hittites. ²They were from nations about which the LORD had told the Israelites, "You must not intermarry with them, because they will surely turn your hearts after their gods." Nevertheless, Solomon held fast to them in love. ³He had seven hundred wives of royal birth and three hundred concubines, and his wives led him astray. ⁴As Solomon grew old, his wives turned his heart after other gods, and his heart was not fully devoted to the LORD his God, as the heart of David his father had been. ⁵He followed Ashtoreth the goddess of the Sidonians, and Molech the detestable god of the Ammonites. ⁶So Solomon did evil in the eyes of the LORD; he did not follow the LORD completely, as David his father had done.

⁷On a hill east of Jerusalem, Solomon built a high place for Chemosh the detestable god of Moab, and for Molech the detestable god of the Ammonites. ⁸He did the same for all his foreign wives, who burned incense and offered sacrifices to their gods.

⁹The Lord became angry with Solomon because his heart had turned away from the Lord, the God of Israel, who had appeared to him twice. ¹⁰Although he had forbidden Solomon to follow other gods, Solomon did not keep the Lord's command. ¹¹So the Lord said to Solomon, "Since this is your attitude and you have not kept my covenant and my decrees, which I commanded you, I will most certainly tear the kingdom away from you and give it to one of your subordinates. ¹²Nevertheless, for the sake of David your father, I will not do it during your lifetime. I will tear it out of the hand of your son. ¹³Yet I will not tear the whole kingdom from him, but will give him one tribe for the sake of David my servant and for the sake of Jerusalem, which I have chosen."

At the creation God announced that in marriage one man and one woman would become one flesh for life (Genesis 2:24). Before his people entered the land of Canaan, God warned them not to intermarry with the heathen (Exodus 34:16). Solomon ignored God's warning and despised the sanctity of marriage.

These sinful actions were not pleasing to God. They brought about great spiritual harm, to say nothing of the family problems which inevitably followed.

In Exodus 34:16 God had said, "When you choose some of their daughters as wives for your sons and those daughters prostitute themselves to their gods, they will lead your sons to do the same." God was right. Solomon began to worship heathen gods.

Medal of Ashtoreth (1 Kings 11:15)

One of these goddesses was Ashtoreth, or Astarte. She is pictured with the horns of a bull protruding from her head.

Her picture is also surrounded by stars since she was worshiped as "the queen of heaven." It is possible that the people also worshiped the moon under the name Ashtoreth.

Milcom (or Molech) and Chemosh are two other gods who were worshiped by Israel's heathen neighbors. Children were offered to these gods as burnt sacrifices. "Milcom" is similar to the Hebrew word for "king." Instead of worshiping the Lord as King and Creator of the universe, Solomon now gave that honor to this detestable idol.

At first the heathen altars at Jerusalem were only for the convenience of Solomon's heathen wives. But in verse 5 we see Solomon himself taking part in the worship, and in verse 33 we see the Israelites also giving themselves to these idols.

Look ahead to verse 33. David kept God's statutes and ordinances. This does not mean that he was perfect. It means that he had regard for God's word. David let God's word define sin, and he believed God's words and promises regarding the coming of a Savior from sin. Solomon, unfortunately, no longer shared the attitude of his father. He did not pay attention to God's "statutes and laws." He ignored the warning God gave in chapter 9:4,5. When Solomon left God's word, he began to serve false gods. The two go hand in hand.

It is difficult to believe that the man who once wrote, "The fear of the LORD is the beginning of wisdom" (Proverbs 9:10), should fall so deeply into idolatry.

God's people sometimes make the same combination of mistakes today. Many of God's people consider the hearing of God's word to be of little importance. Many Christian men and women declare that marrying a heathen will not affect their faith. When that attitude prevails, God's people are in danger of becoming idolaters just like King Solomon.

"From everyone who has been given much, much will be demanded" (Luke 12:48). God will not continue to bless those who rebel against him. Solomon's family would not continue to rule all twelve tribes of Israel. After Solomon's death ten of the tribes would be given to a man named Jeroboam. To show his displeasure with Solomon's idolatry and to call the king to repentance, God now raised up adversaries who threatened to disrupt Solomon's reign of peace.

Solomon's Adversaries

¹⁴Then the LORD raised up against Solomon an adversary, Hadad the Edomite, from the royal line of Edom. ¹⁵Earlier when David was fighting with Edom, Joab the commander of the army, who had gone up to bury the dead, had struck down all the men in Edom. ¹⁶Joab and all the Israelites stayed there for six months, until they had destroyed all the men in Edom. ¹⁷But Hadad, still only a boy, fled to Egypt with some Edomite officials who had served his father. ¹⁸They set out from Midian and went to Paran. Then taking men from Paran with them, they went to Egypt, to Pharaoh king of Egypt, who gave Hadad a house and land and provided him with food.

¹⁹Pharaoh was so pleased with Hadad that he gave him a sister of his own wife, Queen Tahpenes, in marriage. ²⁰The sister of Tahpenes bore him a son named Genubath, whom Tahpenes brought up in the royal palace. There Genubath lived with Pharaoh's own children.

²¹While he was in Egypt, Hadad heard that David rested with his fathers and that Joab the commander of the army was also dead. Then Hadad said to Pharaoh, "Let me go, that I may return to my own country."

²²"What have you lacked here that you want to go back to your own country?" Pharaoh asked.

"Nothing," Hadad replied, "but do let me go!"

In 2 Samuel 8:14 we read how David defeated Edom (south of the Dead Sea) and put garrisons throughout the land. Although he was only a boy at the time, Hadad escaped. After staying for a while in the Wilderness of Paran (west of Edom in the Sinai Peninsula), he and some of his men lived as exiles in Egypt.

When David and Joab were dead, Hadad returned to his homeland. He had personal reasons to seek revenge against the people of Jerusalem. According to Josephus, a Jewish secular historian, he then went up north to Aram where he became a friend of Rezon, a second adversary of Solomon.

23 And God raised up against Solomon another adversary, Rezon son of Eliada, who had fled from his master, Hadadezer king of Zobah. 24He gathered men around him and became the leader of a band of rebels when David destroyed the forces ⌊of Zobah⌋ ; the rebels went to Damascus, where they settled and took control. 25Rezon was Israel's adversary as long as Solomon lived, adding to the trouble caused by Hadad. So Rezon ruled in Aram and was hostile toward Israel.

In 2 Samuel 10:6-14 we read how David and Joab defeated the Syrians of Zobah, north of Damascus. At the time when Hadad came to Aram, Rezon, who hailed from Zobah, was leading a band of robbers.

It is likely that when Rezon died, Hadad became the chief ruler of Aram, for the kings of Aram who gave Israel trouble later on are called "Ben-Hadad," that is, "Son of Hadad."

Those who are familiar with the King James Bible will note that the NIV translators do not use the name "Syria." Actually, Syria was the later name of the country which was Israel's neighbor to the north, whose capital is Damascus. That country's name during the centuries of the Old Testament was Aram. "Aram" is the word from which we get the word "Aramaic," a language similar to Hebrew spoken in many areas throughout the ancient world. Parts of the books of Ezra and Daniel are written in Aramaic.

Jeroboam Rebels Against Solomon

²⁶Also, Jeroboam son of Nebat rebelled against the king. He was one of Solomon's officials, an Ephraimite from Zeredah, and his mother was a widow named Zeruah.

²⁷Here is the account of how he rebelled against the king: Solomon had built the supporting terraces and had filled in the gap in the wall of the city of David his father. ²⁸Now Jeroboam was a man of standing, and when Solomon saw how well the young man did his work, he put him in charge of the whole labor force of the house of Joseph.

²⁹About that time Jeroboam was going out of Jerusalem, and Ahijah the prophet of Shiloh met him on the way, wearing a new cloak. The two of them were alone out in the country, ³⁰and Ahijah took hold of the new cloak he was wearing and tore it into twelve pieces. ³¹Then he said to Jeroboam, "Take ten pieces for yourself, for this is what the LORD, the God of Israel, says: 'See, I am going to tear the kingdom out of Solomon's hand and give you ten tribes. ³²But for the sake of my servant David and the city of Jerusalem, which I have chosen out of all the tribes of Israel, he will have one tribe. ³³I will do this because they have forsaken me and worshiped Ashtoreth the goddess of the Sidonians, Chemosh the god of the Moabites, and Molech the god of the Ammonites, and have not walked in my ways, nor done what is right in my eyes, nor kept my statutes and laws as David, Solomon's father, did.

³⁴" 'But I will not take the whole kingdom out of Solomon's hand; I have made him ruler all the days of his life for the sake of David my servant, whom I chose and who observed my commands and statutes. ³⁵I will take the kingdom from his son's hands and give you ten tribes. ³⁶I will give one tribe to his son so that David my servant may always have a lamp before me in Jerusalem, the city where I chose to put my Name. ³⁷However, as for you, I will take you, and you will rule over all that your heart desires; you will be king over Israel. ³⁸If you do whatever I command you and walk in my ways and do what is right in my eyes by keeping my statutes and commands, as David my servant

did, I will be with you. I will build you a dynasty as enduring as the one I built for David and will give Israel to you. ³⁹I will humble David's descendants because of this, but not forever.' "
⁴⁰Solomon tried to kill Jeroboam, but Jeroboam fled to Egypt, to Shishak the king, and stayed there until Solomon's death.

Solomon's third adversary was Jeroboam. He was an industrious man who supervised the work of strengthening the walls of Jerusalem and building the supporting terraces (the King James Version calls it "the Millo," verse 28), that is, the fortress in Jerusalem. In graphic fashion God's prophet Ahijah showed him that he would one day rule over ten of Israel's twelve tribes.

When God's people turn their backs on his word, when they bring their incense and their offerings to false gods, when they no longer want to do the work their Lord gives to them, then the Lord chooses others to carry out his plans.

Solomon's sons would continue to rule one (actually two) of the tribes, the tribe of Judah and the much smaller tribe of Benjamin.

It is important to note the reason for God's actions. Ten tribes were given to Jeroboam because of Solomon's unfaithfulness. Two tribes would remain with the family of Solomon "for the sake of my servant David and the city of Jerusalem, which I have chosen" (verse 32). Fifty years earlier God had told David that one of his descendants would be a King who would rule forever. That King is the Lord Jesus, who was born to the Virigin Mary. Despite, Solomon's unfaithfulness, God would fulfill his promise. Two tribes would remain with Solomon's family "so that David my servant may always have a lamp before me in Jerusalem, the city where I chose to put my Name" (verse 36). David's "lamp," that is, David's influence in Jerusalem, would not be extinguished until the "Light of the world" himself would come to Jerusalem. In this city of Jerusalem, where God chose to put his Name, the Messiah would teach, perform miracles, die and rise again.

Solomon was unfaithful to God; but the Lord would *never* be unfaithful to his promises. "If we are faithless, he will remain faithful, for he cannot disown himself" (2 Timothy 2:13).

Just as God blessed an undeserving Solomon "for the sake of David my servant," so the Lord blesses us undeserving individuals for the sake of Jesus, great David's greater Son. For Jesus's sake God loves us, forgives us, and grants us eternal life.

Solomon tried to kill Jeroboam just as he had killed other men who threatened his power. But God would not permit it.

We will meet the prophet Ahijah again in chapter 14. There he condemned Jeroboam's idolatry and announced the extinction of the new king's family.

Solomon's Death

⁴¹As for the other events of Solomon's reign—all he did and the wisdom he displayed—are they not written in the book of the annals of Solomon? ⁴²Solomon reigned in Jerusalem over all Israel forty years. ⁴³Then he rested with his fathers and was buried in the city of David his father. And Rehoboam his son succeeded him as king.

Did Solomon ever repent of his idolatry? Many Christians read this peaceful account of his death and burial and conclude that he did. Many view the Book of Ecclesiastes as Solomon's hymn of repentance. However the Scripture nowhere tells us specifically that we will see Solomon at the Lord's right hand on judgment day.

What a warning for us! If even a man like Solomon can fall away at least for a time; if even a man like the Apostle

Paul can mention the possibility of being "disqualified for the prize" (1 Corinthians 9:27), then faithful Christians today and the children of faithful Christians are capable of making that same tragic mistake. There is no such thing as "too much Christian education" or "too much Christian training" for our children. There are no fathers or mothers who pray too much or too often for their children.

"Train a child in the way he should go, and when he is old he will not turn from it" (Proverbs 22:6). This is the general rule, but here and there we find an exception. Solomon may have been one of them.

"The book of the annals of Solomon" is a secular record that has been lost. It seems to have been one in a series of books of official records later referred to as "The Book of the Chronicles of the Kings of Israel (or Judah)."

PART II

THE KINGS OF ISRAEL REJECT THE **KING** WHO DESIRED TO BLESS THEM
1 KINGS 12:1-22:53

For seventy-three years Israel and Judah had been united under the rulership of David and then Solomon. Now that united kingdom was about to become a divided kingdom.

Jeroboam

Israel Rebels Against Rehoboam

12 Rehoboam went to Shechem, for all the Israelites had gone there to make him king. ²When Jeroboam son of Nebat heard this (he was still in Egypt, where he had fled from King Solomon), he returned from Egypt. ³So they sent for Jeroboam, and he and the whole assembly of Israel went to Rehoboam and said to him: ⁴"Your father put a heavy yoke on us, but now lighten the harsh labor and the heavy yoke he put on us, and we will serve you."

⁵Rehoboam answered, "Go away for three days and then come back to me." So the people went away.

The city of Shechem, in the dead center of the land of Canaan, had an important history. Nestled in the valley between Mount Gerizim and Mount Ebal, it is the place where Abraham stopped when he entered the promised land of Canaan and built an altar to the Lord (Genesis 12:6,7). It is also the place where Joshua assembled the Israelites and encouraged them once again to serve the Lord faithfully (Joshua 24). At this central location some thirty miles north of Jerusalem Solomon's son Rehoboam planned a festive coronation and anointing.

The people of Israel, however, wanted to settle one item first, the matter of taxation and forced labor. Solomon had hundreds of household servants. It took a lot of money to support them. Solomon had carried on an extensive building program in Jerusalem. That required a large labor force and a lot of tax money. According to chapter 5:13 Solomon had 30,000 Israelite men working in the lumber camps in Lebanon. These men worked only one month out of three, but they had become tired of donating their services to the king. Remember also that Solomon had 1,000 wives. It takes a lot of money to support a family that size. According to 1 Kings 4:22,23 Solomon's provisions for a single day included 300 bushels of fine flour, 30 oxen, and 100 sheep.

6 Then King Rehoboam consulted the elders who had served his father Solomon during his lifetime. "How would you advise me to answer these people?" he asked.

7 They replied, "If today you will be a servant to these people and serve them and give them a favorable answer, they will always be your servants."

8 But Rehoboam rejected the advice the elders gave him and consulted the young men who had grown up with him and were serving him. 9 He asked them, "What is your advice? How should we answer these people who say to me, 'Lighten the yoke your father put on us'? "

10 The young men who had grown up with him replied, "Tell these people who have said to you, 'Your father put a heavy yoke on us, but make our yoke lighter'—tell them, 'My little finger is thicker than my father's waist. 11 My father laid on you a heavy yoke; I will make it even heavier. My father scourged you with whips; I will scourge you with scorpions.' "

Discussing matters with the older men, the fathers, is generally a wise idea (Proverbs 4:1). Happy is the congregation that has elders who have a lifetime of Bible study and Christian service behind them, elders who are happy to share their wisdom and counsel with the pastor and others.

But the younger men suggested a different answer. They said, "Tell them, 'My father used an ordinary whip to keep you people in line but I will use a whip that stings like a scorpion.' "

¹²Three days later Jeroboam and all the people returned to Rehoboam, as the king had said, "Come back to me in three days." ¹³The king answered the people harshly. Rejecting the advice given him by the elders, ¹⁴he followed the advice of the young men and said, "My father made your yoke heavy; I will make it even heavier. My father scourged you with whips; I will scourge you with scorpions." ¹⁵So the king did not listen to the people, for this turn of events was from the LORD, to fulfill the word the LORD had spoken to Jeroboam son of Nebat through Ahijah the Shilonite.

¹⁶When all Israel saw that the king refused to listen to them, they answered the king:

"What share do we have in David,
what part in Jesse's son?
To your tents, O Israel!
Look after your own house,
O David!"

So the Israelites went home. ¹⁷But as for the Israelites who were living in the towns of Judah, Rehoboam still ruled over them.

Rehoboam should have known better. He was already forty-one years old (1 Kings 14:21). His own father had written, "A gentle answer turns away wrath, but a harsh word stirs up anger" (Proverbs 15:1). Unfortunately, Rehoboam ignored the advice of the fathers and looked at himself as a master who could demand whatever he wanted. He viewed the people as though their only purpose in life was to serve him.

By taking the advice of the young men, Rehoboam showed himself to be a ruler totally unlike our Savior. The

Lord Jesus once said to the people, "Come to me, all you who are weary and burdened, and I will give you rest. Take my yoke upon you and learn from me, for I am gentle and humble in heart, and you will find rest for your souls. For my yoke is easy and my burden is light" (Matthew 11:28-30).

Perhaps we can think of a time or two when we gave our parents a harsh answer, a time when we talked back to a teacher, a time when we lost our temper. Perhaps we husbands can think of a time or two when we abused our headship in the home, viewing ourselves as lords and masters, viewing the other family members as servants who exist only to please the man. Perhaps we can think of times when our harsh words to fellow Christians did nothing at all to "keep the unity of the Spirit" (Ephesians 4:3) in the church but served only to anger others and to divide the body.

The Lord Jesus is our greatest example of patience. When he was abused, he did not retaliate. Instead he prayed, "Father, forgive them." May that same Lord forgive the sins of our tongues also!

In Rehoboam's case the result was a bloodless revolution. With the words, "To your tents, O Israel!" the ten northern tribes prepared to go back home to establish an independent nation of their own.

But God used even the foolish answer of Rehoboam and the rebellious attitude of the people to accomplish what he had foretold. *God* had made Solomon king and had given him power and glory (1 Chronicles 29:25). When Solomon began to turn away from the Lord, it was *God* who raised up adversaries against him. Now *God* was taking ten of the twelve tribes away from Rehoboam.

Politicians do not control world history today either. God does. If God's people today decide they no longer want to give their hearts to their Lord, then God may well remove from our midst the national freedoms, the personal blessings, and even the religious blessings and opportunities that we enjoy.

The tribe of Judah remained faithful to Rehoboam. This also was part of God's plan, for the Messiah would be born from this tribe. Rehoboam himself would be one of the Savior's ancestors. In all things God continues to work "for the good of those who love him" (Romans 8:28).

18 King Rehoboam sent out Adoniram, who was in charge of forced labor, but all Israel stoned him to death. King Rehoboam, however, managed to get into his chariot and escape to Jerusalem. 19 So Israel has been in rebellion against the house of David to this day.

20 When all the Israelites heard that Jeroboam had returned, they sent and called him to the assembly and made him king over all Israel. Only the tribe of Judah remained loyal to the house of David.

21 When Rehoboam arrived in Jerusalem, he mustered the whole house of Judah and the tribe of Benjamin—a hundred and eighty thousand fighting men—to make war against the house of Israel and to regain the kingdom for Rehoboam son of Solomon.

22 But this word of God came to Shemaiah the man of God: 23 "Say to Rehoboam son of Solomon king of Judah, to the whole house of Judah and Benjamin, and to the rest of the people, 24 'This is what the LORD says: Do not go up to fight against your brothers, the Israelites. Go home, every one of you, for this is my doing.'" So they obeyed the word of the LORD and went home again, as the LORD had ordered.

Adoniram is the man Solomon had appointed over the forced labor forty years earlier. When the rebels stoned him to death, Rehoboam hurried to his chariot (without much royal ceremony, it seems) and fled to Jerusalem.

To his credit Rehoboam submitted to the word of God spoken by the prophet Shemaiah and sent his soldiers back home.

91

This division into a northern and a southern kingdom continued until the time when our inspired author wrote this account, that is, until 586 B.C., when the Jews were carried into captivity in Babylon.

Golden Calves at Bethel and Dan

²⁵Then Jeroboam fortified Shechem in the hill country of Ephraim and lived there. From there he went out and built up Peniel.

²⁶Jeroboam thought to himself, "The kingdom will now likely revert to the house of David. ²⁷If these people go up to offer sacrifices at the temple of the LORD in Jerusalem, they will again give their allegiance to their lord, Rehoboam king of Judah. They will kill me and return to King Rehoboam."

²⁸After seeking advice, the king made two golden calves. He said to the people, "It is too much for you to go up to Jerusalem. Here are your gods, O Israel, who brought you up out of Egypt." ²⁹One he set up in Bethel, and the other in Dan. ³⁰And this thing became a sin; the people went even as far as Dan to worship the one there.

³¹Jeroboam built shrines on high places and appointed priests from all sorts of people, even though they were not Levites. ³²He instituted a festival on the fifteenth day of the eighth month, like the festival held in Judah, and offered sacrifices on the altar. This he did in Bethel, sacrificing to the calves he had made. And at Bethel he also installed priests at the high places he had made. ³³On the fifteenth day of the eighth month, a month of his own choosing, he offered sacrifices on the altar he had built at Bethel. So he instituted the festival for the Israelites and went up to the altar to make offerings.

Jeroboam's first act as the new leader of the northern tribes was to solidify control over his people. He chose to locate his headquarters at Shechem, where the Israelites had met earlier with Rehoboam. Not only does Shechem enjoy a central location, but it is known for its many springs of water and for its abundance of fruit trees. Jacob's well is also at Shechem, the place where Jesus later talked to the woman of Samaria. Jeroboam rebuilt the city that had been there. He also rebuilt Penuel (or, Peniel). This is about twenty-five miles directly east of Shechem on the other side of the Jordan River. It is the place where Jacob had wrestled with the angel (Genesis 32:30).

Fortifications, however, could not command the hearts of the people. Since the temple was in Jerusalem and since Jerusalem was not part of Jeroboam's territory, Jeroboam decided to make certain changes in the religious laws and practices of the people.

Bethel and Dan were located at the southern and northern ends of Jeroboam's kingdom. By asking the people to worship here, he was contradicting God, who had chosen to place the temple in Jerusalem. By asking the people to worship golden calves, he was breaking the first commandment. By ordaining priests from outside the tribe of Levi, Jeroboam rejected the plan God had established at Mount Sinai. By asking the people to celebrate the Feast of Tabernacles on the fifteenth day of the *eighth* month instead of the fifteenth day of the *seventh* month, the king again contradicted God's clear instructions.

Jeroboam, however, did not view his innovations as idolatry. When the calves were finished, he announced, "Here are your gods, O Israel, who brought you up out of Egypt." Jeroboam's religion claimed to offer the same blessings as the old religion. Jeroboam viewed his religion as a progressive step, for it eliminated the need for the Israelites in the north to make the long journey to Jerusalem.

God, however, viewed Jeroboam's religion as a sin. God says through the prophet Hosea, "Throw out your calf-idol, O Samaria! . . . a craftsman has made it; it is not God" (Hosea 8:5,6).

93

In our day many are still tampering with God's word. They talk about "creation," but they do not believe that God made all things out of nothing in six ordinary days. They talk about "salvation," but they are thinking about how people might be saved from poverty and from political oppression. Because they give new definitions to old, familiar terms, they may be hard to recognize. They are wolves in sheep's clothing.

Others suggest ways to make the Bible easier for people to accept. They suggest that we not talk so much about sin or that we change our "close communion" practice.

To all of these suggestions and new definitions God says no. If people worship a false god like Buddha or Allah, they are committing idolatry. If people tamper with God's word and worship a god different from the one revealed in Scriptures, they are committing idolatry.

God did not turn his back on Jeroboam and the people of the northern kingdom. The prophet Amos warned the people: "Jeroboam will die by the sword, and Israel will surely go into exile" (Amos 7:11). Here an unidentified man of God came from Judah with another warning.

The Man of God From Judah

13 **By the word of the LORD a man of God came from Judah to Bethel, as Jeroboam was standing by the altar to make an offering. ²He cried out against the altar by the word of the LORD: "O altar, altar! This is what the LORD says: 'A son named Josiah will be born to the house of David. On you he will sacrifice the priests of the high places who now make offerings here, and human bones will be burned on you.' "³That same day the man of God gave a sign: "This is the sign the LORD has declared: The altar will be split apart and the ashes on it will be poured out."**

⁴When King Jeroboam heard what the man of God cried out against the altar at Bethel, he stretched out his hand from the altar

and said, "Seize him!" But the hand he stretched out toward the man shriveled up, so that he could not pull it back. ⁵Also, the altar was split apart and its ashes poured out according to the sign given by the man of God by the word of the LORD.

⁶Then the king said to the man of God, "Intercede with the LORD your God and pray for me that my hand may be restored." So the man of God interceded with the LORD, and the king's hand was restored and became as it was before.

⁷The king said to the man of God, "Come home with me and have something to eat, and I will give you a gift."

⁸But the man of God answered the king, "Even if you were to give me half your possessions, I would not go with you, nor would I eat bread or drink water here. ⁹For I was commanded by the word of the LORD: 'You must not eat bread or drink water or return by the way you came.' "¹⁰So he took another road and did not return by the way he had come to Bethel.

This unidentified man of God foretold even the name of the king who would inflict God's judgment. It would be Josiah, a man who would reign over Judah some 300 years later. We will read the fulfillment of this prophecy in 2 Kings 23:15,16.

This is not the only time a prophet foretold the name of a man who had not yet been born. In Isaiah 44:28 God's prophet foretold the name of Cyrus, the Persian king who would permit the Jews to return home from their captivity in Babylon.

When idolatrous King Jeroboam became angry, God did not permit him or anyone else to lay a hand on his prophet. The calf they worshiped was a powerless idol. But the Lord is the almighty God who splits apart heathen altars and who decides when and how far heathen men may stretch out their arms against God's spokesmen.

Note that Jeroboam in his predicament did not call on the golden calf for help. He asked the prophet to call on "the

LORD your God." The Lord gave his healing even to this idolatrous king.

King Jeroboam's repentance was, however, short-lived. He, his successors, and the people in general continued to worship the golden calves throughout the history of the Northern Kingdom (see 2 Kings 17:16).

Because God's people have nothing in common with the unbelievers and because God had given specific directions to this prophet, the man of God wisely declined King Jeroboam's dinner invitation.

¹¹**Now there was a certain old prophet living in Bethel, whose sons came and told him all that the man of God had done there that day. They also told their father what he had said to the king. ¹²Their father asked them, "Which way did he go?" And his sons showed him which road the man of God from Judah had taken. ¹³So he said to his sons, "Saddle the donkey for me." And when they had saddled the donkey for him, he mounted it ¹⁴and rode after the man of God. He found him sitting under an oak tree and asked, "Are you the man of God who came from Judah?"**

"I am," he replied.

¹⁵**So the prophet said to him, "Come home with me and eat."**

¹⁶**The man of God said, "I cannot turn back and go with you, nor can I eat bread or drink water with you in this place. ¹⁷I have been told by the word of the LORD: 'You must not eat bread or drink water there or return by the way you came.' "**

¹⁸**The old prophet answered, "I too am a prophet, as you are. And an angel said to me by the word of the LORD: 'Bring him back with you to your house so that he may eat bread and drink water.' "(But he was lying to him.) ¹⁹So the man of God returned with him and ate and drank in his house.**

The context implies that this "certain old prophet" had at one time been a faithful spokesman for the true God. Perhaps he had been trained in one of Samuel's schools of the prophets. But now he acted as an enemy of God and of the truth.

The sin of the first prophet was very much like that of Adam and Eve. In each case the subjects knew God's will but deliberately acted contrary to it. Jesus, on the other hand, is our example of one who knew God's words and refused to budge from them (Matthew 4:1-11).

Some of the greatest dangers for the church today continue to come from within the visible church. The Apostle John writes that many antichrists "went out from us, but they did not really belong to us" (1 John 2:19). Today's false prophets often pose as fellow Christians. They come to us "in sheep's clothing" (Matthew 7:15). They may claim that God has spoken to them directly or through an angel. But in spite of their disguise we can recognize them, for their words contradict God's clear word.

Following the words of a false prophet does not result in a blessing. It leads only to death and judgment, as it did here.

20 While they were sitting at the table, the word of the LORD came to the old prophet who had brought him back. 21 He cried out to the man of God who had come from Judah, "This is what the LORD says: 'You have defied the word of the LORD and have not kept the command the LORD your God gave you. 22 You came back and ate bread and drank water in the place where he told you not to eat or drink. Therefore your body will not be buried in the tomb of your fathers.' "

23 When the man of God had finished eating and drinking, the prophet who had brought him back saddled his donkey for him. 24 As he went on his way, a lion met him on the road and killed him, and his body was thrown down on the road, with both the donkey and the lion standing beside it. 25 Some people who passed by saw the body thrown down there, with the lion standing beside the body, and they went and reported it in the city where the old prophet lived.

26 When the prophet who had brought him back from his journey heard of it, he said, "It is the man of God who defied the word

of the LORD. The LORD has given him over to the lion, which has mauled him and killed him, as the word of the LORD had warned him."

Because of his deliberate disobedience the man of God would suffer the disgrace of not being buried in the family plot. His death was an evident judgment from God, for the lion did not devour the man nor did the lion harm the donkey. Later others saw both the lion and the donkey standing together looking at the body of the dead prophet.

Those who disobey God's law earn death for themselves. Those who disregard the gospel message of forgiveness in Christ will suffer also the pains of eternal death.

[27] The prophet said to his sons, "Saddle the donkey for me," and they did so. [28] Then he went out and found the body thrown down on the road, with the donkey and the lion standing beside it. The lion had neither eaten the body nor mauled the donkey. [29] So the prophet picked up the body of the man of God, laid it on the donkey, and brought it back to his own city to mourn for him and bury him. [30] Then he laid the body in his own tomb, and they mourned over him and said, "Oh, my brother!"

[31] After burying him, he said to his sons, "When I die, bury me in the grave where the man of God is buried; lay my bones beside his bones. [32] For the message he declared by the word of the LORD against the altar in Bethel and against the shrines on the high places in the towns of Samaria will certainly come true."

[33] Even after this, Jeroboam did not change his evil ways, but once more appointed priests for the high places from all sorts of people. Anyone who wanted to become a priest he consecrated for the high places. [34] This was the sin of the house of Jeroboam that led to its downfall and to its destruction from the face of the earth.

The old prophet believed the warning that the bones of the false prophets would be burned on Jeroboam's altar. In order to escape that shameful judgment, he instructed his sons to bury him in the same grave with the man of God. When King Josiah carried out God's judgment 300 years later, the bones of the man of God and of the old prophet were not disturbed (2 Kings 23:18).

There is no fool like an old fool. There is no unbeliever like a hardened, old unbeliever. The miracles, the prophecies and the fulfillment of those prophecies did nothing at all to change the hardened heart of King Jeroboam. Let no one think he can postpone his repentance to a time when he is old.

Although Jeroboam worshiped idols, he did not turn to one of his golden calves or to one of his own priests when he wanted to learn the future. Instead he went to the Lord, the God who had made a covenant with Israel.

Ahijah's Prophecy Against Jeroboam

14 **At that time Abijah son of Jeroboam became ill, ²and Jeroboam said to his wife, "Go, disguise yourself, so you won't be recognized as the wife of Jeroboam. Then go to Shiloh. Ahijah the prophet is there—the one who told me I would be king over this people. ³Take ten loaves of bread with you, some cakes and a jar of honey, and go to him. He will tell you what will happen to the boy." ⁴So Jeroboam's wife did what he said and went to Ahijah's house in Shiloh.**

Now Ahijah could not see; his sight was gone because of his age. ⁵But the LORD had told Ahijah, "Jeroboam's wife is coming to ask you about her son, for he is ill, and you are to give her such and such an answer. When she arrives, she will pretend to be someone else."

"At that time," that is, at the time when King Jeroboam was living in idolatry, the king's son became ill. Because Abijah was, apparently, the heir to the throne, Jeroboam had a consuming desire to learn whether his son would recover. He hoped that Ahijah, the man who had foretold his rulership over the ten tribes, would have more good news for him.

But Jeroboam did not want to meet the prophet face to face. He did not want to be reminded again of his sin nor did he want to repent. He hoped to hear a message of good news without repentance or faith.

It may also be significant that Jeroboam sent his wife to the prophet. Like many another man who has relinquished his God-given headship, Jeroboam evidently put his wife in charge of religious matters and the welfare of the children.

Like many an unbeliever the king tried to play games with God. He pretended to be someone other than the rebellious sinner he really was. But Jeroboam's charades did not fool God. If we say that we have no sin, we deceive only ourselves. God told his aged and blind prophet exactly what to expect and what to say.

⁶So when Ahijah heard the sound of her footsteps at the door, he said, "Come in, wife of Jeroboam. Why this pretense? I have been sent to you with bad news. ⁷Go, tell Jeroboam that this is what the Lᴏʀᴅ, the God of Israel, says: 'I raised you up from among the people and made you a leader over my people Israel. ⁸I tore the kingdom away from the house of David and gave it to you, but you have not been like my servant David, who kept my commands and followed me with all his heart, doing only what was right in my eyes. ⁹You have done more evil than all who lived before you. You have made for yourself other gods, idols made of metal; you have provoked me to anger and thrust me behind your back.

¹⁰" 'Because of this, I am going to bring disaster on the house of Jeroboam. I will cut off from Jeroboam every last male in Israel—slave or free. I will burn up the house of Jeroboam as one burns dung, until it is all gone. ¹¹Dogs will eat those belonging to Jeroboam who die in the city, and the birds of the air will feed on those who die in the country. The Lᴏʀᴅ has spoken!'

¹²"As for you, go back home. When you set foot in your city, the boy will die. ¹³All Israel will mourn for him and bury him. He

is the only one belonging to Jeroboam who will be buried, because he is the only one in the house of Jeroboam in whom the LORD, the God of Israel, has found anything good. ¹⁴"The LORD will raise up for himself a king over Israel who will cut off the family of Jeroboam. This is the day! What? Yes, even now. ¹⁵And the LORD will strike Israel, so that it will be like a reed swaying in the water. He will uproot Israel from this good land that he gave to their forefathers and scatter them beyond the River, because they provoked the LORD to anger by making Asherah poles. ¹⁶And he will give Israel up because of the sins Jeroboam has committed and has caused Israel to commit."

¹⁷Then Jeroboam's wife got up and left and went to Tirzah. As soon as she stepped over the threshold of the house, the boy died. ¹⁸They buried him, and all Israel mourned for him, as the LORD had said through his servant the prophet Ahijah.

¹⁹The other events of Jeroboam's reign, his wars and how he ruled, are written in the book of the annals of the kings of Israel. ²⁰He reigned for twenty-two years and then rested with his fathers. And Nadab his son succeeded him as king.

"Come in, wife of Jeroboam. Why do you pretend to be another person?" (New KJV). God sees through every disguise of self-righteousness. That includes Adam who, clothed in fig leaves, tried to blame his wife for his predicament. It includes the Pharisee in the temple who tried to impress God with his piety. It includes the unbelievers who, even on judgment day, will continue to proclaim their innocence.

"From everyone who has been given much, much will be demanded"(Luke 12:48). God had given Jeroboam much— ten of the twelve tribes to be exact. But the king did not walk in the ways of David, who repented of his sins. Instead Jeroboam ignored God's words and lived in idolatry. Therefore God's judgment would rest on him. A future king (Baasha, as we learn in 1 Kings 15:28-30) would destroy all of Jeroboam's descendants. Jeroboam's son Abijah would die the moment his mother returned to the palace. Because the sins of Jeroboam would continue in the land, the nation of Israel would finally be carried away into captivity by the Assyrians.

Note that the death of Abijah was not a judgment against that child. It was God's judgment against Jeroboam. In his grace God took that child from this world to himself in heaven before he could begin to walk in the sins of his father. Any suggestion, however, that God might do the same with aborted or battered children today is pure speculation.

In due time God's other judgments will also be fulfilled. That includes the ones threatened in this chapter and God's final judgment on all unbelievers at the end of time.

In verse 15 we have the first reference to Asherah poles or "groves" as they are called in the King James Version. The Asherah pole evidently had the face of a female goddess carved on it. We will read more about the idolatry connected with Asherah poles in later chapters.

Verse 19 contains the first reference to "the annals of the kings." Evidently the kings of Israel and the kings of Judah kept written records describing in detail activities of their reigns. These annals (or, chronicles) were available to the readers when our books were being written, but they have disappeared long ago. They are evidently not to be equated with the Books of Chronicles in our Bible.

Rehoboam King of Judah

²¹ Rehoboam son of Solomon was king in Judah. He was forty-one years old when he became king, and he reigned seventeen years in Jerusalem, the city the LORD had chosen out of all the tribes of Israel in which to put his Name. His mother's name was Naamah; she was an Ammonite.

²² Judah did evil in the eyes of the LORD. By the sins they committed they stirred up his jealous anger more than their

fathers had done. ²³They also set up for themselves high places, sacred stones and Asherah poles on every high hill and under every spreading tree. ²⁴There were even male shrine prostitutes in the land; the people engaged in all the detestable practices of the nations the LORD had driven out before the Israelites.

²⁵In the fifth year of King Rehoboam, Shishak king of Egypt attacked Jerusalem. ²⁶He carried off the treasures of the temple of the LORD and the treasures of the royal palace. He took everything, including all the gold shields Solomon had made. ²⁷So King Rehoboam made bronze shields to replace them and assigned these to the commanders of the guard on duty at the entrance to the royal palace. ²⁸Whenever the king went to the LORD's temple, the guards bore the shields, and afterward they returned them to the guardroom.

²⁹As for the other events of Rehoboam's reign, and all he did, are they not written in the book of the annals of the kings of Judah? ³⁰There was continual warfare between Rehoboam and Jeroboam. ³¹And Rehoboam rested with his fathers and was buried with them in the City of David. His mother's name was Naamah; she was an Ammonite. And Abijah his son succeeded him as king.

Rehoboam was born one year before his father Solomon became king. For forty-one years he had enjoyed the splendor of the Israelite kingdom. But his seventeen-year reign was nothing compared to that of his father.

During his reign even more idolatry was introduced into the land of Judah. The Asherah pole, this wooden statue of a female goddess, was worshiped through the performance of fertility rites (fornication). Long before the Israelites entered their land of Canaan, God had told his people to cut down the Asherah poles (Exodus 34:13) and burn them (Deuteronomy 12:3). Rehoboam paid no attention to those warnings.

Since it is mentioned twice that Rehoboam's mother was from the people of Ammon and since Solomon had already introduced the worship of Molech, god of the Ammonites (1 Kings 11:5), we are not surprised to see Rehoboam walking in the ways of his father and mother.

Sometimes we hear people saying of a wayward son or daughter, "Don't worry, pastor. They will come back." Sometimes they do come back. Perhaps even Solomon repented. But by that time the damage had already been done. Thanks to Solomon's carelessness, his own son and the entire land of Judah were now firmly entrenched in idolatry.

When God's people deliberately reject their Lord, then God sends a judgment. Even the fortified cities that Rehoboam had built around Jerusalem (2 Chronicles 12) could not stop the Egyptian conqueror, Thutmose III (a half-brother of Solomon's wife), from entering Jerusalem. "Unless the LORD watches over the city, the watchmen stand guard in vain" (Psalm 127:1). God withdrew his protecting hand as Shishak helped himself to the temple treasures and the golden shields which Solomon had placed in the Palace of the Forest of Lebanon (1 Kings 10:17). Pictures of Solomon's treasures can be seen on the walls of Thutmose III's temple in Egypt. The bronze shields that replaced the golden ones were a visible reminder that the glory had departed from Judah. Those bronze shields were as phony as the gods worshiped by the king.

The success of the Egyptian armies reminds us that *our* country needs penitent people kneeling before the Lord's throne of grace even more than we need the plans of the politician or the weapons of modern warfare.

Jeroboam's Unworthy Successors (15:1-16:34)

The kingdom ruled by David and then by Solomon was now permanently divided. The Northern Kingdom, which now took the name, "The Kingdom of Israel," consisted of ten tribes. The Kingdom of Judah, the Southern Kingdom, had only two of the twelve tribes.

Our inspired writer now tells us about the men who succeeded King Jeroboam in the north and King Rehoboam in the south. Each of the kings of Israel continued "in the sins of Jeroboam," that is, they continued to worship the golden calves. Some of the kings of Judah worshiped the Lord. Others were idolaters like Rehoboam.

The remainder of 1 Kings is, in a general way, the story of how the kings of Israel and Judah continued to reject the King of kings.

We refer the reader to the list of kings in the appendix.

Abijah King of Judah

15 In the eighteenth year of the reign of Jeroboam son of Nebat, Abijah became king of Judah, ²and he reigned in Jerusalem three years. His mother's name was Maacah daughter of Abishalom.

³He committed all the sins his father had done before him; his heart was not fully devoted to the LORD his God, as the heart of David his forefather had been. ⁴Nevertheless, for David's sake the LORD his God gave him a lamp in Jerusalem by raising up a son to succeed him and by making Jerusalem strong. ⁵For David had done what was right in the eyes of the LORD and had not failed to keep any of the LORD's commands all the days of his life—except in the case of Uriah the Hittite.

⁶There was war between Rehoboam and Jeroboam throughout ⌊Abijah's⌋ lifetime. ⁷As for the other events of Abijah's reign, and all he did, are they not written in the book of the annals of the kings of Judah? There was war between Abijah and Jeroboam. ⁸And Abijah rested with his fathers and was buried in the City of David. And Asa his son succeeded him as king.

Chapter 13 of 2 Chronicles tells us how Abijah and his soldiers trusted in the Lord and waged a successful military campaign against the Northern Kingdom. It seems, however, that his obedience to the Lord was short-lived. Abijah's heart was not right with the Lord.

Here our writer impresses on us the grace and faithfulness of the Lord. God had said earlier that David would continue to have "a lamp in Jerusalem" (1 Kings 11:36). That is, David's influence would continue in Jerusalem until the Messiah himself would be born. God kept that promise. Back in Exodus 20:6 God promised to show his steadfast love to thousands of generations for the sake of one believing ancestor. For David's sake God continued to show mercy even to a man like Abijah.

David committed sins in addition to adultery and murder. His adultery with Bathsheba is singled out because it marked a short time in David's life when he was impenitent, a time when he refused to let God's word define sin.

Asa King of Judah

9In the twentieth year of Jeroboam king of Israel, Asa became king of Judah, 10and he reigned in Jerusalem forty-one years. His grandmother's name was Maacah daughter of Abishalom.

11Asa did what was right in the eyes of the LORD, as his father David had done. 12He expelled the male shrine prostitutes from the land and got rid of all the idols his fathers had made. 13He even deposed his grandmother Maacah from her position as queen mother, because she had made a repulsive Asherah pole. Asa cut the pole down and burned it in the Kidron Valley. 14Although he did not remove the high places, Asa's heart was fully committed to the LORD all his life. 15He brought into the temple of the LORD the silver and gold and the articles that he and his father had dedicated.

When someone's heart is right with the Lord, he will actively serve the Lord. Asa showed his faith by his actions.

He even deposed his grandmother from her position of influence. There are times, Jesus tell us, when faithfulness to him will mean hating our own parents (Luke 14:26).

Asa did not come from a family of believers. But our gracious God is able to create faith even in the hearts of children of godless parents.

16There was war between Asa and Baasha king of Israel throughout their reigns. 17Baasha king of Israel went up against Judah and fortified Ramah to prevent anyone from leaving or entering the territory of Asa king of Judah.

18Asa then took all the silver and gold that was left in the treasuries of the LORD's temple and of his own palace. He entrusted it to his officials and sent them to Ben-Hadad son of Tabrimmon, the son of Hezion, the king of Aram, who was ruling in Damascus. 19"Let there be a treaty between me and you," he said, "as there was between my father and your father. See, I am sending you a gift of silver and gold. Now break your treaty with Baasha king of Israel so he will withdraw from me."

20Ben-Hadad agreed with King Asa and sent the commanders of his forces against the towns of Israel. He conquered Ijon, Dan, Abel Beth Maacah and all Kinnereth in addition to Naphtali. 21When Baasha heard this, he stopped building Ramah and withdrew to Tirzah. 22Then King Asa issued an order to all Judah—no one was exempt—and they carried away from Ramah the stones and timber Baasha had been using there. With them King Asa built up Geba in Benjamin, and also Mizpah.

23As for all the other events of Asa's reign, all his achievements, all he did and the cities he built, are they not written in the book of the annals of the kings of Judah? In his old age, however, his feet became diseased. 24Then Asa rested with his fathers and was buried with them in the city of his father David. And Jehoshaphat his son succeeded him as king.

The author of 1 Kings does not pass judgment on the propriety of taking silver and gold from the temple and giving it to Ben-Hadad, the king of Aram. In 2 Chronicles 16:7, however, the writer scolds Asa because he "relied on the king of Aram and not on the LORD your God." The disease that Asa suffered in his feet was apparently part of the judgment God sent on him because of his lack of trust. Even in that sickness Asa looked to the physicians rather than to the Lord for help (2 Chronicles 16:12).

By relying on a heathen king, Asa ignored the word of the prophet Azariah, who assured Asa that "The LORD is with you when you are with him" (2 Chronicles 15:2).

Asa's mistake is frequently repeated today. When the church looks to the unbelieving world instead of to the Lord, when the church relies on the heathen instead of on the Lord for assistance in carrying out its mission of reaching out, the church is weakened and God is displeased. The Lord may well send on that church also a "disease in the feet" so that it begins to totter.

We can assume that Asa repented of his sins of weakness before his death, for our writer has already noted that Asa's heart was "fully committed to the LORD all his life" (verse 14). God is patient with his elect and restores them when they wander.

In the case of unbelievers, however, God's patience finally comes to an end.

Nadab King of Israel

25Nadab son of Jeroboam became king of Israel in the second year of Asa king of Judah, and he reigned over Israel two years. 26He did evil in the eyes of the LORD, walking in the ways of his father and in his sin, which he had caused Israel to commit.

27Baasha son of Ahijah of the house of Issachar plotted against him, and he struck him down at Gibbethon, a Philistine town, while Nadab and all Israel were besieging it. 28Baasha killed Nadab in the third year of Asa king of Judah and succeeded him as king.

²⁹As soon as he began to reign, he killed Jeroboam's whole family. He did not leave Jeroboam anyone that breathed, but destroyed them all, according to the word of the Lord given through his servant Ahijah the Shilonite—³⁰because of the sins Jeroboam had committed and had caused Israel to commit, and because he provoked the Lord, the God of Israel, to anger. ³¹As for the other events of Nadab's reign, and all he did, are they not written in the book of the annals of the kings of Israel? ³²There was war between Asa and Baasha king of Israel throughout their reigns.

When Jeroboam's wife came to Ahijah to ask about the fate of their son, Ahijah announced God's judgment on the entire house of Jeroboam (1 Kings 14:10). Even though Baasha also worshiped the golden calves, God used him as his arm of vengeance.

Baasha and the three kings who succeeded him in Israel were idolaters. They refused to follow the example of their God-fearing counterpart and contemporary, King Asa, in Jerusalem.

Baasha King of Israel

³³In the third year of Asa king of Judah, Baasha son of Ahijah became king of all Israel in Tirzah, and he reigned twenty-four years. ³⁴He did evil in the eyes of the Lord walking in the ways of Jeroboam and in his sin, which he had caused Israel to commit.

16 Then the word of the Lord came to Jehu son of Hanani against Baasha: ²"I lifted you up from the dust and made you leader of my people Israel, but you walked in the ways of Jeroboam and caused my people Israel to sin and to provoke me to anger by their sins. ³So I am about to consume Baasha and his house, and I will make your house like that of Jeroboam son of Nebat. ⁴Dogs will eat those belonging to Baasha who die in the city, and the birds of the air will feed on those who die in the country."

⁵As for the other events of Baasha's reign, what he did and his achievements, are they not written in the book of the annals of the kings of Israel? ⁶Baasha rested with his fathers and was buried in Tirzah. And Elah his son succeeded him as king.

⁷Moreover, the word of the LORD came through the prophet Jehu son of Hanani to Baasha and his house, because of all the evil he had done in the eyes of the LORD, provoking him to anger by the things he did, and becoming like the house of Jeroboam— and also because he destroyed it.

Baasha was crowned as king in Tirzah, a beautiful city several miles northeast of Samaria, a city where Jeroboam also had lived (1 Kings 14:17).

Those to whom God has given positions of trust and leadership have a solemn responsibility toward God. Since Baasha was not faithful, his house also would be destroyed. Even his slaying of Jeroboam's family was now counted as sin. That massacre had been carried out for the sake of personal gain, not to honor the Lord.

Elah King of Israel

⁸In the twenty-sixth year of Asa king of Judah, Elah son of Baasha became king of Israel, and he reigned in Tirzah two years.

⁹Zimri, one of his officials, who had command of half his chariots, plotted against him. Elah was in Tirzah at the time, getting drunk in the home of Arza, the man in charge of the palace at Tirzah. ¹⁰Zimri came in, struck him down and killed him in the twenty-seventh year of Asa king of Judah. Then he succeeded him as king.

¹¹As soon as he began to reign and was seated on the throne, he killed off Baasha's whole family. He did not spare a single male, whether relative or friend. ¹²So Zimri destroyed the whole family of Baasha, in accordance with the word of the LORD spoken against Baasha through the prophet Jehu—¹³because of all the sins Baasha and his son Elah had committed and had caused

Israel to commit, so that they provoked the LORD, the God of Israel, to anger by their worthless idols.

[14] As for the other events of Elah's reign, and all he did, are they not written in the book of the annals of the kings of Israel?

We do not expect to see Elah in heaven. The only thing God's writer records is that he was assassinated in a drunken orgy. "Those who live like this," Paul tells us in Galatians 5:21, "will not inherit the kingdom of God." Arza and any others who support and contribute to the sins of others are no better.

In a positive way Paul encourages each Christian to "live by the Spirit" (Galatians 5:16) lest we give free reign to the flesh and die in our sins.

God often uses one heathen man or nation to bring his revenge on another heathen man or nation. Zimri became God's arm of vengeance to destroy the family of Baasha. At the end of 2 Kings we will see how God used the heathen Babylonians to bring judgment on his own people of Judah.

Zimri King of Israel

[15] In the twenty-seventh year of Asa king of Judah, Zimri reigned in Tirzah seven days. The army was encamped near Gibbethon, a Philistine town. [16] When the Israelites in the camp heard that Zimri had plotted against the king and murdered him, they proclaimed Omri, the commander of the army, king over Israel that very day there in the camp. [17] Then Omri and all the Israelites with him withdrew from Gibbethon and laid siege to Tirzah. [18] When Zimri saw that the city was taken, he went into the citadel of the royal palace and set the palace on fire around him. So he died, [19] because of the sins he had committed, doing evil in the eyes of the LORD and walking in the ways of Jeroboam and in the sin he had committed and had caused Israel to commit.

20 As for the other events of Zimri's reign, and the rebellion he carried out, are they not written in the book of the annals of the kings of Israel?

Gibbethon is a town in the extreme southern part of Israel, east of Ekron, near the Mediterranean Sea. It is the place where Baasha had assassinated Nadab when the armies of Israel were besieging Gibbethon some twenty-five years earlier. The army of Israel was not willing to accept Zimri as their king. It took the soldiers only seven days to receive word of Zimri's rule, march the fifty or so miles up to Tirzah, and frighten Zimri into taking his own life.

Zimri's rule of only seven days is the shortest of any king of Israel or Judah.

The Bible does not discuss cremation. But the death of Zimri is generally cited whenever the subject is brought up. There may be reasons for a Christian, under certain circumstances, to choose cremation rather than a customary earth burial. Zimri's death, however, is an example of a heathen man taking his own life and then attempting to destroy all that remained of his earthly existence.

From time to time a whole congregation copies Zimri's sinful example. The members refuse to do God's will, that is, they refuse to share the gospel with others in their community. They prefer instead to hide themselves within the walls of their building until the last member passes away. They would rather burn their building, they would rather die, than have outsiders enter their sanctuary. By such an attitude a congregation commits spiritual suicide.

Omri King of Israel

21 Then the people of Israel were split into two factions; half supported Tibni son of Ginath for king, and the other half supported Omri. 22 But Omri's followers proved stronger than those of Tibni son of Ginath. So Tibni died and Omri became king.

²³In the thirty-first year of Asa king of Judah, Omri became king of Israel, and he reigned twelve years, six of them in Tirzah. ²⁴He bought the hill of Samaria from Shemer for two talents of silver and built a city on the hill, calling it Samaria, after Shemer, the name of the former owner of the hill.

²⁵But Omri did evil in the eyes of the LORD and sinned more than all those before him. ²⁶He walked in all the ways of Jeroboam son of Nebat and in his sin, which he had caused Israel to commit, so that they provoked the LORD, the God of Israel, to anger by their worthless idols.

²⁷As for the other events of Omri's reign, what he did and the things he achieved, are they not written in the book of the annals of the kings of Israel? ²⁸Omri rested with his fathers and was buried in Samaria. And Ahab his son succeeded him as king.

It was only after a four-year struggle against Tibni (see verses 10 and 23) that Omri became the undisputed ruler over Israel.

The tragic deaths of his predecessors Nadab, Elah, and Zimri did nothing to bring Omri to repentance. He ignored God's warnings just as the heathen often do today and became the king who "sinned more than all those before him."

The prophet Micah scolded the Israelites when he wrote, "You have observed the statutes of Omri and all the practices of Ahab's house, and you have followed their traditions. Therefore I will give you over to ruin and your people to derision; you will bear the scorn of the nations" (Micah 6:16).

Omri is the man who built the city of Samaria. It was built on a beautiful, strategic site that enabled the people of Israel to repulse attacks from Aram and from Assyria for many generations. It finally fell to the Assyrians in the year 722 B.C., but only after a three-year siege (2 Kings 17:5,6).

Apparently Omri was forced to turn over certain cities to Aram (1 Kings 20:34). From certain Assyrian inscriptions it seems also that Omri was the first Israelite king to pay tribute to the Assyrians.

On the other hand, Omri had success against enemies to the east, across the Jordan. He completely subdued Moab so that they remained in subjection to Israel until after the death of Ahab (2 Kings 3:5).

Ahab Becomes King of Israel

²⁹In the thirty-eighth year of Asa king of Judah, Ahab son of Omri became king of Israel, and he reigned in Samaria over Israel twenty-two years. ³⁰Ahab son of Omri did more evil in the eyes of the LORD than any of those before him. ³¹He not only considered it trivial to commit the sins of Jeroboam son of Nebat, but he also married Jezebel daughter of Ethbaal king of the Sidonians, and began to serve Baal and worship him. ³²He set up an altar for Baal in the temple of Baal that he built in Samaria. ³³Ahab also made an Asherah pole and did more to provoke the LORD, the God of Israel, to anger than did all the kings of Israel before him.

³⁴In Ahab's time, Hiel of Bethel rebuilt Jericho. He laid its foundations at the cost of his firstborn son Abiram, and he set up its gates at the cost of his youngest son Segub, in accordance with the word of the LORD spoken by Joshua son of Nun.

The previous kings of Israel were mentioned only briefly. But our writer uses more than six chapters to record events from the reign of King Ahab and to comment on their spiritual significance.

Ahab has the unfortunate distinction of being the man who "did more evil in the eyes of the LORD than any of those before him." Through marriage he became one flesh with a heathen woman named Jezebel, the daughter of Ethbaal. This makes Jezebel the sister (or at least a close relative) of

Queen Dido, the founder of Carthage. The idolatry practiced by Dido and by Jezebel have similarities (see 2 Kings 23:4-14).

One of the gods Jezebel introduced into Israel was named Baal. The word "baal" simply means "lord." But the Baal mentioned here was considered the god who sent rain and caused the crops to grow. Baal worshipers engaged in a kind of sacred fornication at the temple to praise him as the source of life. At times the people would even offer their children to Baal as burnt sacrifices (Jeremiah 19:5).

Another goddess was Asherah. Although the King James Bible regularly translates this word as "grove," an Asherah was actually a wooden post on which was carved the symbol of a female goddess. Asherah was considered to be the sister as well as the wife of Baal. She was a fertility goddess, the goddess of passion, who was also worshiped by a kind of sacred prostitution.

The reign of Ahab was a time when people in general had no use for God's word, a time when people dared the Lord to carry out his threats. Five hundred years earlier the Israelites had entered Canaan and captured the city of Jericho. At God's direction they burned that city and all it contained. At that time Joshua announced, "Cursed before the LORD is the man who undertakes to rebuild this city, Jericho: At the cost of his firstborn son will he lay its foundations; at the cost of his youngest will he set up its gates" (Joshua 6:26). Jericho was rebuilt during Ahab's reign and God's curse was fulfilled.

Ahab, the Worst King over Israel

Our faithful God was not ready to abandon his unfaithful people. He sent the prophet Elijah, a fearless preacher of repentance, and confirmed his words through miraculous signs.

Elijah Fed by Ravens

17 **Now Elijah the Tishbite, from Tishbe in Gilead, said to Ahab, "As the LORD, the God of Israel, lives, whom I serve, there will be neither dew nor rain in the next few years except at my word."**

2Then the word of the LORD came to Elijah: 3"Leave here, turn eastward and hide in the Kerith Ravine, east of the Jordan. 4You will drink from the brook, and I have ordered the ravens to feed you there."

5So he did what the LORD had told him. He went to the Kerith Ravine, east of the Jordan, and stayed there. 6The ravens brought him bread and meat in the morning and bread and meat in the evening, and he drank from the brook.

Elijah came from Gilead east of the Jordan River. Even his name is significant and is a call to repentance. "Elijah" means "the LORD is my God."

The prophet's first recorded words are not words of comfort or peace or forgiveness. They are words of judgment. To people who thought that Baal sent rain for the crops and that their fertility goddess, Asherah, caused crops to grow and cows to calve and women to become pregnant and bear children, Elijah announced, "The Lord God will shut the heavens so that there will be no more rain." With that announcement a drought began which lasted three and a half years.

John the Baptist, like Elijah, was a bold preacher of repentance.

Faithful pastors today will also announce God's judgments to an unbelieving world. Many an unbeliever will ignore that warning of eternal condemnation. He will prefer to seek advice regarding dating and marriage from counsellors who approve of fornication, divorce, and abortion. If God should send serious drought into the world today, he is

Elijah Fed by the Ravens (1 Kings 17:6)

only trying once again to awaken the unbeliever from his spiritual sleep and is leading his own people, as we will see from the next verses, to trust more completely in his promises.

The 3½-year drought God sent upon the whole land of Israel affected believers as well as unbelievers, but the faithful covenant God provided for his prophet in a miraculous way. The raven is ordinarily a scavenger and is not willing to share his food with anyone. Proverbs 30:17 says, "The eye that mocks a father, that scorns obedience to a mother, will be pecked out by the ravens of the valley." But here God caused the ravens to act contrary to their nature.

Ordinarily God provides for his people through natural means. That is, he sends seedtime and harvest according to his promise to Noah in Genesis 8:22. But the God who fed the Israelites with manna in the wilderness five hundred years earlier and fed 5,000 in the wilderness nine hundred years later can still provide for his people through miracles. Because we have the sure promises of almighty God, we need not fear drought, famine, sickness, or even nuclear war. "All depends on our possessing God's abundant grace and blessing" (TLH 425:1).

The Widow at Zarephath

⁷Some time later the brook dried up because there had been no rain in the land. ⁸Then the word of the LORD came to him: ⁹"Go at once to Zarephath of Sidon and stay there. I have commanded a widow in that place to supply you with food." ¹⁰So he went to Zarephath. When he came to the town gate, a widow was there gathering sticks. He called to her and asked, "Would you bring me a little water in a jar so I may have a drink?" ¹¹As she was going to get it, he called, "And bring me, please, a piece of bread."

¹²"As surely as the LORD your God lives," she replied, "I don't have any bread—only a handful of flour in a jar and a little oil in a

jug. I am gathering a few sticks to take home and make a meal for myself and my son, that we may eat it—and die."

[13]Elijah said to her, "Don't be afraid. Go home and do as you have said. But first make a small cake of bread for me from what you have and bring it to me, and then make something for yourself and your son. [14]For this is what the LORD, the God of Israel, says: 'The jar of flour will not be used up and the jug of oil will not run dry until the day the LORD gives rain on the land.' "

[15]She went away and did as Elijah had told her. So there was food every day for Elijah and for the woman and her family. [16]For the jar of flour was not used up and the jug of oil did not run dry, in keeping with the word of the LORD spoken by Elijah.

Zarephath was outside Israel, near Sidon, the hometown of Queen Jezebel. Would someone from that idolatrous land really provide for a prophet of the Lord? Could a woman (a widow at that) feed another mouth during a famine?

Once again Elijah passed God's test of faith by doing exactly as God had said.

There in Zarephath God would also test the faith of the widow he had chosen. God's promise to her was this: The bowl of flour and the jar of oil will not be exhausted until the famine is over. The widow also passed God's test. By preparing bread for Elijah, the widow acted as though the flour and oil would last forever. And that is the very essence of faith. Faith is "being certain of what we do not see" (Hebrews 11:1).

A familiar hymn refers to this incident and is a prayer that God would bless all who are troubled:

> And if their home be dark and drear,
> The cruse be empty, hunger near,
> All hope within them dying,
> Let them despair not in distress;
> Lo, Christ is there the bread to bless,
> The fragments multiplying. (TLH 624:3)

Jesus refers to the widow of Zarephath in Luke 4:26. There were many widows in Israel who, theoretically, could have provided for Elijah. But God pronounced judgment on his people's unbelief by sending his prophet to a Gentile woman. When God's own people worship idols instead of the Lord, then God sends his prophets and his blessings to others.

In spite of her poverty the widow of Zarephath brought a cake of bread to God's prophet. In spite of her poverty the widow in Mark 12:42 brought to the Lord two mites, all that she had. Poverty does not excuse any Christian from worshiping the Lord. The offerings of Christians, rich and poor, are a demonstration of their love and trust. The command to "love the Lord your God with all your heart and with all your soul and with all your mind" (Matthew 22:37) applies to rich and poor, in good times and bad.

But the widow of Zarephath did not live happily ever after.

¹⁷Some time later the son of the woman who owned the house became ill. He grew worse and worse, and finally stopped breathing. ¹⁸She said to Elijah, "What do you have against me, man of God? Did you come to remind me of my sin and kill my son?"

¹⁹"Give me your son," Elijah replied. He took him from her arms, carried him to the upper room where he was staying, and laid him on his bed. ²⁰Then he cried out to the LORD, "O LORD my God, have you brought tragedy also upon this widow I am staying with, by causing her son to die?" ²¹Then he stretched himself out on the boy three times and cried to the LORD, "O LORD my God, let this boy's life return to him!"

²²The LORD heard Elijah's cry, and the boy's life returned to him, and he lived. ²³Elijah picked up the child and carried him down from the room into the house. He gave him to his mother and said, "Look, your son is alive!"

²⁴Then the woman said to Elijah, "Now I know that you are a man of God and that the word of the LORD from your mouth is the truth."

The widow's response to her son's death is not unusual. At first she was angry—angry with God and God's prophet. Her conscience bothered her, and she wondered whether her son's death was God's punishment for a particular sin from her past.

The Bible assures us that God never punishes his people for sins they have committed. "There is now no condemnation for those who are in Christ Jesus" (Romans 8:1). But there is a direct connection between sin and death. Sickness and death are constant reminders that we live in a sinful world, that the perfectness of Eden is gone, that we personally need a Savior from sin.

Elijah responded to the woman's anger with gentleness. He asked God whether, after sparing this family from starvation, he really intended to take the life of this boy. Then Elijah boldly asked God to perform a work such as the world had never seen before. The boy died when his soul left his body, when "there was no breath left in him" (verse 17, KJV). Elijah asked God to raise that boy from the dead, to join the boy's soul and body together again.

God, who is the source of all life, heard that prayer. The God who gave life to Adam at the beginning of time gave new life to the dead body lying on Elijah's bed.

The miracle provided further proof that the word of God spoken by Elijah was the truth. Here was proof that God would also keep his other promises, that God would send a Savior who would defeat Satan, the one "who holds the power of death" (Hebrews 2:14), a Savior who would bring "life and immortality to light" (2 Timothy 1:10).

Elijah could announce, "Look, your son is alive." God's spokesmen in the New Testament can announce something greater. They can tell others, "Look, God's Son is alive! His death was a payment for sin. His resurrection proves that even death has lost its sting."

Elijah was not the only believer left in Israel. Other prophets also faithfully proclaimed God's word. And their work was not without fruit. Obadiah, for example, worked for King Ahab himself but continued to confess his faith publicly. Even in a time of persecution the angel of the everlasting gospel continues to do his work here on earth (Revelation 14:6).

Elijah and Obadiah

18 After a long time, in the third year, the word of the LORD came to Elijah: "Go and present yourself to Ahab, and I will send rain on the land." ²So Elijah went to present himself to Ahab.

Now the famine was severe in Samaria, ³and Ahab had summoned Obadiah, who was in charge of his palace. (Obadiah was a devout believer in the LORD. ⁴While Jezebel was killing off the LORD's prophets, Obadiah had taken a hundred prophets and hidden them in two caves, fifty in each, and had supplied them with food and water.) ⁵Ahab had said to Obadiah, "Go through the land to all the springs and valleys. Maybe we can find some grass to keep the horses and mules alive so we will not have to kill any of our animals." ⁶So they divided the land they were to cover, Ahab going in one direction and Obadiah in another.

⁷As Obadiah was walking along, Elijah met him. Obadiah recognized him, bowed down to the ground, and said, "Is it really you, my lord Elijah?"

⁸"Yes," he replied, "Go tell your master, 'Elijah is here.' "

⁹"What have I done wrong," asked Obadiah, "that you are handing your servant over to Ahab to be put to death? ¹⁰As surely as the LORD your God lives, there is not a nation or kingdom where my master has not sent someone to look for you. And whenever a nation or kingdom claimed you were not there, he made them swwear they could not find you. ¹¹But now you tell me to go to my master and say, 'Elijah is here.' ¹²I don't know where the Spirit of the LORD may carry you when I leave you. If I go and

tell Ahab and he doesn't find you, he will kill me. Yet I your servant have worshiped the LORD since my youth. [13]Haven't you heard, my lord, what I did while Jezebel was killing the prophets of the LORD? I hid a hundred of the LORD's prophets in two caves, fifty in each, and supplied them with food and water. [14]And now you tell me to go to my master and say, 'Elijah is here.' He will kill me!"

[15]Elijah said, "As the LORD Almighty lives, whom I serve, I will surely present myself to Ahab today."

Ordinarily it is a good thing when people seek God's prophets, but Ahab did not look for a prophet because he wanted to hear God's word or repent of his sin. He wanted to kill Elijah.

After Elijah had assured his friend Obadiah that he would certainly appear before the king that day, Obadiah put away his fear and obeyed the words of Elijah. In a similar way God's people today will trust the promises of their God even when a heathen king threatens to take their lives.

Elijah on Mount Carmel

[16]So Obadiah went to meet Ahab and told him, and Ahab went to meet Elijah. [17]When he saw Elijah, he said to him, "Is that you, you troubler of Israel?"

[18]"I have not made trouble for Israel," Elijah replied. "But you and your father's family have. You have abandoned the LORD's commands and have followed the Baals. [19]Now summon the people from all over Israel to meet me on Mount Carmel. And bring the four hundred and fifty prophets of Baal and the four hundred prophets of Asherah, who eat at Jezebel's table."

Elijah and Ahab had not seen each other for three years. During that time Ahab's heart had not changed one bit. The king's first words to the prophet were a bold accusation, "Is that you, you troubler of Israel?"

If a prophet or a pastor is a faithful preacher of repentance, he will step on a few toes. Unbelievers will accuse God's pastors of causing trouble. Because Christians have a sinful heart, even they occasionally speak out against the man who instructs them in God's word.

This should not surprise us. Even Jesus was accused of being in league with the devil.

The real troublemaker is not God or God's messengers but Satan. He brought sin into this world and desires to lead us into eternal death, the greatest trouble.

Even though King Ahab and the people had given themselves over to the worship of idols, God would attempt once again to lead his people to repentance. The contest proposed by Elijah would take place at Mount Carmel. This was near the Mediterranean Sea, northeast of Ahab's summer palace in Jezreel, near the present-day city of Haifa.

20So Ahab sent word throughout all Israel and assembled the prophets on Mount Carmel. 21Elijah went before the people and said, "How long will you waver between two opinions? If the Lord is God, follow him; but if Baal is God, follow him."

But the people said nothing.

22Then Elijah said to them, "I am the only one of the Lord's prophets left, but Baal has four hundred and fifty prophets. 23Get two bulls for us. Let them choose one for themselves, and let them cut it into pieces, and put it on the wood but not set fire to it. I will prepare the other bull and put it on the wood but not set fire to it. 24Then you call on the name of your god, and I will call on the name of the Lord. The god who answers by fire—he is God."

Then all the people said, "What you say is good."

Because God wanted to make a public display of his power, he moved King Ahab, unknowingly, to give his full cooperation.

Elijah directed his first words to the people, asking them to stop sitting on the fence and to take a stand either for the

Savior-God or against him. In Revelation 3:16 Jesus also condemns halfheartedness. He says, "Because you are luke-warm—neither hot nor cold—I am about to spit you out of my mouth."

Perhaps you have been at a meeting where the chairman asked for volunteers to help with a project but received only silence and downcast eyes in reply. That silence probably meant that the people did not oppose the project but that they were unwilling to offer any of their own time and energy. That is what happened to Elijah. His challenge to the people was greeted with silence.

Then Elijah issued a challenge to the prophets of Baal. The Lord, the mighty Creator, and Baal, the bloodthirsty fertility god of the Sidonians, would each have an opportunity to show his power.

25 Elijah said to the prophets of Baal, "Choose one of the bulls and prepare it first, since there are so many of you. Call on the name of your god, but do not light the fire." 26 So they took the bull given them and prepared it.

Then they called on the name of Baal from morning till noon. "O Baal, answer us!" they shouted. But there was no response; no one answered. And they danced around the altar they had made.

27 At noon Elijah began to taunt them. "Shout louder!" he said. "Surely he is a god! Perhaps he is deep in thought, or busy, or traveling. Maybe he is sleeping and must be awakened." 28 So they shouted louder and slashed themselves with swords and spears, as was their custom, until their blood flowed. 29 Midday passed, and they continued their frantic prophesying until the time for the evening sacrifice. But there was no response, no one answered, no one paid attention.

At noon Elijah did something that many would consider impolite. He began to mock the prophets of Baal and the idol they worshiped.

At evening we see some exhausted prophets of Baal. But we see no fire. Obviously Baal was not the winner of this contest.

Very few people today still worship a god named Baal. But thousands in our country still delight in sacrificing children (unborn children) on his altar. A million and a half children are sacrificed to Baal every year in our own country, to a Baal who has been renamed "pleasure" or "convenience." We see a powerful priesthood for Baal, powerful national organizations which spend huge amounts of time and money so that their bloody worship may not be forbidden, that no laws may be passed to restrict abortion on demand.

Today we find many who hesitate between two opinions. Many wish to retain membership in a Christian congregation but are in reality strangers to the house of God. Comparatively few will step forward, dedicating themselves body and soul with their time and treasure to the service of the Lord.

If people have given their hearts to a modern Baal, they are worshiping a powerless god who will give no answer in a time of trouble, who will give no reply on our deathbed, who will give no help on the great judgment day.

Now it was Elijah's turn.

30Then Elijah said to all the people, "Come here to me." They came to him, and he repaired the altar of the LORD, which was in ruins. 31Elijah took twelve stones, one for each of the tribes descended from Jacob, to whom the word of the LORD had come, saying, "Your name shall be Israel." 32With the stones he built an altar in the name of the LORD, and he dug a trench around it large enough to hold two seahs of seed. 33He arranged the wood, cut the bull into pieces and laid it on the wood. Then he said to them, "Fill four large jars with water and pour it on the offering and on the wood."

Fire from Heaven Consumes the Sacrifice (1 Kings 18:38)

³⁴"Do it again," he said, and they did it again.

"Do it a third time," he ordered, and they did it the third time.
³⁵The water ran down around the altar and even filled the trench.

³⁶At the time of sacrifice, the prophet Elijah stepped forward and prayed: "O LORD, God of Abraham, Isaac and Israel, let it be known today that you are God in Israel and that I am your servant and have done all these things at your command. ³⁷Answer me, O LORD, answer me, so these people will know that you, O LORD, are God, and that you are turning their hearts back again."

³⁸Then the fire of the LORD fell and burned up the sacrifice, the wood, the stones and the soil, and also licked up the water in the trench.

³⁹When all the people saw this, they fell prostrate and cried, "The LORD—he is God! The LORD—he is God!"

⁴⁰Then Elijah commanded them, "Seize the prophets of Baal. Don't let anyone get away!" They seized them, and Elijah had them brought down to the Kishon Valley and slaughtered there.

It was now evening, the time when God's faithful people would bring the evening sacrifice to the Lord at Solomon's temple. Elijah deliberately chose twelve stones to rebuild the altar, one stone for each of the twelve tribes of Israel. After drenching the sacrifice and the altar, he deliberately called on the God of Israel, the God who had promised to send a Savior into the world through the nation of Israel. The prophet who had asked God to stop sending rain and who had asked God to raise the widow's son now asked God to show his mighty power once again.

Notice that Elijah does not even use the word "fire" in his prayer. He asks only that God would glorify his name, that God would convince the people that he is the true God, and that God would show the people that he, Elijah, is a true prophet. Elijah desires the conversion and the salvation of the people of Israel.

When fire fell from heaven, what else could the people say except, "The LORD—he is God!"

The prophet who had mocked the prophets of Jezebel now supervised their execution in the Kishon Valley.

When Jesus came into the world eight hundred years later, the people challenged him to prove his words by performing miracles, but the Savior would not accept that challenge. It is not necessary for God to repeat such dramatic proof of his mighty power, for we can read the record in the Scriptures.

There will come a time, however, when God will again show his mighty power. That will be on the last day. Then Jesus will say to every false prophet and unbeliever, "Depart from me, you who are cursed, into the eternal fire prepared for the devil and his angels" (Matthew 25:41). Then the mighty Creator will destroy this world with a fire that burns even stone and water.

We pray that all people would recognize the Lord as the true God and through that faith gain eternal life.

41 And Elijah said to Ahab, "Go, eat and drink, for there is the sound of a heavy rain." 42 So Ahab went off to eat and drink, but Elijah climbed to the top of Carmel, bent down to the ground and put his face between his knees.

43 "Go and look toward the sea," he told his servant. And he went up and looked.

"There is nothing there," he said.

Seven times Elijah said, "Go back."

44 The seventh time the servant reported, "A cloud as small as a man's hand is rising from the sea."

So Elijah said, "Go and tell Ahab, 'Hitch up your chariot and go down before the rain stops you.' "

45 Meanwhile, the sky grew black with clouds, the wind rose, a heavy rain came on and Ahab rode off to Jezreel. 46 The power of the LORD came upon Elijah and, tucking his cloak into his belt, he ran ahead of Ahab all the way to Jezreel.

It had not rained for three years and six months (Luke 4:25). But now that the real troublers of Israel were dead, God would once again send rain on the parched ground.

James was thinking of this chapter when he wrote, "The prayer of a righteous man is powerful and effective. Elijah was a man just like us. He prayed earnestly that it would not rain, and it did not rain on the land for three and a half years. Again he prayed, and the heavens gave rain, and the earth produced its crops" (James 5:16-18).

When God's people turn their backs on him and on his word, it is not unusual for God to withdraw his blessings. At the same time, God blesses an entire nation for the sake of his faithful people who live there.

Note also the physical strength God was pleased to give to his prophet. Elijah ran the entire twenty miles back to Jezreel and arrived there before the king. To each of his messengers God says, "My power is made perfect in [your] weakness" (2 Corinthians 12:9).

In Luke 16:31 Jesus said that if someone will not believe the words of Moses and the prophets, then even the mightiest miracles will not convert his stubborn heart. The actions of Queen Jezebel now show us what Jesus meant.

Elijah Flees to Horeb

19 **Now Ahab told Jezebel everything Elijah had done and how he had killed all the prophets with the sword. ²So Jezebel sent a messenger to Elijah to say, "May the gods deal with me, be it ever so severely, if by this time tomorrow I do not make your life like that of one of them."**

³Elijah was afraid and ran for his life. When he came to Beersheba in Judah, he left his servant there, ⁴while he himself went a day's journey into the desert. He came to a broom tree, sat down under it and prayed that he might die. "I have had enough, LORD," he said. "Take my life; I am no better than my ancestors." ⁵Then he lay down under the tree and fell asleep.

All at once an angel touched him and said, "Get up and eat." [6]He looked around, and there by his head was a cake of bread baked over hot coals, and a jar of water. He ate and drank and then lay down again.

[7]The angel of the LORD came back a second time and touched him and said, "Get up and eat, for the journey is too much for you." [8]So he got up and ate and drank. Strengthened by that food, he traveled forty days and forty nights until he reached Horeb, the mountain of God. [9]There he went into a cave and spent the night.

God's mighty miracles did not change the heart of Jezebel. This wicked woman, who had already killed many of the Lord's prophets, now swore to avenge the death of the 450 prophets of Baal. She swore by her gods that Elijah would die within twenty-four hours.

Eight hundred years later Jesus warned his apostles that the unbelieving world would continue to hate God's messengers. The time would come, Jesus said, "when anyone who kills you will think he is offering a service to God." All this will happen, Jesus added, "because they have not known the Father or me" (John 16:2,3).

Elijah therefore fled for his life. He went toward the south, leaving the land of Israel and passing through the Kingdom of Judah. Finally he came to Beersheba at the southern end of Judah, some seventy-five miles from his home. He left his servant there and continued another twenty miles south. Alone, at night, under a broom tree, Elijah poured out his heart to God. The prophet was disappointed, discouraged, and depressed. He wanted to die. It seemed that his preaching, his warnings, even his miracles had been a waste of time.

Elijah was not the last man of God to be threatened with death by his government. Jesus foretold how his apostles would stand before kings and governors (Matthew 10:18).

Elijah Dwells in a Cave (1 Kings 19:9)

132

Herod put the Apostle James to death with the sword (Acts 12:2). Martin Luther was excommunicated by his church and was threatened with death by the emperor.

If God's people today confess that the Lord is the only God and that Jesus is the only Savior, they can expect the same kind of treatment from the unbelieving world.

But even here God did not forsake his prophet. When the Old Testament talks about "*the* angel of the Lord" (verse 7), it is not describing one of God's created angels. It is referring to that Messenger of God who is equal with the Father and who deserves our worship, namely, the Lord Jesus. That Lord who told his disciples, "Surely I am with you always" (Matthew 28:20), was with Elijah in the wilderness.

We will meet that angel again in 2 Kings 1:3 and 19:35.

The Lord who fed Elijah miraculously at the Kerith Ravine (1 Kings 17:5) and has numbered the hair on our heads acted once again. When Elijah opened his eyes, there was some freshly baked bread and some water.

Mount Horeb, better known as Mount Sinai, was a journey of another 200 miles. This is the place where God had given the Ten Commandments to Moses some 700 years earlier. Just imagine: the discouraged prophet had now traveled 300 miles on foot, most of it through inhospitable desert country!

The writer of the Letter to the Hebrews takes note of heroes of faith who wandered "in deserts and mountains, and in caves and holes in the ground" (Hebrews 11:38) and remarks that "the world was not worthy of them." This was true of God's prophet Elijah.

The Lord Appears to Elijah

And the word of the Lord came to him: "What are you doing here, Elijah?"

[10]He replied, "I have been very zealous for the LORD God Almighty. The Israelites have rejected your covenant, broken down your altars, and put your prophets to death with the sword. I am the only one left, and now they are trying to kill me too."

[11]The LORD said, "Go out and stand on the mountain in the presence of the LORD, for the LORD is about to pass by."

Then a great and powerful wind tore the mountains apart and shattered the rocks before the LORD, but the LORD was not in the wind. After the wind there was an earthquake, but the LORD was not in the earthquake. [12]After the earthquake came a fire, but the LORD was not in the fire. And after the fire came a gentle whisper. [13]When Elijah heard it, he pulled his cloak over his face and went out and stood at the mouth of the cave.

Then a voice said to him. "What are you doing here, Elijah?"

[14]He replied, "I have been very zealous for the LORD God Almighty. The Israelites have rejected your covenant, broken down your altars, and put your prophets to death with the sword. I am the only one left, and now they are trying to kill me too."

[15]The LORD said to him, "Go back the way you came, and go to the Desert of Damascus. When you get there, anoint Hazael king over Aram. [16]Also, anoint Jehu son of Nimshi king over Israel, and anoint Elisha son of Shaphat from Abel Meholah to succeed you as prophet. [17]Jehu will put to death any who escape the sword of Hazael, and Elisha will put to death any who escape the sword of Jehu. [18]Yet I reserve seven thousand in Israel—all whose knees have not bowed down to Baal and all whose mouths have not kissed him."

Unfortunately Elijah was right—almost right. Elijah had done everything that we would expect from a faithful confirmand. The other Israelites, however, did not share his enthusiasm. It seemed that Elijah was the only believer left in Israel.

The God who gave physical strength to Elijah now gave him spiritual strength as well. God invited Elijah to step out of his cave while the LORD, the Savior-God, showed him three tremendous displays of natural forces—a powerful wind, an earthquake, and a fire.

Would God use that mighty wind, the earthquake, or the fire to send revenge on his enemies? God had done that before. He had used a mighty wind to separate the waters of the Red Sea and had then drowned the Egyptian soldiers when the water came crashing back together. God had sent fire from heaven to destroy the people of Sodom and Gomorrah. But God was not yet about to deal with his people according to the law. Instead God came and spoke to Elijah in a gentle whisper, "a still small voice" (KJV).

Seven hundred years earlier God had appeared at Mount Sinai with fire, smoke, and an earthquake. When God gave the Ten Commandments, his voice was like thunder (Exodus 19:18-20). Now God was not coming to Elijah with threats and anger but with patience and love, with gentleness and mercy. Through a quiet voice God gave spiritual strength to Elijah. Through that same quiet word God still today continues to save sinners and to restore the souls of his troubled people.

As a matter of fact, Elijah had not been a failure. The God who sees into our hearts and who "knows those who are his" (2 Timothy 2:19) still had 7,000 faithful followers in Israel.

To encourage Elijah, God also gave him a threefold assignment. He was to head north and anoint the next king of Aram, who would be God's scourge on Israel. He was also to anoint a new king over Israel, who would wipe out the dynasty of Ahab and destroy Baal-worship in Israel. Finally, Elijah was to anoint the man who would succeed him as prophet. The mission of Elijah was to be continued in Elisha.

The true God—that is, the Angel of the Lord who was with Elijah, the Holy Spirit who brings people to faith through the "still small voice" of the gospel, and the Father who passed by Elijah on the mountain—has promised that the church of true believers will be in the world until the end of time. The Apostle Paul assures us that, despite the vicious efforts of Satan, God will always have his "7,000" faithful people in Israel (Romans 11:1-5).

When Elijah asked to die, God did not grant his request. Elijah's death would not come until his work was finished. Then God would give Elijah something much better than the death he had prayed for. God would send a fiery chariot to take him bodily to heaven (2 Kings 2).

God alone will determine when our work on earth is finished. Until that time he will continue to console us through the "still small voice" of his word and sacrament.

The Call of Elisha

[19] So Elijah went from there and found Elisha son of Shaphat. He was plowing with twelve yoke of oxen, and he himself was driving the twelfth pair. Elijah went up to him and threw his cloak around him. [20] Elisha then left his oxen and ran after Elijah. "Let me kiss my father and mother goodby," he said, "and then I will come with you."

"Go back," Elijah replied. "What have I done to you?"

[21] So Elisha left him and went back. He took his yoke of oxen and slaughtered them. He burned the plowing equipment to cook the meat and gave it to the people, and they ate. Then he set out to follow Elijah and became his attendant.

Evidently Elisha was a farmer—and fairly well-to-do, since he and his servants were at work with twelve teams of oxen. When Elijah removed his cloak, the symbol of his prophetic office, and placed it on Elisha's shoulders, Elisha understood immediately that God was appointing him as a prophet, to take Elijah's place.

We hear about that cloak again in 2 Kings 2. Elijah threw it down from the fiery chariot. Elijah and Elisha both used it to part the waters of the Jordan River.

When Jesus called Peter, James, and John to become his full-time followers, they left their fishing business and their families (Luke 5:11). Elisha responded in a similar way. He said good-bye to his parents. By his actions he showed that he would not need oxen or farm implements in his new calling.

God has also called us. In baptism God put his name on us and called us to be children in his family, clothing us not with the prophet's mantle but with the robe of Christ's righteousness. At that time God also asked us to turn our backs on our former way of living. God did not ask us to quit our jobs or leave our parents, but God does ask us to give our hearts, our souls, and our bodies to him.

God continues to call men to serve in the public ministry. Even though a call to become a pastor or Christian day school teacher is issued by human beings, it is God who makes men overseers to feed the flock of the Savior (Acts 20:28).

One of our hymns is based on this incident. In it we pray for our pastors and sing,

> God of the prophets, bless the prophets' sons;
> Elijah's mantle o'er Elisha cast.
> Each age its solemn task may claim but once;
> Make each one nobler, stronger, than the last.
>
> (TLH 483:1)

Baal had not been able to send fire from heaven at Mount Carmel, and he could offer no help now when King Ahab found himself surrounded by heathen soldiers.

Ben-Hadad Attacks Samaria

20 Now Ben-Hadad king of Aram mustered his entire army. Accompanied by thirty-two kings with their horses and chariots, he went up and besieged Samaria and attacked it. ²He sent messengers into the city to Ahab king of Israel, saying, "This is what Ben-Hadad says: ³'Your silver and gold are mine, and the best of your wives and children are mine.' "

⁴The king of Israel answered. "Just as you say, my lord the king. I and all I have are yours."

⁵The messengers came again and said, "This is what Ben-Hadad says: 'I sent to demand your silver and gold, your wives and your children. ⁶But about this time tomorrow I am going to send my officials to search your palace and the houses of your officials. They will seize everything you value and carry it away.' "

⁷The king of Israel summoned all the elders of the land and said to them, "See how this man is looking for trouble! When he sent for my wives and my children, my silver and my gold, I did not refuse him."

⁸The elders and the people all answered, "Don't listen to him or agree to his demands."

⁹So he replied to Ben-Hadad's messengers, "Tell my lord the king, 'Your servant will do all you demanded the first time, but this demand I cannot meet.' " They left and took the answer back to Ben-Hadad.

¹⁰Then Ben-Hadad sent another message to Ahab: "May the gods deal with me, be it ever so severely, if enough dust remains in Samaria to give each of my men a handful."

¹¹The king of Israel answered, "Tell him: 'One who puts on his armor should not boast like one who takes it off.' "

¹²Ben-Hadad heard this message while he and the kings were drinking in their tents, and he ordered his men: "Prepare to attack." So they prepared to attack the city.

Ben-Hadad II was the son of the Ben-Hadad whom we read about back in chapter 15:18. During his reign Aram, Israel's powerful neighbor to the northeast, continued to threaten God's chosen people. Ben-Hadad II, together with thirty-two vassal kings, invaded the land of Israel and laid siege to the capital city of Samaria. Ahab was powerless. He did not have adequate military power. Because he was an unbeliever, he did not turn to the Lord for help.

King Ben-Hadad took advantage of Ahab's weakness by sending arrogant messages to him. Solomon had written, "Pride goes before destruction, a haughty spirit before a fall" (Proverbs 16:18). In a short time Ben-Hadad also would learn that God's words are the truth.

Ahab Defeats Ben-Hadad

¹³Meanwhile a prophet came to Ahab king of Israel and announced, "This is what the LORD says: 'Do you see this vast army? I will give it into your hand today, and then you will know that I am the LORD.' "

¹⁴"But who will do this?" asked Ahab.

The prophet replied, "This is what the LORD says: 'The young officers of the provincial commanders will do it.' "

"And who will start the battle?" he asked.

The prophet answered, "You will."

¹⁵So Ahab summoned the young officers of the provincial commanders, 232 men. Then he assembled the rest of the Israelites, 7,000 in all. ¹⁶They set out at noon while Ben-Hadad and the 32 kings allied with him were in their tents getting drunk. ¹⁷The young officers of the provincial commanders went out first.

Now Ben-Hadad had dispatched scouts, who reported, "Men are advancing from Samaria."

¹⁸He said, "If they have come out for peace, take them alive; if they have come out for war, take them alive."

¹⁹The young officers of the provincial commanders marched out of the city with the army behind them ²⁰and each one struck down his opponent. At that, the Arameans fled, with the Israelites in pursuit. But Ben-Hadad king of Aram escaped on horseback with some of his horsemen. ²¹The king of Israel advanced and overpowered the horses and chariots and inflicted heavy losses on the Arameans.

A gracious God offered his help to Ahab even though this unbelieving king did not deserve it and was not seeking it. This is God's undeserved love, his grace.

God's actions here are similar to the way in which he has dealt with us. By nature we also were in a predicament. We were captives of Satan and were doomed to death. By nature we did not call out to God for help. How could we when we were dead in trespasses and sins! But our gracious God showed his undeserved love for us by rescuing us. God won a victory for Ahab in a way which seems weak and foolish. Sending his Son into the world to die on a cross seems to be an equally weak and foolish way to win a victory for us.

But that first victory was not the end of Ahab's trouble. Ben-Hadad would return.

[22] Afterward, the prophet came to the king of Israel and said, "Strengthen your position and see what must be done, because next spring the king of Aram will attack you again."

[23] Meanwhile, the officials of the king of Aram advised him, "Their gods are gods of the hills. That is why they were too strong for us. But if we fight them on the plains, surely we will be stronger than they. [24] Do this: Remove all the kings from their commands and replace them with other officers. [25] You must also raise an army like the one you lost—horse for horse and chariot for chariot—so we can fight Israel on the plains. Then surely we will be stronger than they." He agreed with them and acted accordingly.

[26] The next spring Ben-Hadad mustered the Arameans and went up to Aphek to fight against Israel. [27] When the Israelites were also mustered and given provisions, they marched out to meet them. The Israelites camped opposite them like two small flocks of goats, while the Arameans covered the countryside.

[28] The man of God came up and told the king of Israel, "This is what the LORD says: 'Because the Arameans think the LORD is a god of the hills and not a god of the valleys, I will deliver this vast army into your hands, and you will know that I am the LORD.' "

[29] For seven days they camped opposite each other, and on the seventh day the battle was joined. The Israelites inflicted a

hundred thousand casualties on the Aramean foot soldiers in one day. ³⁰The rest of them escaped to the city of Aphek, where the wall collapsed on twenty-seven thousand of them. And Ben-Hadad fled to the city and hid in an inner room.

Israel's heathen neighbors believed in many gods. They believed that each of them had power over a certain part of the world. They did not believe in one almighty God who is the Creator of heaven and earth. Therefore Ben-Hadad was back a year later more determined than ever to win a victory over Israel.

Ben-Hadad not only chose a different place to fight. He also replaced the thirty-two kings with thirty-two professional soldiers, men who were veterans of the battlefield.

Our enemy does not give up easily either. Peter tells us that Satan is like a roaring lion constantly seeking victims to devour. The hymn writer reminds us that we "walk in danger all the way" (TLH 413:1). Therefore, just as the prophet asked Ahab to strengthen himself for the next battle, so God instructs us to strengthen ourselves through his word and sacrament so that we will be prepared for tomorrow's battle.

The armies of Aram and Israel met at Aphek, east of the Sea of Galilee. Here God would show that he controls not only the hills but the valleys as well.

Once again God kept his promise and fought for that little army of Israel. Even when Ben-Hadad fled to the city of Aphek and took refuge on and behind the city walls, God's hand was against them. No one can escape God's avenging hand.

³¹His officials said to him, "Look, we have heard that the kings of the house of Israel are merciful. Let us go to the king of Israel with sackcloth around our waists and ropes around our heads. Perhaps he will spare your life."

³²Wearing sackcloth around their waists and ropes around their heads, they went to the king of Israel and said, "Your servant Ben-Hadad says: 'Please let me live.' "

The king answered, "Is he still alive? He is my brother."

³³The men took this as a good sign and were quick to pick up his word. "Yes, your brother Ben-Hadad!" they said.

"Go and get him," the king said. When Ben-Hadad came out, Ahab had him come up into his chariot.

³⁴"I will return the cities my father took from your father," Ben-Hadad offered. "You may set up your own market areas in Damascus, as my father did in Samaria."

⌊Ahab said,⌋ "On the basis of a treaty I will set you free." So he made a treaty with him, and let him go.

God's grace is free, but it is not cheap. It is not given to sinners so that we might squander it as we please. This is where King Ahab made another mistake. He did not take advantage of the victory God had freely given to him. In Ahab's own chariot, the enemy Ben-Hadad had the nerve to propose the terms of peace: he would return certain cities to Israel, and he would permit Ahab to establish trade centers in Damascus; Ahab in turn would give Ben-Hadad his freedom.

A Prophet Condemns Ahab

³⁵By the word of the LORD one of the sons of the prophets said to his companion, "Strike me with your weapon," but the man refused.

³⁶So the prophet said, "Because you have not obeyed the LORD, as soon as you leave me a lion will kill you." And after the man went away, a lion found him and killed him.

³⁷The prophet found another man and said, "Strike me, please." So the man struck him and wounded him. ³⁸Then the prophet went and stood by the road waiting for the king. He disguised himself with his headband down over his eyes. ³⁹As the king passed by, the prophet called out to him, "Your servant went

into the thick of the battle, and somone came to me with a captive and said, 'Guard this man. If he is missing, it will be your life for his life, or you must pay a talent of silver.' [40]While your servant was busy here and there, the man disappeared."

"That is your sentence," the king of Israel said. "You have pronounced it yourself."

[41]Then the prophet quickly removed the headband from his eyes, and the king of Israel recognized him as one of the prophets. [42]He said to the king, "This is what the LORD says: 'You have set free a man I had determined should die. Therefore it is your life for his life, your people for his people.' "[43]Sullen and angry, the king of Israel went to his palace in Samaria.

Striking another human being in anger or for revenge is clearly a sin against God. In this case, however, the man who refused to strike God's prophet was deliberately acting against God's unusual but clear command.

It was foolish for Ahab to make peace with his arch-enemy. Therefore God sent another prophet to him. This unnamed prophet was perhaps Micaiah, the man we will hear about in chapter 22.

When Satan's direct attacks against us meet with failure, he uses different tactics. He may well come to us with a smiling face, just as Ben-Hadad came to Ahab. Satan will stretch out his hand and say, "Let's be friends!" Therefore Christians need to encourage each other with the hymn,

> Oh, watch and fight and pray,
> The battle ne'er give o'er;
> Renew it boldly ev'ry day
> And help divine implore. (TLH 449:2)

The Christian who dares to make friends with the enemy of God and to put himself on the side of the enemy, will find himself condemned with the enemy on the last day.

Jezebel Advises Ahab (1 Kings 21:7)

144

Secular historians would probably not take time to recount the incident recorded in chapter 21. Neither Naboth nor his vineyard has any political significance. But our inspired writer records this event to show us how "a bad tree bears bad fruit" (Matthew 7:17). In the case of an unbeliever like Ahab we will see the works of the flesh in full control of his life. The fruit of the Spirit will be absent.

Naboth's Vineyard

21 **Some time later there was an incident involving a vineyard belonging to Naboth the Jezreelite. The vineyard was in Jezreel, close to the palace of Ahab king of Samaria.** **²Ahab said to Naboth, "Let me have your vineyard to use for a vegetable garden, since it is close to my palace. In exchange, I will give you a better vineyard or, if you prefer, I will pay you whatever it is worth."**

³But Naboth replied, "The LORD forbid that I should give you the inheritance of my fathers."

⁴So Ahab went home, sullen and angry because Naboth the Jezreelite had said, "I will not give you the inheritance of my fathers." He lay on his bed sulking and refused to eat.

The valley of Jezreel begins at Mount Carmel on the Mediterranean Sea and stretches toward the south and east down to the Jordan River. It is one of the richest areas of the land of Palestine. Isaiah referred to it as "a fertile valley" (Isaiah 28:1). The valley was sheltered from the coldest weather. The rich soil and a good supply of water from the surrounding hills make it an ideal place to raise grapes and other crops. That's how it got its name, "Jezreel," a Hebrew word meaning, "God will sow."

The city of Jezreel was located at the top of a steep slope that descended into the valley. From this point, especially from the tower of Jezreel, it is possible to see for many miles.

It was from this tower that the watchman saw Jehu coming when he was still a great distance away (2 Kings 9:17).

Caravans of merchants crisscrossed the valley. Military leaders also saw its importance.

Ahab's capital and his palace were in Samaria. For the reasons just mentioned he chose Jezreel, twenty-five miles north of Samaria, as the location of his summer palace. Ahab's famous ivory house was likely here in Jezreel (1 Kings 22:39).

And it was here, close to the palace, that a man named Naboth owned a vineyard. Since that vineyard had been in his family for generations, Naboth did not care to sell it. That was God's plan from the beginning. He wanted the land to remain with each Israelite family perpetually (Leviticus 25:23).

It is not a sin to offer to buy a piece of property, but in this case Ahab would not take "no" for an answer. Ahab became "sullen and angry." In Deuteronomy 21:18-21 Moses uses the same word to describe a stubborn child who refuses to obey his mother or father. Hosea uses it to describe a stubborn heifer who will not obey her owner (Hosea 4:16). The Hebrew word "angry" is used to describe a raging sea in Jonah 1:15. A storm was raging in Ahab's heart.

The Bible has yet another word to describe Ahab's attitude—"covetous." "Covet" means to want something God clearly does not want us to have, to want something so badly that one is willing to break one of God's other commandments to get it.

The unbeliever knows that it is wrong to kill or to rob a bank or to take another man's wife. But the world generally does not use the word "covet." The world does not agree that even thoughts can be morally wrong. Although man looks at the outward appearance, "the LORD looks at the heart" (1 Samuel 16:7). Jesus puts evil thoughts on the same level with murder and adultery (Matthew 15:19). God has given us not one but two commandments in which he forbids coveting.

Because coveting takes place in the heart, we will ordinarily not be able to see that sin in someone else's life. But we will recognize it when it enters our own heart. The sin of coveting begins when we are not content with the food, clothing, and other earthly blessings that God has given to us.

⁵His wife Jezebel came in and asked him, "Why are you so sullen? Why won't you eat?"

⁶He answered her, "Because I said to Naboth the Jezreelite, 'Sell me your vineyard; or if you prefer, I will give you another vineyard in its place.' But he said, 'I will not give you my vineyard.' "

⁷Jezebel his wife said, "Is this how you act as king over Israel? Get up and eat! Cheer up. I'll get you the vineyard of Naboth the Jezreelite."

⁸So she wrote letters in Ahab's name, placed his seal on them, and sent them to the elders and nobles who lived in Naboth's city with him. ⁹In those letters she wrote:

"Proclaim a day of fasting and seat Naboth in a prominent place among the people. ¹⁰But seat two scoundrels opposite him and have them testify that he has cursed both God and the king. Then take him out and stone him to death."

¹¹So the elders and nobles who lived in Naboth's city did as Jezebel directed in the letters she had written to them. ¹²They proclaimed a fast and seated Naboth in a prominent place among the people. ¹³Then two scoundrels came and sat opposite him and brought charges against Naboth before the people, saying, "Naboth has cursed both God and the king." So they took him outside the city and stoned him to death. ¹⁴Then they sent word to Jezebel: "Naboth has been stoned and is dead."

¹⁵As soon as Jezebel heard that Naboth had been stoned to death, she said to Ahab, "Get up and take possession of the

vineyard of Naboth the Jezreelite that he refused to sell you. He is no longer alive, but dead." 16When Ahab heard that Naboth was dead, he got up and went down to take possession of Naboth's vineyard.

If Ahab had remained unmarried or if he had married a God-fearing woman, this might have been the end of the story. But Ahab had married a heathen princess named Jezebel, a daughter of the king of neighboring Phoenicia. "His wife Jezebel," "Jezebel his wife"—those words are emphasized in verses, 5,7 and 25. She devised a devilish plan to get what the king wanted.

Through forged letters Jezebel asked the city leaders to proclaim a fast, an indication that something terrible had happened. When Naboth was found guilty of cursing both God and the king, he was stoned to death outside the city in strict compliance with God's law (Leviticus 24:14-16).

The woman who had put many of God's prophets to death thought nothing of seizing power for herself and putting to death another innocent man.

It is not unusual today for a Christian man or woman to marry an unbelieving spouse. Sometimes the Christian is convinced that this will cause only a minor conflict, perhaps only on Sunday mornings. The example before us shows that much more is involved. A heathen woman like Jezebel is thoroughly different from a Christian woman. The Christian and the heathen view life in different ways, they have different goals, they are willing to do different things in order to acquire property. Jezebel's philosophy was "me first." Jezebel would say, "If I or someone in my family wants something, I will see to it that we get it." Christian husbands and wives have tasted the unselfish love of Christ. As Christians our motto is "God first." Like Paul, we are learning to be content with the conditions in life that God has assigned to us.

¹⁷Then the word of the LORD came to Elijah the Tishbite: ¹⁸"Go down to meet Ahab king of Israel, who rules in Samaria. He is now in Naboth's vineyard, where he has gone to take possession of it. ¹⁹Say to him, 'This is what the LORD says: Have you not murdered a man and seized his property?' Then say to him, 'This is what the LORD says: In the place where dogs licked up Naboth's blood, dogs will lick up your blood—yes, yours!' "

²⁰Ahab said to Elijah, "So you have found me, my enemy!"

"I have found you," he answered, "because you have sold yourself to do evil in the eyes of the LORD. ²¹'I am going to bring disaster to you. I will consume your descendants and cut off from Ahab every last male in Israel—slave or free. ²²I will make your house like that of Jeroboam son of Nebat and that of Baasha son of Ahijah, because you have provoked me to anger and have caused Israel to sin.'

²³"And also concerning Jezebel the LORD says: 'Dogs will devour Jezebel by the wall of Jezreel.'

²⁴"Dogs will eat those belonging to Ahab who die in the city, and the birds of the air will feed on those who die in the country."

²⁵(There was never a man like Ahab, who sold himself to do evil in the eyes of the LORD, urged on by Jezebel his wife. ²⁶He behaved in the vilest manner by going after idols, like the Amorites the LORD drove out before Israel.)

²⁷When Ahab heard these words, he tore his clothes, put on sackcloth and fasted. He lay in sackcloth and went around meekly.

²⁸Then the word of the LORD came to Elijah the Tishbite: ²⁹"Have you noticed how Ahab has humbled himself before me? Because he has humbled himself, I will not bring this disaster in his day, but I will bring it on his house in the days of his son."

God has established that the man is the head of the family. Just as God came looking for Adam and held him responsible when things went wrong in the Garden of Eden, so God's prophet now came looking for Ahab. God held him accountable for the actions of his wife.

When Elijah met the king in Naboth's vineyard (note that it is still called *Naboth's* vineyard), Ahab's first words were, "So you have found me, my enemy!" Here is the key to the problem. Ahab viewed God and God's prophet as his enemies. Ahab was still a child of the devil. Because Ahab deliberately remained in unbelief and had led others away from the Lord, God's judgment on him would be severe.

When Ahab showed signs of penitence, a gracious God delayed the judgment he had threatened. But that penitence was short-lived. In the following chapters we see how a just God carried out his threat.

This incident from Ahab's life is similar to an incident in the life of King David. Both kings were guilty of coveting. Ahab wanted another man's property; David wanted another man's wife (2 Samuel 11-12). Both kings received a visit from God's prophet.

But here the similarity ends. David did not greet his pastor with the words, "So you have found me, my enemy!" David repented of his sin. He wrote Psalm 51: "Have mercy on me, O God, according to your unfailing love; according to your great compassion blot out my transgressions" (Psalm 51:1). David lived and died as a believer in the Lord. Ahab lived and died as an unbeliever.

Death is the consequence of sin for all people. Eternal death is the punishment for unbelief.

A young man named Jehu was present and overheard the prophecy spoken against King Ahab. Jehu was destined to become the commander-in-chief of Israel's armies at the time of King Joram, Ahab's son. Acting as God's avenger Jehu would slay Ahab's wife Jezebel (2 Kings 9:33-37), as well as the entire family of Ahab (2 Kings 9:26).

How quickly we forget! Back in chapter 20 we heard how *the LORD*, the faithful Savior-God, gave Ahab a victory over Aram and how *the LORD* was displeased when Ahab permitted King Ben-Hadad to slip through his fingers. In the next chapter we see the Lord pushed into the background while Ahab relies instead on Judah's King Jehoshaphat for help and seeks counsel from his troop of false prophets.

Micaiah Prophesies Against Ahab

22 For three years there was no war between Aram and Israel. ²But in the third year Jehoshaphat king of Judah went down to see the king of Israel. ³The king of Israel had said to his officials, "Don't you know that Ramoth Gilead belongs to us and yet we are doing nothing to retake it from the king of Aram?"

⁴So he asked Jehoshaphat, "Will you go with me to fight against Ramoth Gilead?"

Jehoshaphat replied to the king of Israel, "I am as you are, my people as your people, my horses as your horses." ⁵But Jehoshaphat also said to the king of Israel, "First seek the counsel of the LORD."

⁶So the king of Israel brought together the prophets—about four hundred men—and asked them, "Shall I go to war against Ramoth Gilead, or shall I refrain?"

"Go," they answered, "for the Lord will give it into the king's hand."

⁷But Jehoshaphat asked, "Is there not a prophet of the LORD here whom we can inquire of?"

⁸The king of Israel answered Jehoshaphat, "There is still one man through whom we can inquire of the LORD, but I hate him because he never prophesies anything good about me, but always bad. He is Micaiah son of Imlah."

"The king should not say that," Jehoshaphat replied.

⁹So the king of Israel called one of his officials and said, "Bring Micaiah son of Imlah at once."

¹⁰Dressed in their royal robes, the king of Israel and Jehoshaphat king of Judah were sitting on their thrones at the threshing floor by the entrance of the gate of Samaria, with all the prophets prophesying before them. ¹¹Now Zedekiah son of Kenaanah had

made iron horns and he declared, "This is what the LORD says: 'With these you will gore the Arameans until they are destroyed.' "

¹²All the other prophets were prophesying the same thing. "Attack Ramoth Gilead and be victorious," they said, "for the LORD will give it into the king's hand."

We learn from 2 Chronicles 18:1,2 that there was a marital alliance between Ahab and Jehoshaphat. Jehoshaphat, the God-fearing king of Judah, had made the mistake of arranging a marriage between his son Jehoram and Athaliah, the wicked daughter of Ahab and Jezebel.

A summit meeting of the two kings took place in Samaria, where Ahab entertained his guests with a lavish feast. At that meeting Ahab suggested that they attempt to regain Ramoth Gilead, a city east of the Jordan on the border between Israel and Aram. Ramoth Gilead was one of the six cities of refuge which God had appointed when Israel took possession of their promised land (Deuteronomy 4:43; Joshua 20:8). The fact that heathen people had captured and occupied this important Israelite city was apparently viewed with embarrassment by both Israel and Judah. Therefore Jehoshaphat agreed to give military help.

Zedekiah is a classic example of a false prophet. Using iron horns, he graphically appealed to the pride and power of his hearers. He flattered his king and the royal advisers and soothed their impenitent hearts with a message of peace and safety. Pious King Jehoshaphat, however, was not impressed with this foolishness.

God's prophet Micaiah, on the other hand, like the prophet Ahijah back in chapter 14, refused to announce good news to an impenitent king. The gospel is intended only for the penitent. Verses 26 and 27 imply that Micaiah was at this time already in prison for giving unfavorable reports to the king. Wicked hearts like that of King

Ahab enjoy the flattering words of false prophets but dislike the word of truth.

¹³The messenger who had gone to summon Micaiah said to him, "Look, as one man the other prophets are predicting success for the king. Let your word agree with theirs, and speak favorably."

¹⁴But Micaiah said, "As surely as the LORD lives, I can tell him only what the LORD tells me."

¹⁵When he arrived, the king asked him, "Micaiah, shall we go to war against Ramoth Gilead, or shall I refrain?"

"Attack and be victorious," he answered, "for the LORD will give it into the king's hand."

¹⁶The king said to him, "How many times must I make you swear to tell me nothing but the truth in the name of the LORD?"

¹⁷Then Micaiah answered, "I saw all Israel scattered on the hills like sheep without a shepherd, and the LORD said, 'These people have no master. Let each one go home in peace.' "

¹⁸The king of Israel said to Jehoshaphat, "Didn't I tell you that he never prophesies anything good about me, but only bad?"

¹⁹Micaiah continued, "Therefore hear the word of the LORD: I saw the LORD sitting on his throne with all the host of heaven standing around him on his right and on his left. ²⁰And the LORD said, 'Who will entice Ahab into attacking Ramoth Gilead and going to his death there?'

"One suggested this, and another that. ²¹Finally, a spirit came forward, stood before the LORD and said, 'I will entice him.'

²²" 'By what means?' the LORD asked.

" 'I will go out and be a lying spirit in the mouths of all his prophets,' he said.

" 'You will succeed in enticing him,' said the LORD. 'Go and do it.'

²³"So now the LORD has put a lying spirit in the mouths of all these prophets of yours. The LORD has decreed disaster for you."

²⁴Then Zedekiah son of Kenaanah went up and slapped Micaiah in the face. "Which way did the spirit from the LORD go when he went from me to speak to you?" he asked.

²⁵Micaiah replied, "You will find out on the day you go to hide in an inner room."

²⁶The king of Israel then ordered, "Take Micaiah and send him back to Amon the ruler of the city and to Joash the king's son ²⁷and say, 'This is what the king says: Put this fellow in prison and give him nothing but bread and water until I return safely.' "

²⁸Micaiah declared, "If you ever return safely, the LORD has not spoken through me." Then he added, "Mark my words, all you people!"

Here is one of the few examples of irony and sarcasm in the Bible—sarcasm but not deceit, for Ahab understood Micaiah's position very well. The brief role reversal of the king and the prophet in verses 15 and 16 would be humorous if it were not so serious.

As a matter of fact, Israel would be soundly defeated by Aram. King Ahab would die just as Elijah had foretold earlier (1 Kings 21:19).

The "lying spirit" who stood before God's throne and filled the hearts of the false prophets is Satan himself, the "father of lies" (John 8:44). The Bible does not reveal to us how much access Satan has to the throne of God, but in Job 1:6 we hear of another time when Satan appeared before God with the other angels. In each case God was fully in control. In each case Satan's power was limited to carrying out God's gracious plans.

When people continue, intentionally, to reject God and his word, the time finally comes when God abandons them to the control of Satan. Something similar had already happened to King Saul (1 Samuel 16:14,15). False prophets like Zedekiah and wicked kings like Ahab might continue to use the name of the Lord, but Ahab's unbelief had become a deliberate, inexcusable rejection of what he knew to be God's word.

In our day we frequently see clergymen of different denominations worshiping together. The participants, some of whom may claim to be Lutheran, often express the desire that they "want to learn from one another." Micaiah was not that kind of man. Micaiah did not shake hands with the false prophets, hoping to learn something from them. He spoke the words of God boldly, decisively, and without apology. May God bless our church with pastors and lay people who have that same determination!

Ahab Killed at Ramoth Gilead

²⁹So the king of Israel and Jehoshaphat king of Judah went up to Ramoth Gilead. ³⁰The king of Israel said to Jehoshaphat, "I will enter the battle in disguise, but you wear your royal robes." So the king of Israel disguised himself and went into battle.

³¹Now the king of Aram had ordered his thirty-two chariot commanders, "Do not fight with anyone, small or great, except the king of Israel." ³²When the chariot commanders saw Jehoshaphat, they thought, "Surely this is the king of Israel." So they turned to attack him, but when Jehoshaphat cried out, ³³the commanders saw that he was not the king of Israel and stopped pursuing him.

³⁴But someone drew his bow at random and hit the king of Israel between the sections of his armor. The king told his chariot driver, "Wheel around and get me out of the fighting, I've been wounded." ³⁵All day long the battle raged, and the king was propped up in his chariot facing the Arameans. The blood from his wound ran onto the floor of the chariot, and that evening he died. ³⁶As the sun was setting, a cry spread through the army: "Every man to his town; everyone to his land!"

³⁷So the king died and was brought to Samaria, and they buried him there. ³⁸They washed the chariot at a pool in Samaria (where the prostitutes bathed), and the dogs licked up his blood, as the word of the LORD had declared.

³⁹As for the other events of Ahab's reign, including all he did, the palace he built and inlaid with ivory, and the cities he fortified,

Ahab Wounded in Battle (1 Kings 22:34)

are they not written in the book of the annals of the kings of Israel? **40**Ahab rested with his fathers. And Ahaziah his son succeeded him as king.

Ahab's disguise in battle demonstrates that the children of this world are often wiser than the children of God (Luke 16:8). But Ahab's cleverness would not prevent God from carrying out the threat he had made through Elijah and Micaiah. A random arrow inflicted a deadly wound on King Ahab. The details of prophecy were fulfilled, and Ahab's earthly life came to a shameful end. Eternal shame awaits all those who follow his example of unbelief.

The God of history still uses what appear as random happenings to carry out his plans. St. Paul assures us that "in all things God works for the good of those who love him" (Romans 8:28).

Jehoshaphat King of Judah

41Jehoshaphat son of Asa became king of Judah in the fourth year of Ahab king of Israel. **42**Jehoshaphat was thirty-five years old when he became king, and he reigned in Jerusalem twenty-five years. His mother's name was Azubah daughter of Shilhi. **43**In everything he walked in the ways of his father Asa and did not stray from them; he did what was right in the eyes of the LORD. The high places, however, were not removed, and the people continued to offer sacrifices and burn incense there. **44**Jehoshaphat was also at peace with the king of Israel.

45As for the other events of Jehoshaphat's reign, the things he achieved and his military exploits, are they not written in the book of the annals of the kings of Judah? **46**He rid the land of the rest of the male shrine prostitutes who remained there even after the reign of his father Asa. **47**There was then no king in Edom; a deputy ruled.

48Now Jehoshaphat built a fleet of trading ships to go to Ophir for gold, but they never set sail—they were wrecked at Ezion

Geber. ⁴⁹At that time Ahaziah son of Ahab said to Jehoshaphat, "Let my men sail with your men," but Jehoshaphat refused.

⁵⁰Then Jehoshaphat rested with his fathers and was buried with them in the city of David his father. And Jehoram his son succeeded him.

When King Jehoshaphat returned safely to Jerusalem, the prophet Jehu came to him and announced that God's wrath was burning against him (2 Chronicles 19:1-3). Jehu is the same man who announced the destruction of Baasha and his family (1 Kings 16:3); he should not be confused with the man who later became king over Israel. The reason for God's anger is that Jehoshaphat loved those whom God hated. He had made a family alliance with Ahab and had stood at his side in battle.

This is a dangerous road for anyone to travel. Whoever runs with the world is compelled to sin with the world. "If anyone loves the world, the love of the Father is not in him" (1 John 2:15). "Anyone who chooses to be a friend of the world becomes an enemy of God" (James 4:4).

Christians and Christian denominations need to be cautioned lest they become unequally yoked with unbelievers. At times the Christians and the unbelievers may appear to have a common goal. But their reasons for reaching out to that goal and even their methodology will be entirely different.

The writer of 1 Kings, however, recounts only the good things that Jehoshaphat did, how he removed the idolatrous practices set up by previous kings.

The glory days of King Solomon were gone forever. God did not permit Jehoshaphat's ships to bring back costly treasures.

Although we will read more about Jehoshaphat and Ahaziah in 2 Kings 3, the obituaries of both men are recorded here.

Ahaziah King of Israel

[51]Ahaziah son of Ahab became king of Israel in Samaria in the seventeenth year of Jehoshaphat king of Judah, and he reigned over Israel two years. [52]He did evil in the eyes of the LORD, because he walked in the ways of his father and mother and in the ways of Jeroboam son of Nebat, who caused Israel to sin. [53]He served and worshiped Baal and provoked the LORD, the God of Israel, to anger, just as his father had done.

"Like father, like son." No one should be surprised to learn that Ahaziah worshiped Baal "just as his father had done."

If parents today do not care whether their spouse is Christian or heathen, if they do not worship the Lord with their whole heart, they should not be surprised to see their children grow up with the same attitudes and finally perish eternally.

THE **KING** AND THE KINGS
2 KINGS
THE **KING** REJECTS THE KINGS

In their original form 1 and 2 Kings were counted as one book. 2 Kings begins in the middle of a story exactly where 1 Kings ended.

PART I

THE KING REJECTS ISRAEL
2 KINGS 1:1-17:41

The Ministry of Elijah and Elisha

The Lord's Judgment on Ahaziah

1 After Ahab's death, Moab rebelled against Israel. ²Now Ahaziah had fallen through the lattice of his upper room in Samaria and injured himself. So he sent messengers, saying to them, "Go and consult Baal-Zebub, the god of Ekron, to see if I will recover from this injury."

³But the angel of the Lord said to Elijah the Tishbite, "Go up and meet the messengers of the king of Samaria and ask them, 'Is it because there is no God in Israel that you are going off to consult Baal-Zebub, the god of Ekron?' ⁴Therefore this is what the Lord says: 'You will not leave the bed you are lying on. You will certainly die!' " So Elijah went.

⁵When the messengers returned to the king, he asked them, "Why have you come back?"

⁶"A man came to meet us," they replied. "And he said to us, 'Go back to the king who sent you and tell him, "This is what the Lord says: Is it because there is no God in Israel that you are sending men to consult Baal-Zebub, the god of Ekron? Therefore you will not leave the bed you are lying on. You will certainly die!' "

⁷The king asked them, "What kind of man was it who came to meet you and told you this?"

⁸They replied, "He was a man with a garment of hair and with a leather belt around his waist."

The king said, "That was Elijah the Tishbite."

Ahaziah, son and successor of wicked King Ahab, ruled over Israel for two years, and his reign was filled with political and personal troubles. When the Moabites saw that Ahaziah's father, Ahab, was not able to control the Arameans, they decided that they also would stop bringing tribute. From 2 Kings 3:4 we learn that the king of Moab had been paying the king of Israel tribute amounting to 100,000 lambs and the wool of 100,000 rams. The second part of a divine judgment came when Ahaziah was seriously injured in a fall.

When people are sick, they often turn to God. Since Ahaziah was an unbeliever, he turned to Baal-Zebub, the god of the Philistines.

Baal-Zebub means "lord of the flies." That title sounds unusual to us, but Ahaziah and the Philistines did not think it was one bit funny. They were convinced that Baal-Zebub could not only keep flies and insects away from the crops, but could foretell the future as well.

The messengers never had an opportunity to consult with "the lord of the flies." The angel of the Lord, that is, the Lord Jesus himself (whom we met in 1 Kings 19:5) had just brought a message to Elijah.

Elijah had not won any popularity contest with Ahaziah's parents, Ahab and Jezebel. Ahaziah did not like God's prophet either. We can almost hear the king saying with a disgusted tone of voice, "It is Elijah the Tishbite!"

In Luke 1:17 Gabriel announced that our Lord's fore-runner, John the Baptist, would go before the Lord Jesus "in the spirit and power of Elijah." There is a striking similarity between the two. When John was preaching in the wilderness at the Jordan River, he also was wearing a garment of camel's hair and had a leather belt around his waist. The messages of Elijah and of John were also similar. Both men talked to people face to face, even to kings and kings' messengers. Both of them talked about real, specific sins which they saw in the lives of the people. Both of them incurred the wrath of their king.

God's faithful messengers must continue to talk about specific sins as they call people to repentance. As they do that work, they will be viewed with contempt by the impenitent. Disgusted voices will continue to say, "That Pastor So-and-so!" If people fail to see their sin, they will see no need for a Savior. And if people die in impenitence, they will not escape God's judgment, as the following verses show us.

⁹Then he sent to Elijah a captain with his company of fifty men. The captain went up to Elijah, who was sitting on the top of a hill, and said to him, "Man of God, the king says, 'Come down!' "

¹⁰Elijah answered the captain, "If I am a man of God, may fire come down from heaven and consume you and your fifty men!" The fire fell from heaven and consumed the captain and his men.

¹¹At this the king sent to Elijah another captain with his fifty men. The captain said to him, "Man of God, this is what the king says, 'Come down at once!' "

¹²"If I am a man of God," Elijah replied, "may fire come down from heaven and consume you and your fifty men!" Then the fire of God fell from heaven and consumed him and his fifty men.

¹³So the king sent a third captain with his fifty men. This third captain went up and fell on his knees before Elijah. "Man of God," he begged, "please have respect for my life and the lives of these fifty men, your servants! ¹⁴See, fire has fallen from heaven and consumed the first two captains and all their men. But now have respect for my life!"

¹⁵The angel of the LORD said to Elijah, "Go down with him; do not be afraid of him." So Elijah got up and went down with him to the king.

¹⁶He told the king, "This is what the LORD says: Is it because there is no God in Israel for you to consult that you have sent messengers to consult Baal-Zebub, the god of Ekron? Because you have done this, you will never leave the bed you are lying on. You will certainly die!" ¹⁷So he died, according to the word of the LORD that Elijah had spoken.

Because Ahaziah had no son, Joram succeeded him as king in the second year of Jehoram son of Jehoshaphat king of Judah. [18] As for all the other events of Ahaziah's reign, and what he did, are they not written in the book of the annals of the kings of Israel?

We can almost hear the tough army captain barking orders at Elijah: "Man of God, the king says, 'Come down! Come down at once!' " The words of God's prophets, however, are more powerful than the words of any captain. St. John may have been thinking of this incident when he wrote, "If anyone tries to harm them, fire comes from their mouths and devours their enemies" (Revelation 11:5).

The fire that consumed Elijah's sacrifice on Mount Carmel was a gracious sign from God. It showed the people that the Lord is almighty and urged the people to repent (1 Kings 18:37). Now God twice sent the fire of judgment—not on innocent soldiers but on people who for many years had rejected his call to repentance.

It is hard to understand how an unbeliever can be so blind to God's hand of vengeance, but King Ahaziah sent a third captain with still another fifty soldiers to arrest Elijah. Scripture does not tell us whether this captain was genuinely repentant, but we do know that God spared his life and the lives of his men. We know also that the Lord is not willing that any should perish but that all should come to repentance (2 Peter 3:9). When sinners come before God on their knees, pleading for his mercy, God is "faithful and just and will forgive us our sins and purify us from all unrighteousness" (1 John 1:9).

King Ahaziah's death—his earthly death as well as his eternal condemnation—were so unnecessary. In the Gospels we read of many sick people who came or were brought to Jesus, and the Savior healed them all. But when people come before God with an impenitent, idolatrous heart, they reject God's help and healing. They receive only death and judgment. Elijah's message to the king was emphatic: "You will certainly die!" Elijah's prophecy came true.

Many years later James and John wanted to call down fire from heaven on a certain Samaritan village because they would not receive Jesus (Luke 9:54,55). Jesus, however, would have nothing to do with it. Our work also is to proclaim the gospel of forgiveness to the penitent. Any judgments God will send, he will send at the appropriate time.

Since Ahaziah had no son, he was succeeded on the throne by his brother Joram, another son of Ahab and Jezebel.

In the Old Testament we read of two men who did not die but were taken bodily to heaven. One was Enoch, the other Elijah.

Elijah Taken Up to Heaven

2 When the LORD was about to take Elijah up to heaven in a whirlwind, Elijah and Elisha were on their way from Gilgal. **2** Elijah said to Elisha, "Stay here; the LORD has sent me to Bethel."

But Elisha said, "As surely as the LORD lives and you live, I will not leave you." So they went down to Bethel.

3 The company of the prophets at Bethel came out to Elisha and asked, "Do you know that the LORD is going to take your master from you today?"

"Yes, I know," Elisha replied, "but do not speak of it."

4 Then Elijah said to him, "Stay here, Elisha; the LORD has sent me to Jericho."

And he replied, "As surely as the LORD lives and as you live, I will not leave you." So they went to Jericho.

5 The company of the prophets at Jericho went up to Elisha and asked him, "Do you know that the LORD is going to take your master from you today?"

"Yes, I know," he replied, "but do not speak of it."

⁶Then Elijah said to him, "Stay here; the LORD has sent me to the Jordan."

And he replied, "As surely as the LORD lives and as you live, I will not leave you." So the two of them walked on.

Back in 1 Kings 19 we read how Elijah was thoroughly discouraged and wanted to die. At that time, however, God was not ready to grant Elijah's request. God still had work for his prophet to accomplish.

Now Elijah's work was finished. The time came when the Lord was ready to take Elijah up to heaven.

From time to time God's people today are discouraged and ask, "Why doesn't the Lord take me home?" The answer to that question is, "God will surely take us home when God determines that our earthly work is finished."

We can say the same thing of the Lord Jesus. Like Elijah, he ascended bodily into heaven only after his saving work was completed, only after he had paid for all sin, destroyed the power of Satan, and broken the bonds of death.

Elijah's last work was to visit the "companies of prophets" in Gilgal, Bethel, and Jericho. Evidently these groups of "sons of the prophets" (that is the literal translation of the Hebrew) were schools of music and religion conducted by one of God's inspired prophets (1 Samuel 10:5; 19:20), to provide a regular supply of messengers through whom God would speak to his people. Somehow God had revealed to these students also that Elijah would soon be taken into heaven.

⁷Fifty men of the company of the prophets went and stood at a distance, facing the place where Elijah and Elisha had stopped at the Jordan. ⁸Elijah took his cloak, rolled it up and struck the water with it. The water divided to the right and to the left, and the two of them crossed over on dry ground.

⁹When they had crossed, Elijah said to Elisha, "Tell me, what can I do for you before I am taken from you?"

"Let me inherit a double portion of your spirit," Elisha replied. [10]"You have asked a difficult thing," Elijah said, "yet if you see me when I am taken from you, it will be yours—otherwise not." [11]As they were walking along and talking together, suddenly a chariot of fire and horses of fire appeared and separated the two of them, and Elijah went up to heaven in a whirlwind. [12]Elisha saw this and cried out, "My father! My father! The chariots and horsemen of Israel!" And Elisha saw him no more. Then he took hold of his own clothes and tore them apart.

In Bible days a father customarily gave his oldest son or his favorite son a double share of the inheritance. By requesting a double portion of Elijah's spirit, Elisha was asking for that share which belonged to him as Elijah's successor. Like King Solomon, he wanted a practical gift to use in serving God's people. Only God could grant that request, but Elijah could give his successor a sign that God would do so.

Elijah had previously brought down fire from heaven, on Mount Carmel and again when King Ahaziah had ordered his arrest. Now a chariot and horses of fire took Elijah into heaven. There God gave Elijah a glorified body, the body in which he appeared with Jesus on the Mount of the Transfiguration (Matthew 17:3).

Elisha's exclamation, "The chariots and horsemen of Israel," refers to Elijah, his father in the faith. Just as mighty horses and chariots are emblems of a king's strength, so Elijah had been the spiritual bulwark of God's people. King Jehoash later addressed Elisha with that same title of respect (2 Kings 13:14). May God continue to give us faithful pastors and teachers who can rightly be called "the chariots and horsemen of Israel"!

[13]He picked up the cloak that had fallen from Elijah and went back and stood on the bank of the Jordan. [14]Then he took the

Elijah Ascends in a Chariot of Fire (2 Kings 2:11)

cloak that had fallen from him and struck the water with it. "Where now is the LORD, the God of Elijah?" he asked. When he struck the water, it divided to the right and to the left, and he crossed over.

15 The company of the prophets from Jericho, who were watching, said, "The spirit of Elijah is resting on Elisha." And they went to meet him and bowed to the ground before him. 16 "Look," they said, "we your servants have fifty able men. Let them go and look for your master. Perhaps the Spirit of the LORD has picked him up and set him down on some mountain or in some valley."

"No," Elisha replied, "do not send them."

17 But they persisted until he was too ashamed to refuse. So he said, "Send them." And they sent fifty men, who searched for three days but did not find him. 18 When they returned to Elisha, who was staying in Jericho, he said to them, "Didn't I tell you not to go?"

Elisha's prayer was granted. Not only did he see Elijah taken up into heaven, but the cloak, the symbol of Elijah's office, was once again delivered to him (see 1 Kings 19:19). God would be with Elisha just as he had been with Elijah.

When the waters of the Jordan River parted miraculously, the sons of the prophets, the seminary students there in Jericho, realized that Elisha was one of those men who "spoke from God as they were carried along by the Holy Spirit" (2 Peter 1:21). Unfortunately even the sons of the prophets refused to believe all of Elisha's words until their search party returned empty-handed three days later.

Healing of the Water

19 The men of the city said to Elisha, "Look, our lord, this town is well situated, as you can see, but the water is bad and the land is unproductive."

20 "Bring me a new bowl," he said, "and put salt in it." So they brought it to him.

171

²¹Then he went out to the spring and threw the salt into it, saying, "This is what the LORD says: 'I have healed this water. Never again will it cause death or make the land unproductive.' " ²²And the water has remained wholesome to this day, according to the word Elisha had spoken.

Parting the waters of the Jordan River was only the first of a dozen miracles performed by Elisha. In spite of its fine location near the Jordan, the well at Jericho was bad, and much of the land was unfruitful. Through Elisha the water there was made sweet—not because of the salt, but by the powerful word of God, "I have healed this water" (verse 21).

It is noteworthy that Isaiah later used the same Hebrew word for "heal." "By his wounds we are healed" (Isaiah 53:5). There is a similarity. The spring in Jericho had produced death and unfruitfulness. So also we were by nature impure, worthy of death, unable to produce the fruit of good works (see Romans 6:21,22). But just as God healed the spring of water in Jericho, so the wounds of our Savior have healed us from the impurity of sin. And having been healed from sin, we begin to please God by producing the fruits of good works.

Elisha Is Jeered

²³From there Elisha went up to Bethel. As he was walking along the road, some youths came out of the town and jeered at him. "Go on up, you baldhead!" they said. "Go on up, you baldhead!" ²⁴He turned around, looked at them and called down a curse on them in the name of the LORD. Then two bears came out of the woods and mauled forty-two of the youths. ²⁵And he went on to Mount Carmel and from there returned to Samaria.

"Bethel" literally means "house of God." At this time, however, Bethel had become a house of idolatry. Eighty years earlier wicked King Jeroboam had set up a golden calf at Bethel and had encouraged the people to worship it (1 Kings 12:29). For several generations the people had not been worshiping the Lord in Jerusalem. Because human nature is so perverse, it does not surprise us that the next generation publicly mocked those who taught God's word.

That is what happened to Elisha.

Such mocking is not unusual. The Jews mocked Jesus when he was on trial before Caiaphas. Some mocked the apostles on the day of Pentecost, accusing them of being drunk. Peter assures us that there will be scoffers in the world until the end of time (2 Peter 3:3).

But this time something unusual did happen. Elisha turned around and cursed that group of young people in the name of the Lord. The LORD, the faithful God of the covenant, immediately gave power to that curse. Two female bears came out of the woods and literally "tore apart" forty-two of the mockers.

The unbelieving world continues to hold the office of the public ministry in contempt. Television and movies routinely present the minister as a hypocrite, a comedian, an ignoramus, an unscrupulous fund raiser, an adulterer, or a combination of all five. This incident reminds us that God means business. As he sent his disciples out on a missionary journey, Jesus said to them, "He who listens to you listens to me; he who rejects you rejects me; but he who rejects me rejects him who sent me" (Luke 10:16). Those who will not listen to the word of God proclaimed by the apostles and prophets are rejecting God. Those who taunt God's prophets will rest under God's judgment, if not now then certainly on judgment day.

What a warning this is for our generation!

On the other hand, God's faithful people, like Elisha, find comfort in knowing that the Lord stands at our side to

173

protect us from the attacks of Satan and from the mockery of every unbeliever.

The bloody judgment which we see in this chapter is a shadow of a greater judgment to come. Because of Israel's continued impenitence, God later threatened, "Like a bear robbed of her cubs, I will attack them and rip them open" (Hosea 13:8).

Each of the twenty kings who ruled over the northern kingdom of Israel was an idolater. But God continued to be with these men and continued to call them to repentance. This is evidence of God's grace.

Moab Revolts

3 **Joram son of Ahab became king of Israel in Samaria in the eighteenth year of Jehoshaphat king of Judah, and he reigned twelve years. ²He did evil in the eyes of the LORD, but not as his father and mother had done. He got rid of the sacred stone of Baal that his father had made. ³Nevertheless he clung to the sins of Jeroboam son of Nebat, which he had caused Israel to commit; he did not turn away from them.**

In chapter 1 (verse 17) we read that Ahab's son Joram became king when Jehoram was in the second year of his reign over Judah. But in the verses before us we read that Ahab's son Joram became king of Israel when Jehoshaphat was king over Judah.

Which date is correct? Both are! It was not unusual for the king's son to be crowned before his father died. That is what happened here. During the last eight years of Jehoshaphat's reign both he and his son Jehoram were counted as kings over Judah. The eighteenth year of Jehoshaphat was the second year of his son Jehoram.

⁴Now Mesha king of Moab raised sheep, and he had to supply the king of Israel with a hundred thousand lambs and with the

wool of a hundred thousand rams. 5But after Ahab died, the king of Moab rebelled against the king of Israel. 6So at that time King Joram set out from Samaria and mobilized all Israel. 7He also sent this message to Jehoshaphat king of Judah: "The king of Moab has rebelled against me. Will you go with me to fight against Moab?"

"I will go with you," he replied. "I am as you are, my people as your people, my horses as your horses."

8"By what route shall we attack?" he asked.

"Through the Desert of Edom," he answered.

Back in 2 Samuel 8:2 we learned that David had conquered the land of Moab. For 150 years the people of Moab paid tribute to David, to Solomon, and then to the kings of Israel. The land of Moab east of the Dead Sea was suited for raising cattle. Some of the tax came in the form of sheep and wool. The writer does not specify that the 100,000 lambs and wool of 100,000 rams was an annual payment. Perhaps this exhorbitant tax was a one-time levy demanded by King Ahab. Therefore we are not surprised to hear that Mesha the king of Moab stopped sending tribute when Ahab died in battle.

Ahaziah, the son and successor of King Ahab, did nothing to bring Moab back into subjection during his two-year reign. But King Joram, Ahaziah's brother, wanted that tribute and was willing to go to war for it. After he had prepared his own army, Joram asked for assistance from Jehoshaphat, the king of Judah. Jehoshaphat had helped Ahab fight a losing battle against Ramoth-Gilead two years earlier. Now he again promised to help his neighbor. Jehoshaphat also suggested that they march directly south through Edom and attack Moab from the rear. Along the way they also picked up the assistance of the "king of Edom," who, according to 1 Kings 22:47, was merely a deputy under the control of Jehoshaphat.

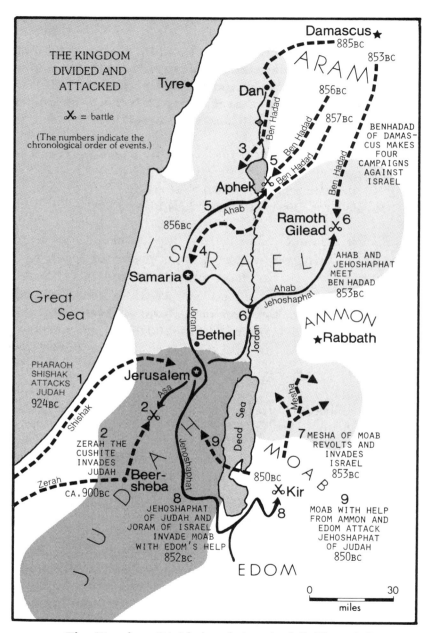

The Kingdom Divided and Attacked (2 Kings 3:8)

176

⁹So the king of Israel set out with the king of Judah and the king of Edom. After a roundabout march of seven days, the army had no more water for themselves or for the animals with them.

¹⁰"What!" exclaimed the king of Israel. "Has the LORD called us three kings together only to hand us over to Moab?"

¹¹But Jehoshaphat asked, "Is there no prophet of the LORD here, that we may inquire of the LORD through him?"

An officer of the king of Israel answered, "Elisha son of Shaphat is here. He used to pour water on the hands of Elijah."

¹²Jehoshaphat said, "The word of the LORD is with him." So the king of Israel and Jehoshaphat and the king of Edom went down to him.

¹³Elisha said to the king of Israel, "What do we have to do with each other? Go to the prophets of your father and the prophets of your mother."

"No," the king of Israel answered, "because it was the LORD who called us three kings together to hand us over to Moab."

¹⁴Elisha said, "As surely as the LORD Almighty lives, whom I serve, if I did not have respect for the presence of Jehoshaphat king of Judah, I would not look at you or even notice you. ¹⁵But now bring me a harpist."

While the harpist was playing, the hand of the LORD came upon Elisha ¹⁶and he said "This is what the LORD says: Make this valley full of ditches. ¹⁷For this is what the LORD says: You will see neither wind nor rain, yet this valley will be filled with water, and you, your cattle and your other animals will drink. ¹⁸This is an easy thing in the eyes of the LORD; he will also hand Moab over to you. ¹⁹You will overthrow every fortified city and every major town. You will cut down every good tree, stop up all the springs, and ruin every good field with stones."

The kings planned their attack route and their food supply carefully. They took along herds of cattle to be used as meat. But someone made a serious miscalculation. When the armies had marched seven days into the wilderness west of the Dead Sea, they discovered that they did not have enough water for the soldiers or for the cattle.

Outwardly the king of Israel, the king of Judah, and the king of Edom were united in their plan against Moab. Inwardly, however, they were deeply divided. When troubles came, the king of Israel quickly forgot that this military campaign had been his own idea, and he accused God of leading them all into certain death. In this way Joram was like his father King Ahab. During his life he worshiped Baal and the golden calves. But when trouble came, he blamed God (1 Kings 18:17). "The sinful mind is hostile to God" (Romans 8:7).

Jehoshaphat, however, was a believer in the Lord. When trouble came, he turned to the true God. According to God's plan Elisha, the man who had been Elijah's personal servant, was there among the soldiers. Jehoshaphat knew that Elisha was a man of God, and the three kings immediately went to his tent.

People sometimes tell us never to criticize another person's religion. Elisha, however, did not follow that advice. He looked at the unbelieving king of Israel and asked, "What do the two of us have in common?" The answer, of course, was nothing at all. Faith and unbelief, light and darkness, life and death have nothing in common.

We can hear the sarcasm in Elisha's voice as he says to Joram, "Why don't you consult the prophets of your father Ahab or the prophets of your mother Jezebel? Don't you remember what a great job they did at Mount Carmel when they tried to call down fire from heaven?" We can hear the anger in Elisha's voice when he says to the unbelieving king, "I swear that if it were not for the presence of Jehoshaphat, I would not even look at your face!"

Most of us would have trouble speaking kind words when our hearts are full of righteous anger. Perhaps it was for this reason that Elisha now called for a minstrel, a musician, to play on the harp. Music is a powerful gift from God. Sacred

178

music is a special gift which has the ability to calm our troubled hearts, to direct our attention away from earthly things to heavenly things. While the musician was playing, perhaps singing psalms from the Bible, the hand of the Lord did come on Elisha with a two-part message of deliverance and victory: God would provide water, and God would give his people a victory.

²⁰The next morning, about the time for offering the sacrifice, there it was—water flowing from the direction of Edom! And the land was filled with water.

²¹Now all the Moabites had heard that the kings had come to fight against them; so every man, young and old, who could bear arms was called up and stationed on the border. ²²When they got up early in the morning, the sun was shining on the water. To the Moabites across the way, the water looked red—like blood. ²³"That's blood!" they said. "Those kings must have fought and slaughtered each other. Now to the plunder, Moab!"

²⁴But when the Moabites came to the camp of Israel, the Israelites rose up and fought them until they fled. And the Israelites invaded the land and slaughtered the Moabites. ²⁵They destroyed the towns, and each man threw a stone on every good field until it was covered. They stopped up all the springs and cut down every good tree. Only Kir Hareseth was left with its stones in place, but men armed with slings surrounded it and attacked it as well.

²⁶When the king of Moab saw that the battle had gone against him, he took with him seven hundred swordsmen to break through to the king of Edom, but they failed. ²⁷Then he took his firstborn son, who was to succeed him as king, and offered him as a sacrifice on the city wall. The fury against Israel was great; they withdrew and returned to their own land.

God fulfilled his promise immediately. The very next morning, at the time when the priests in Jerusalem were offering the morning sacrifice, water came flowing out of the hills of Edom and filled the trenches dug by the soldiers.

The soldiers of Moab also saw the water from a distance. Reason told them that there could not be any water in that part of the land at that time of the year. Certainly not without any rain clouds! When the soldiers of Moab rushed in to collect the spoil, the Israelite soldiers were waiting. The army of Moab fled in disarray.

Now the three kings invaded and destroyed the land of Moab just as Elisha had foretold. By destroying the trees, they devastated the land for a good time to come. When the king of Moab knew that he could not escape, he tried a desperate appeal to his god. At the top of the city wall, in a place where he could be seen by friend and foe alike, he sacrificed his son to the bloodthirsty god Chemosh. God's people were so appalled and disgusted by what they saw that they packed up and returned home without having achieved the purpose of the campaign.

There are three periods in Bible history when we read about the performance of many miracles. The first is at the time of Moses when God delivered his people from bondage in Egypt and established them in their promised land. The last is at the time when our Savior lived here on earth. The second period is here at the time of Elijah and Elisha, a time when the people of Israel had sunk into the deepest, darkest idolatry and God was trying to recall them. In chapters 4, 5 and 6 our writer recounts several miracles of Elisha. In each case God showed his kindness to his people and delivered them from trouble.

The Widow's Oil

4 **The wife of a man from the company of the prophets cried out to Elisha, "Your servant my husband is dead, and you know that he revered the LORD. But now his creditor is coming to take my boys as his slaves."**

²Elisha replied to her, "How can I help you? Tell me, what do you have in your house?"

"Your servant has nothing there at all," she said, "except a little oil."

³Elisha said, "Go around and ask all your neighbors for empty jars. Don't ask for just a few. ⁴Then go inside and shut the door behind you and your sons. Pour oil into all the jars, and as each is filled, put it to one side."

⁵She left him and afterward shut the door behind her and her sons. They brought the jars to her and she kept pouring. ⁶When all the jars were full, she said to her son, "Bring me another one."

But he replied, "There is not a jar left." Then the oil stopped flowing.

⁷She went and told the man of God, and he said, "Go, sell the oil and pay your debts. You and yours sons can live on what is left."

This gracious miracle reminds us how God provided food for the widow of Zarephath at the time of Elijah (1 Kings 17:14-16).

Throughout the Scripture God shows a special concern for the widows and fatherless. He still answers their prayers and provides for them even though he generally does it in less spectacular ways. God wants his people to have a special concern for the needy. "Religion that God our Father accepts as pure and faultless is this: to look after orphans and widows in their distress. . . . " (James 1:27).

According to this example it is good that we as a church have a continuing concern for all widows, including those of our pastors and teachers.

The Shunammite's Son Restored to Life

⁸One day Elisha went to Shunem. And a well-to-do woman was there, who urged him to stay for a meal. So whenever he came by, he stopped there to eat. ⁹She said to her husband, "I know that this man who often comes our way is a holy man of God. ¹⁰Let's

make a small room on the roof and put in it a bed and a table, a chair and a lamp for him. Then he can stay there whenever he comes to us."

[11]One day when Elisha came, he went up to his room and lay down there. [12]He said to his servant Gehazi, "Call the Shunammite." So he called her, and she stood before him. [13]Elisha said to him, "Tell her, 'You have gone to all this trouble for us. Now what can be done for you? Can we speak on your behalf to the king or the commander of the army?' "

She replied, "I have a home among my own people."

[14]"What can be done for her?" Elisha asked.

Gehazi said, "Well, she has no son and her husband is old."

[15]Then Elisha said, "Call her." So he called her, and she stood in the doorway. [16]"About this time next year," Elisha said, "you will hold a son in your arms."

"No, my lord," she objected. "Don't mislead your servant, O man of God!"

[17]But the woman became pregnant, and the next year about that same time she gave birth to a son, just as Elisha had told her.

As Elisha made his rounds, he often passed through Shunem, a village near Jezreel, where the king had his summer palace (1 Kings 21:1). Although the king "did evil in the sight of the LORD" (2 Kings 3:2) and many of the people followed his bad example, certain faithful individuals still worked to support the preaching of God's word.

A woman of Shunem recognized Elisha as "a holy man of God," that is, a man who spoke as he was "moved by the Holy Ghost" (2 Peter 1:21 KJV). Just as certain wealthy women supported Jesus and his disciples during our Lord's time on earth (Luke 8:1-3), so this woman also provided room and board for God's prophet.

Thank God for the faithful services Christian women continue to perform in the church today!

When Elisha announced that she would bear a child, the woman thought at first that Elisha was mocking her because of her barrenness. The birth of a child at this time of life seemed impossible also to Sarah, wife of Abraham, and to Zechariah and Elizabeth.

When God created our first parents, he "blessed them and said to them, 'Be fruitful and increase in number' " (Genesis 1:28). When Adam and Eve later had children, this was because of God's creative word of blessing. The son born at Shunem was likewise a gift and a blessing from God. His birth came about according to God's word, "just as Elisha had told her."

It is not unusual for God to give more wealth to one than to another. The same is true of children. God gives many to one couple, only one to another, and for his own reasons withholds children from still another couple. In each case *God* gives (or withholds) the blessing. And in each case *God* is the one who requires that parents care for that blessing. Parents are responsible to "bring them up in the training and instruction of the Lord" (Ephesians 6:4).

The God who graciously blessed the woman of Shunem now permitted serious troubles to enter her home.

18 The child grew, and one day he went out to his father, who was with the reapers. 19 "My head! My head!" he said to his father.

His father told a servant, "Carry him to his mother." 20 After the servant had lifted him up and carried him to his mother, the boy sat on her lap until noon, and then he died. 21 She went up and laid him on the bed of the man of God, then shut the door and went out.

22 She called her husband and said, "Please send me one of the servants and a donkey so I can go to the man of God quickly and return."

23 "Why go to him today?" he asked. "It's not the New Moon or the Sabbath."

"It's all right," she said.

When the lad was perhaps eight years old, he suffered what appears to have been a sunstroke and died the same day.

The death of a child is a solemn reminder that even children are born with sinful hearts. Even though we were not present personally in the Garden of Eden, nevertheless "death came upon all men, because all sinned" (Romans 5:12). Death is powerful evidence that people are sinners.

Satan wants us to forget these facts. He wants us to think that children can safely go through a "stage" when they turn their backs on God's word and sow their wild oats. God, however, has not promised that we or our children will live to see our next birthday.

The other details demonstrate the mother's faith in God and indicate that the boy's father must have been an unbeliever. It was the woman's idea to provide meals for the prophet and to build an addition to their house for Elisha's use. When her son died, she laid his body on the prophet's bed and went to seek God's prophet. She followed Peter's advice literally to "cast all your anxiety on him because he cares for you" (1 Peter 5:7).

The boy's father did not bother to inquire about his son's health. He continued to work in the field. His only question was, "Why would you want to visit the man of God if it is neither a Sabbath day nor the festival of the new moon?" He could not understand why someone would want to "go to church" when there was no legal requirement. We are not surprised therefore that the mother preferred to discuss this spiritual crisis with God's prophet rather than with her husband.

Many husbands today follow this example. They work hard to provide material benefits for their families but abdicate their position as the spiritual and religious head of the family.

If a Christian woman today marries an unbelieving man, she cannot expect her husband to understand her faith. Her husband will not be able to comfort her when death enters the home, he will be unable to pray for her in a time of trouble, he will be unable to offer real comfort or encouragement as she labors in a sinful world (Genesis 3:16).

[24] She saddled the donkey and said to her servant, "Lead on; don't slow down for me unless I tell you." [25] So she set out and came to the man of God at Mount Carmel.

When he saw her in the distance the man of God said to his servant Gehazi, "Look! There's the Shunammite! [26] Run to meet her and ask her, 'Are you all right? Is your husband all right? Is your child all right?' "

"Everything is all right," she said.

[27] When she reached the man of God at the mountain, she took hold of his feet. Gehazi came over to push her away, but the man of God said, "Leave her alone! She is in bitter distress, but the LORD has hidden it from me and has not told me why."

[28] "Did I ask you for a son, my lord?" she said. "Didn't I tell you, 'Don't raise my hopes'?"

[29] Elisha said to Gehazi, "Tuck your cloak into your belt, take my staff in your hand and run. If you meet anyone, do not greet him, and if anyone greets you, do not answer. Lay my staff on the boy's face."

[30] But the child's mother said, "As surely as the LORD lives and as you live, I will not leave you." So he got up and followed her.

[31] Gehazi went on ahead and laid the staff on the boy's face, but there was no sound or response. So Gehazi went back to meet Elisha and told him, "The boy has not awakened."

[32] When Elisha reached the house, there was the boy lying dead on his couch. [33] He went in, shut the door on the two of them and prayed to the LORD. [34] Then he got on the bed and lay upon the boy, mouth to mouth, eyes to eyes, hands to hands. As he stretched himself out upon him, the boy's body grew warm. [35] Elisha turned away and walked back and forth in the room and

then got on the bed and stretched out upon him once more. The boy sneezed seven times and opened his eyes.

36 Elisha summoned Gehazi and said, "Call the Shunammite." And he did. When she came, he said, "Take your son." **37** She came in, fell at his feet and bowed to the ground. Then she took her son and went out.

The woman and her servant hurried some twenty miles through the valley of Jezreel. Before her son was born, she had accepted the idea that she would die childless. Now the untimely death of this special child seemed like a cruel joke.

At the same time this woman showed herself to be a real daughter of Abraham. Like Abraham, she believed that God could raise her son from the dead (Hebrews 11:19).

When Elisha arrived at Shunem, he did not administer CPR or begin other emergency procedures. His first act was to pray to God behind closed doors, just as Jesus later instructed his disciples (Matthew 6:6). Then he placed his body over the body of the boy just as Elijah had done at Zarephath (1 Kings 17:21). God tested also the faith of Elisha as he paced back and forth in the room. Finally God responded and gave life to this body a second time.

Here again God showed himself to be the giver of life, the one who would deliver his people from the death they had earned when they fell into sin. That Savior desires to give life also to us and to our children. In baptism he has raised us from spiritual death to spiritual life. Someday he will escort us also into the joys of eternal life. May God bless all Christian parents as we bring our children to their Savior.

Once again the boy's father is conspicuous by his absence.

Death in the Pot

38 Elisha returned to Gilgal and there was a famine in that region. While the company of the prophets was meeting with him, he said to his servant, "Put on the large pot and cook some stew for these men."

³⁹One of them went out into the fields to gather herbs and found a wild vine. He gathered some of its gourds and filled the fold of his cloak. When he returned, he cut them up into the pot of stew, though no one knew what they were. ⁴⁰The stew was poured out for the men, but as they began to eat it, they cried out, "O man of God, there is death in the pot!" And they could not eat it.

⁴¹Elisha said, "Get some flour." He put it into the pot and said, "Serve it to the people to eat." And there was nothing harmful in the pot.

During Elijah's ministry God had sent a famine as a judgment on the unbelievers (1 Kings 17:1). Now, a generation later, the land was again in the grip of a famine that would last seven years (2 Kings 8:1). During this time the men who attended the school of the prophets at Gilgal received God's special care.

The wild gourds were perhaps wild cucumbers which gave the stew a strong, bitter taste.

Elijah's miracle is similar to the one we read about in chapter 2. There Elisha threw salt into the bitter spring at Jericho and declared, "This is what the LORD says: 'I have healed this water. Never again will it cause death'" (2:21). Here also the almighty God, using the flour as a visible sign, neutralized the poison stew so that no one who ate of it suffered any ill effects.

God cursed the ground when our first parents fell into sin. Therefore we should not be surprised to learn that the ground produces poisonous gourds. Perhaps we should not be surprised to learn that many foods today, if eaten in excess, may be harmful to our bodies. Yet our gracious Lord chooses to use food which comes from a ground cursed by sin to preserve the lives of his people during their time of grace here on earth.

On another occasion God provided for the men at the school of the prophets by multiplying the food.

Feeding of a Hundred

⁴²A man came from Baal Shalishah, bringing the man of God twenty loaves of barley bread from the first ripe grain, along with some heads of new grain. "Give it to the people to eat," Elisha said.

⁴³"How can I set this before a hundred men?" his servant asked.

But Elisha answered, "Give it to the people to eat. For this is what the LORD says: 'They will eat and have some left over.'"

⁴⁴Then he set it before them, and they ate and had some left over, according to the word of the LORD.

Just as the Shunammite woman provided for Elisha, so an unnamed man from Baal Shalishah, some thirteen miles northwest of Gilgal, showed his concern for Christian education by bringing twenty loaves of bread and some grain to the school of the prophets.

This miracle reminds us of how Jesus fed the 5,000 in the wilderness (Matthew 14:15-21). When Jesus asked his disciples to feed that crowd with five loaves and two small fish, they also looked at him in disbelief. But Jesus blessed that food and there was enough for 5,000 men, besides women and children—easily 15,000 in all.

God blessed twenty small loaves of bread, and a hundred had enough to eat. Jesus blessed five loaves and two fish, and 5,000 men had enough. The poet was correct when he wrote,

All depends on our possessing

God's abundant grace and blessing (TLH 425:1).

Without God's blessing people will "earn wages, only to put them into a purse with holes in it" (Haggai 1:6).

Our gracious God did not bless only the descendants of Abraham. He offered his miraculous help even to the heathen, as we shall now see.

Naaman Healed of Leprosy

5 Now Naaman was commander of the army of the king of Aram. He was a great man in the sight of his master and highly regarded, because through him the LORD had given victory to Aram. He was a valiant soldier, but he had leprosy.

2 Now bands from Aram had gone out and had taken captive a young girl from Israel, and she served Naaman's wife. **3** She said to her mistress, "If only my master would see the prophet who is in Samaria! He would cure him of his leprosy."

4 Naaman went to his master and told him what the girl from Israel had said. **5** "By all means, go," the king of Aram replied. "I will send a letter to the king of Israel." So Naaman left, taking with him ten talents of silver, six thousand shekels of gold and ten sets of clothing. **6** The letter that he took to the king of Israel read: "With this letter I am sending my servant Naaman to you so that you may cure him of his leprosy."

7 As soon as the king of Israel read the letter, he tore his robes and said, "Am I God? Can I kill and bring back to life? Why does this fellow send someone to me to be cured of leprosy? See how he is trying to pick a quarrel with me!"

Leprosy was a deadly disease. Not all of Naaman's power, wealth or popularity could obtain healing for him. Humanly speaking, he was doomed to a slow and painful death.

But Naaman was one of God's elect. And God used an unusual chain of events to bring this man to faith.

The king of Israel was probably Jehoram, the son of Ahab. Unfortunately he worshiped the golden calves and did not share the simple faith of the servant girl. He was wise enough to realize, however, that his golden calves could not heal anyone from leprosy.

The Apostle Peter asks God's people always to be "prepared to give an answer to everyone who asks you to give the reason for the hope that you have" (1 Peter 3:15). King

Herod, however, was unable to direct the wise men to the new-born King in Bethlehem. Jehoram also, although he was the leader of God's people, could do nothing more than tear his garments in frustration. What a pathetic situation!

God, however, was determined to bless this avowed enemy of Israel.

8 When Elisha the man of God heard that the king of Israel had torn his robes, he sent him this message: "Why have you torn your robes? Have the man come to me and he will know that there is a prophet in Israel." 9 So Naaman went with his horses and chariots and stopped at the door of Elisha's house. 10 Elisha sent a messenger to say to him, "Go, wash yourself seven times in the Jordan, and your flesh will be restored and you will be cleansed."

11 But Naaman went away angry and said, "I thought that he would surely come out to me and stand and call on the name of the LORD his God, wave his hand over the spot and cure me of my leprosy. 12 Are not Abana and Pharpar, the rivers of Damascus, better than any of the waters of Israel? Couldn't I wash in them and be cleansed?" So he turned and went off in a rage.

13 Naaman's servants went to him and said, "My father, if the prophet had told you to do some great thing, would you not have done it? How much more, then, when he tells you, 'Wash and be cleansed'!" 14 So he went down and dipped himself in the Jordan seven times, as the man of God had told him, and his flesh was restored and became clean like that of a young boy.

If someone hands us a dollar bill, we receive it with our hand and put it into our pocket. If someone gives us a promise, we receive it through our ears and believe it in our heart.

At first Naaman refused to accept God's promise. Everyone knows that the Jordan River contains no medicine that can heal leprosy. What if Naaman washed in the Jordan and remained a leper? He would be the laughingstock of the whole army.

But God kept his promise. There was never any question as to whether God could or would do as he said. The problem was not with God but with Naaman. By his unbelief Naaman at first rejected God's promise and God's blessing. When he believed God's words and dipped himself into the water, the blessing became his own. He received God's blessing by faith.

Some of God's other promises seem just as unreasonable. Who would ever think that the man on the cross is the Son of God and that his blood cleanses us from sin? Many reject that teaching as pure foolishness, and by that unbelief they reject God's promise of eternal life.

In Leviticus God gave many laws regarding those who had leprosy. If it did happen that someone recovered from that disease, he was to wash himself with water just as God commanded Naaman (Leviticus 14:8,9). In that same book God commanded other washings by which those who were ceremonially unclean would become clean. These washings reminded God's people that by nature they are morally unclean in the sight of a holy God. It reminded them also that God alone can cleanse someone from guilt.

King David understood this. Therefore David, using the same words that we find here in verse 10 and throughout Leviticus, wrote in Psalm 51, "*Wash* away all my iniquity. . . . Create in me a *pure* heart, O God" (Psalm 51:2,10). The cleansing God has provided is in the blood of his Son. St. John wrote that "the blood of Jesus, his Son, purifies us from all sin" (1 John 1:7).

It is significant that God asked Naaman to wash in the *Jordan* River. Eight hundred years later another prophet was performing washings, baptisms, in that river. This was John the Baptist. His baptism was "for the forgiveness of sins" (Luke 3:3). The Sacrament of Baptism, which Jesus instituted after his death and resurrection, offers the same blessing. The Bible says, "Get up, be baptized and wash your sins away" (Acts 22:16).

Just as God attached healing to the waters of the Jordan River by means of his word, so God by his promise has attached the forgiveness of sins to the water of baptism. Just as Naaman received God's blessing when he believed God's word and actually dipped himself into the Jordan River, so we receive the blessings of baptism by faith. Faith is a receiving hand. Those who believe God's words have the blessings they offer.

The words of an insignificant slave girl from Israel became instrumental in leading a great man to faith in the Savior.

[15]Then Naaman and all his attendants went back to the man of God. He stood before him and said, "Now I know that there is no God in all the world except in Israel. Please accept now a gift from your servant."

[16]The prophet answered, "As surely as the LORD lives, whom I serve, I will not accept a thing." And even though Naaman urged him, he refused.

[17]"If you will not," said Naaman, "please let me, your servant, be given as much earth as a pair of mules can carry, for your servant will never again make burnt offerings and sacrifices to any other god but the LORD. [18]But may the LORD forgive your servant for this one thing. When my master enters the temple of Rimmon to bow down and he is leaning on my arm and I bow there also—when I bow down in the temple of Rimmon, may the LORD forgive your servant for this."

[19]"Go in peace," Elisha said.

Although Elisha had accepted personal gifts from others (2 Kings 4:8,42), he wisely declined the gratuity offered by Naaman. He wanted no one in Aram to think that the blessings God offers may be purchased for money.

Naaman was now converted; the people back in Aram were not. That would present a conflict. It was the duty of the commander-in-chief to accompany his king when he worshiped in the house of his god, Rimmon. Although Naaman would still accompany King Ben-Hadad to the heathen temple, his bowing down would no longer be an act of worship.

Some have wondered whether Naaman's presence in a heathen temple would compromise his faith in the Lord and violate God's principles of fellowship. The Apostle Paul asks us to have nothing to do with idolaters (2 Corinthians 6:17) and to mark and avoid those who teach contrary to God's word (Romans 16:17). Although our writer does not answer all of our questions, Elisha accepted Naaman's explanation and assured him: "Go in peace."

Because we are Christians, we are as different from the unbelieving world as light is from darkness. We face conflicts every day. There are temptations to bow down to false gods. It is because we have been made clean through baptism that we now have power to turn our backs on sin and to serve the Lord alone. Elisha's peaceful words to Naaman do not give us license to carry on church work with unbelievers.

Evidence from sources outside the Bible indicates that Naaman did faithfully confess the Lord before others. The Amarna Letters (cuneiform tablets discovered in Egypt in 1887) tell us that Naaman was the right-hand man of Pharaoh Ikhnaton and returned to Egypt after being cured from his leprosy. Unlike the other Egyptian pharaohs, Ikhnaton worshiped *one* God, Aton, the Egyptian name for Adonai (which is the Hebrew word for "LORD"). "Rimmon," by the way, was the chief god of Egypt, "Re-Amon."

After Naaman had traveled some distance, [20]Gehazi, the servant of Elisha the man of God, said to himself, "My master was too

easy on Naaman, this Aramean, by not accepting from him what he brought. As surely as the LORD lives, I will run after him and get something from him."

²¹So Gehazi hurried after Naaman. When Naaman saw him running toward him, he got down from the chariot to meet him. "Is everything all right?" he asked.

²²"Everything is all right," Gehazi answered. "My master sent me to say, 'Two young men from the company of the prophets have just come to me from the hill country of Ephraim. Please give them a talent of silver and two sets of clothing.' "

²³"By all means, take two talents," said Naaman. He urged Gehazi to accept them, and then tied up the two talents of silver in two bags, with two sets of clothing. He gave them to two of his servants, and they carried them ahead of Gehazi. ²⁴When Gehazi came to the hill, he took the things from the servants and put them away in the house. He sent the men away and they left. ²⁵Then he went in and stood before his master Elisha.

"Where have you been, Gehazi?" Elisha asked.

"Your servant didn't go anywhere," Gehazi answered.

²⁶But Elisha said to him, "Was not my spirit with you when the man got down from his chariot to meet you? Is this the time to take money, or to accept clothes, olive groves, vineyards, flocks, herds, or menservants and maidservants? ²⁷Naaman's leprosy will cling to you and to your descendants forever." Then Gehazi went from Elisha's presence and he was leprous, as white as snow.

Gehazi had the privilege of living with God's prophet, but he did not share the prophet's joy when a heathen man came to faith. He saw Elisha perform miracles to help people in need, but he himself was not satisfied with the earthly goods God had allotted to him. In certain ways Gehazi and Judas have a lot in common.

How easy it was for Gehazi to steal! Naaman gave him more than he had asked for. Everything went according to plan.

But the thing Gehazi had done displeased the Lord. Because Gehazi had sworn falsely by the Lord's name, because he would not be content with the goods God had given to him, and because he raised questions as to whether God's blessings are really without charge, God sent a severe judgment on him immediately.

Paul wrote that "the love of money is a root of all kinds of evil. Some people, eager for money, have wandered from the faith and pierced themselves with many griefs" (1 Timothy 6:10). This is what happened to Gehazi. This is what happens to others who will not be content.

In times of trouble God continued to give his special blessing to men who attended the schools of the prophets.

An Axhead Floats

6 **The company of the prophets said to Elisha, "Look, the place where we meet with you is too small for us. ²Let us go to the Jordan, where each of us can get a pole; and let us build a place there for us to live."**

And he said, "Go."

³Then one of them said, "Won't you please come with your servants?"

"I will," Elisha replied. ⁴And he went with them.

They went to the Jordan and began to cut down trees. ⁵As one of them was cutting down a tree, the iron axhead fell into the water. "Oh, my lord," he cried out, "it was borrowed!"

⁶The man of God asked, "Where did it fall?" When he showed him the place, Elisha cut a stick and threw it there, and made the iron float. ⁷"Lift it out," he said. Then the man reached out his hand and took it.

In chapter 4 we read how Elisha made a poisoned pot of stew fit to eat and how twenty loaves of bread miraculously fed a hundred men. By causing the axhead to float, God here gave his special, miraculous blessing to their building project.

When we compare the weakness of God's people with the strength of God's enemies, we realize that it is only by a miracle of God's grace that the training of full-time kingdom workers continues in our midst today. Sometimes our Creator even suspends the laws of nature in order to advance the work of his church.

Elisha Traps Blinded Arameans

⁸Now the king of Aram was at war with Israel. After conferring with his officers, he said, "I will set up my camp in such and such a place."

⁹The man of God sent word to the king of Israel: "Beware of passing that place, because the Arameans are going down there." ¹⁰So the king of Israel checked on the place indicated by the man of God. Time and again Elisha warned the king, so that he was on his guard in such places.

¹¹This enraged the king of Aram. He summoned his officers and demanded of them, "Will you not tell me which of us is on the side of the king of Israel?"

¹²"None of us, my lord the king," said one of his officers, "but Elisha, the prophet who is in Israel, tells the king of Israel the very words you speak in your bedroom."

¹³"Go, find out where he is," the king ordered, "so I can send men and capture him." The report came back: "He is in Dothan." ¹⁴Then he sent horses and chariots and a strong force there. They went by night and surrounded the city.

¹⁵When the servant of the man of God got up and went out early the next morning, an army with horses and chariots had surrounded the city. "Oh, my lord, what shall we do?" the servant asked.

¹⁶"Don't be afraid," the prophet answered. "Those who are with us are more than those who are with them."

¹⁷And Elisha prayed, "O LORD, open his eyes so he may see." Then the LORD opened the servant's eyes, and he looked and saw the hills full of horses and chariots of fire all around Elisha.

Although the names of the two kings are not mentioned, we assume they are still King Joram of Israel and King Ben-Hadad II of Aram (see 1 Kings 20:1-12).

King David asked, "Where can I go from your Spirit? Where can I flee from your presence? If I go up to the heavens, you are there; if I make my bed in the depths, you are there. If I say, 'Surely the darkness will hide me and the light become night around me,' even the darkness will not be dark to you" (Psalm 139:7,8,11). God is everywhere and knows everything, even the secrets that Ben-Hadad revealed in his bedroom.

The omniscience of God contains a warning. With God there is no such thing as "secret sin." That omniscience is also a comfort. God knows what our earthly and spiritual enemies are up to and can forewarn and prepare his people.

When the mighty enemy plots to destroy God's people, God defends them through his invisible servants, the angels. "The angel of the LORD encamps around those who fear him, and he delivers them" (Psalm 34:7). The hill on which Dothan was built was full of fiery horses and chariots. Angels of God rescued Lot from the doomed city of Sodom, and now God's angels rescued Elisha and his servant.

We are surrounded by real dangers every day. Nuclear bombs, terrorists, accident and disease threaten to snuff out our lives in a moment. We are tempted to cry out with Elisha's servant, "Alas, my God! What shall we do?" One popular answer for the unbeliever is to commit suicide. Suicide among teenagers has become a national epidemic. But God's prophet says to God's servants today, "Don't be afraid. Those who are with us are more than those who are with them." Our mighty Father "will command his angels concerning you to guard you in all your ways" (Psalm 91:11). "He breaks the bow and cuts the spear in two; He burns the chariot in the fire" (Psalm 46:9 NKJV). Not a hair will fall from our head without God's knowledge and permission. The Lord is a "wall of fire" around his city of Jerusalem (Zechariah 2:5).

The omniscience of God and the protecting hand of God, as they are revealed in this section, nearly cause us to laugh with joyful trust in our God.

18As the enemy came down toward him, Elisha prayed to the LORD, "Strike these people with blindness." So he struck them with blindness, as Elisha had asked.

19Elisha told them, "This is not the road and this is not the city. Follow me, and I will lead you to the man you are looking for." And he led them to Samaria.

20After they entered the city, Elisha said, "LORD, open the eyes of these men so they can see." Then the LORD opened their eyes and they looked, and there they were, inside Samaria.

21When the king of Israel saw them, he asked Elisha, "Shall I kill them, my father? Shall I kill them?"

22"Do not kill them," he answered. "Would you kill men you have captured with your own sword or bow? Set food and water before them so that they may eat and drink and then go back to their master." 23So he prepared a great feast for them, and after they had finished eating and drinking, he sent them away, and they returned to their master. So the bands from Aram stopped raiding Israel's territory.

Trying to arrest one of God's prophets can be a risky business. We learned that in 2 Kings 1, where Elijah called down fire from heaven on the soldiers who were sent to arrest him. The soldiers here at Dothan also ran into trouble. The Lord, who had just opened the eyes of Elisha's servant so that he could see angels, now closed the eyes of the enemy soldiers so that they could see nothing at all.

Elisha led the helpless, blind Aramean army twelve miles south to Samaria.

On a previous occasion God's prophet had condemned King Ahab for permitting the king of Aram to escape with his life (1 Kings 20:35-43). This time the enemy soldiers would be treated differently. There would be no bloodshed, no casualties among the Israelites and none among the Arameans. God spared the lives of many people for the sake of Elisha and a few others in Israel who were still faithful to the true God.

When death finally overtakes us, God will open our eyes, and we will have the thrill of seeing our God face to face. Job foretold it this way: "And after my skin has been destroyed, yet in my flesh I will see God; I myself will see him with my own eyes—I, and not another" (Job 19:26,27). Therefore with holy expectation we sing,

> And then from death awaken me
> That these mine eyes with joy may see,
> O Son of God, thy glorious face,
> My Savior and my Fount of grace. (TLH 429:3)

Until that time we are content to see God (and his protecting angels) with the eyes of faith.

The Arameans soon forgot Elisha's kindness. The aggression which King Ben-Hadad had begun many years earlier when Ahab was king of Israel (1 Kings 20:1) continued through the reign of Ahab's son.

Famine in Besieged Samaria

24Some time later, Ben-Hadad king of Aram mobilized his entire army and marched up and laid siege to Samaria. 25There was a great famine in the city; the siege lasted so long that a donkey's head sold for eighty shekels of silver, and a fourth of a cab of seed pods for five shekels.

26As the king of Israel was passing by on the wall, a woman cried to him, "Help me, my lord the king!"

²⁷The king replied, "If the LORD does not help you, where can I get help for you? From the threshing floor? From the winepress?" ²⁸Then he asked her, "What's the matter?"

She answered, "This woman said to me, 'Give up your son so we may eat him today, and tomorrow we'll eat my son.' ²⁹So we cooked my son and ate him. The next day I said to her, 'Give up your son so we may eat him,' but she had hidden him."

³⁰When the king heard the woman's words, he tore his robes. As he went along the wall, the people looked, and there, underneath, he had sackcloth on his body. ³¹He said, "May God deal with me, be it ever so severely, if the head of Elisha son of Shaphat remains on his shoulders today!"

While the capital city of Samaria was under siege, living conditions in the city were horrible beyond description. The Israelites were dying—not by the sword but from starvation. The people were willing to eat anything. Imagine paying $80 for the head of a donkey and eating that for dinner! Even that was not the worst thing. There were reports of people eating the excrement of animals. ("Dove's dung" is the literal translation in verse 25.) There were even instances of cannibalism.

Even King Joram, that "son of a murderer" (verse 32 KJV), that is, the son of Ahab and his wicked wife Jezebel, was disgusted. At the same time he was utterly helpless, unable to provide food for his people. In anger he put the blame on God's prophet just as his father King Ahab blamed God when the war with Moab was not going well (2 Kings 3:13).

That reaction is typical of our sinful flesh. When things go wrong, we're tempted to blame God or God's spokesman or God's people. Our proud human heart refuses to humble itself before God in repentance.

The physical conditions in Samaria are strikingly similar to the spiritual conditions in the human race. Like the Samaritans, we are helpless against our enemies. Satan gained power over the human race back in the Garden of Eden and holds sinners in his clutches. Death also became a mighty king when our first parents disobeyed their Creator. Luther described that misery when he wrote,

> Fast bound in Satan's chains I lay,
> Death brooded darkly o'er me,
> Sin was my torment night and day,
> In sin my mother bore me;
> Yea, deep and deeper still I fell,
> Life had become a living hell,
> So firmly sin possessed me. (TLH 387:2)

Satan will try to convince us that conditions are not so bad, that paying $80 for the head of a donkey is really living. We know better than that.

32 Now Elisha was sitting in his house, and the elders were sitting with him. The king sent a messenger ahead, but before he arrived, Elisha said to the elders, "Don't you see how this murderer is sending someone to cut off my head? Look, when the messenger comes, shut the door and hold it shut against him. Is not the sound of his master's footsteps behind him?"

33 While he was still talking to them, the messenger came down to him. And ⌊the king⌋ said, "This disaster is from the LORD. Why should I wait for the LORD any longer?"

7 Elisha said, "Hear the word of the LORD. This is what the LORD says: About this time tomorrow, a seah of flour will sell for a shekel and two seahs of barley for a shekel at the gate of Samaria."

2 The officer on whose arm the king was leaning said to the man of God, "Look, even if the LORD should open the floodgates of the heavens, could this happen?"

"You will see it with your own eyes," answered Elisha, "but you will not eat any of it!"

When the king's messenger was on his way to put Elisha to death, God's prophet was consulting with the elders of the city. God warned Elisha that the messenger was on his way. Elisha in turn asked the men to block the door of his house. God also told Elisha that King Joram had already changed his mind about the prophet's death and was coming to his house.

The king was at the point of despair. He knew that this trouble had come from the Lord, but he was not willing to turn to God for help.

It was at this hopeless, helpless moment that God announced a great victory for his people. In twenty-four hours the famine would be gone; the next day bread and grain would be sold at the city gate for their usual price.

Why did God permit the people of Samaria to suffer a famine? Why did God permit the cripple at the pool of Bethesda to suffer for thirty-eight years (John 5:5)? The Bible does not give a full answer to such questions. We do know that at the proper time God delivers his people. He intervenes to deliver his people from death; and, at the proper time, he delivers them from all evil through a blessed death.

The Siege Lifted

³Now there were four men with leprosy at the entrance of the city gate. They said to each other, "Why stay here until we die? ⁴If we say, 'We'll go into the city'—the famine is there, and we will die. And if we stay here, we will die. So let's go over to the camp of the Arameans and surrender. If they spare us, we live; if they kill us, then we die."

⁵At dusk they got up and went to the camp of the Arameans. When they reached the edge of the camp, not a man was there, ⁶for the Lord had caused the Arameans to hear the sound of chariots and horses and a great army, so that they said to one another, "Look, the king of Israel has hired the Hittite and Egyptian kings to attack us!" ⁷So they got up and fled in the dusk

and abandoned their tents and their horses and donkeys. They left the camp as it was and ran for their lives.

⁸The men who had leprosy reached the edge of the camp and entered one of the tents. They ate and drank, and carried away silver, gold and clothes, and went off and hid them. They returned and entered another tent and took some things from it and hid them also.

⁹Then they said to each other, "We're not doing right. This is a day of good news and we are keeping it to ourselves. If we wait until daylight, punishment will overtake us. Let's go at once and report this to the royal palace."

¹⁰So they went and called out to the city gatekeepers and told them, "We went into the Aramean camp and not a man was there—not a sound of anyone—only tethered horses and donkeys, and the tents left just as they were." ¹¹The gatekeepers shouted the news, and it was reported within the palace.

¹²The king got up in the night and said to his officers, "I will tell you what the Arameans have done to us. They know we are starving; so they have left the camp to hide in the countryside, thinking, 'They will surely come out, and then we will take them alive and get into the city.' "

¹³One of his officers answered, "Have some men take five of the horses that are left in the city. Their plight will be like that of all the Israelites left here—yes, they will only be like all these Israelites who are doomed. So let us send them to find out what happened."

¹⁴So they selected two chariots with their horses, and the king sent them after the Aramean army. He commanded the drivers, "Go and find out what has happened." ¹⁵They followed them as far as the Jordan, and they found the whole road strewn with the clothing and equipment the Arameans had thrown away in their headlong flight. So the messengers returned and reported to the king. ¹⁶Then the people went out and plundered the camp of the Arameans. So a seah of flour sold for a shekel, and two seahs of barley sold for a shekel, as the LORD had said.

¹⁷Now the king had put the officer on whose arm he leaned in charge of the gate, and the people trampled him in the gateway,

and he died, just as the man of God had foretold when the king came down to his house. [18] It happened as the man of God had said to the king: "About this time tomorrow, a seah of flour will sell for a shekel and two seahs of barley for a shekel at the gate of Samaria."

[19] The officer had said to the man of God, "Look, even if the LORD should open the floodgates of the heavens, could this happen?" The man of God had replied, "You will see it with your own eyes, but you will not eat any of it!" [20] And that is exactly what happened to him, for the people trampled him in the gateway, and he died.

Several years earlier God had interfered with the eyesight of the Aramean soldiers. He blinded them temporarily so that they could not fight. Now the Creator interfered with their hearing. He convinced them that they were being attacked by the Egyptian armies from the south and the Hittite armies from the north.

The miraculous victory described here resembles the victory won by our Savior on Easter morning. That victory also seemed impossible. Even the Lord's disciples were not expecting him to come out of his grave. Thomas (like King Joram) refused to believe it at first.

Imagine the surprise of the four lepers when they found the Aramean camp deserted! The spoils of victory now belonged to these sick men who were not even fit to serve in the army.

The women who visited our Lord's grave on Easter morning also found an unexpected surprise. The grave was empty! God had won a marvelous victory. The spoils of that victory—the forgiveness of sins, life and salvation—now belonged to these women. Now it was their joyful duty and privilege to run and share the good news with the others in the city.

We Christians have likewise discovered the victory at the empty grave. What are we going to do about it? Will we privately feast on the spoils while others remain in ignorance, starving for the bread of life? Or will we share the good news with the others?

Elisha's other prophecy was also fulfilled. The officer who laughed at the prediction of victory and plenty of food saw the blessing but died without receiving a bit of it. Christian churches dot the American landscape today. Those who laugh at the words proclaimed there will die eternally because they have rejected the spoils won by the Savior.

Elijah and Elisha called the people of Israel back to God. Their success, however, was limited and it was temporary. After Elijah and Elisha died, there were a few political attempts at reform. When those failed to bring the people back to God, the Northern Kingdom (Israel) was ripe for judgment. Chapter 8 is a prelude to these coming events.

The Shunammite's Land Restored

8 **Now Elisha had said to the woman whose son he had restored to life, "Go away with your family and stay for a while wherever you can, because the LORD has decreed a famine in the land that will last seven years." ²The woman proceeded to do as the man of God said. She and her family went away and stayed in the land of the Philistines seven years.**

³At the end of the seven years she came back from the land of the Philistines and went to the king to beg for her house and land. ⁴The king was talking to Gehazi, the servant of the man of God, and had said, "Tell me about the great things Elisha has done." ⁵Just as Gehazi was telling the king how Elisha had restored the dead to life, the woman whose son Elisha had brought back to life came to beg the king for her house and land.

Gehazi said, "This is the woman, my lord the king, and this is her son whom Elisha restored to life." ⁶The king asked the woman about it, and she told him.

Then he assigned an official to her case and said to him, "Give back everything that belonged to her, including all the income from her land from the day she left the country until now."

The goodness of God is intended to lead people to repentance (Romans 2:4). When people do not respond to God's kindness, God tries to lead people to repentance through other means. There had been a three and a half year drought during Elijah's time. There was a famine during Elisha's lifetime that lasted twice as long.

The famine affected believers and unbelievers. The incident involving the poisonous stew and the account of how twenty loaves of bread fed a hundred men probably took place during that famine (2 Kings 4:38-44). Even the woman of Shunem, who apparently was now a widow, lived outside the land of Palestine during the seven years of famine.

According to God's law (Leviticus 25:23) no land was to be sold permanently. It was to remain with the original family forever. The fact that King Joram now ordered the Shunammite woman's land restored to her in accord with God's will does not, however, mean that he had become a believer in the Lord. Even though Joram had benefited from miraculous victories on the battlefield, even though he spoke often with Elisha and Gehazi, he remained an unbeliever even in his old age.

The last time we saw Gehazi was at the end of chapter 5 when Naaman's leprosy was transferred to him. As a leper Gehazi would not have been permitted social contact with others. This leads us to suspect that the incident related here actually took place before Gehazi became a leper.

Hazael Murders Ben-Hadad

⁷Elisha went to Damascus, and Ben-Hadad king of Aram was ill. When the king was told, "The man of God has come all the way

up here,"⁸he said to Hazael, "Take a gift with you and go to meet the man of God. Consult the LORD through him; ask him, 'Will I recover from this illness?' "

⁹Hazael went to meet Elisha, taking with him as a gift forty camel-loads of all the finest wares of Damascus. He went in and stood before him, and said, "Your son Ben-Hadad king of Aram has sent me to ask, 'Will I recover from this illness?' "

¹⁰Elisha answered, "Go and say to him, 'You will certainly recover'; but the LORD has revealed to me that he will in fact die." ¹¹He stared at him with a fixed gaze until Hazael felt ashamed. Then the man of God began to weep.

¹²"Why is my lord weeping?" asked Hazael.

"Because I know the harm you will do to the Israelites," he answered. "You will set fire to their fortified places, kill their young men with the sword, dash their little children to the ground, and rip open their pregnant women."

¹³Hazael said, "How could your servant, a mere dog, accomplish such a feat?"

"The LORD has shown me that you will become king of Aram," answered Elisha.

¹⁴Then Hazael left Elisha and returned to his master. When Ben-Hadad asked, "What did Elisha say to you?" Hazael replied, "He told me that you would certainly recover." ¹⁵But the next day he took a thick cloth, soaked it in water and spread it over the king's face, so that he died. Then Hazael succeeded him as king.

Ben-Hadad surely remembered how Elisha had healed Naaman from his leprosy. Experiences on the battlefield also had shown the king of Aram that Elisha's God has almighty power. When Ben-Hadad became very sick, we are not surprised to see him inquire from the Lord.

It was customary to bring a gift to the prophet. With his huge gift the heathen king perhaps desired also to buy God's favor.

Elisha's answer, however, is not quite so clear. We prefer not to think that Elisha contradicted himself or lied in verse 10. There are several possible explanations for this difficulty:

1. Elisha's first words may be sarcastic just as Micaiah at first gave a sarcastic answer to King Ahab in 1 Kings 22:15.

2. Perhaps Elisha meant, "Ben-Hadad would certainly recover from his illness were it not for his imminent assassination." This is the gist of the King James translation of this passage.

3. There may be a copying mistake. The Hebrew words "not" and "to him" are spelled differently but are pronounced the same. The NIV therefore provides an alternate translation in the footnote: "Go and say, 'You will certainly not recover.' "

Verse 11 offers us another difficult question. Who did the staring and who felt ashamed? The NIV implies that Elisha stared until Hazael felt ashamed. The original Hebrew, however, does not mention any name as the subject. Either Hazael stared as he considered Elisha's cryptic answer, or Elisha stared as God permitted him to see the destruction Hazael would bring on God's people.

A third unanswered question is, "When did Elijah carry out God's direction to anoint Hazael king of Aram?" Although Elijah received that command years earlier (1 Kings 19:15), we are not told how he carried it out. Some have suggested that Elisha did the anointing at this time.

Although Hazael learned from Elisha that he would become king, God did not order Hazael to assassinate the present king. Hazael put on a show of humility when he stood before Elisha. But his heart was full of ruthless ambition. Hazael assassinated King Ben-Hadad II, making the death appear to be accidental suffocation. We have here an example of how God uses even the barbarous sins of godless men to carry out his plans and to fulfill his prophecies.

God would permit Hazael to commit even greater atrocities as he took vengeance on an unbelieving nation of Israel.

Today it is the doctors in the abortion clinics who "rip open their pregnant women" for the sake of personal gain. That modern travesty might (like the actions of Hazael) be a part of God's judgment on a nation whose people have left their God.

Because of Hazael's unspeakable crimes, God would someday "send fire upon the house of Hazael that will consume the fortresses of Ben-Hadad" (Amos 1:4).

Since the beginning of 2 Kings the writer has been telling us about events in the northern kingdom of Israel. Now the scene shifts to Judah, the southern kingdom with its capital in Jerusalem. There things had also deteriorated.

Jehoram King of Judah

16In the fifth year of Joram son of Ahab king of Israel, when Jehoshaphat was king of Judah, Jehoram son of Jehoshaphat began his reign as king of Judah. 17He was thirty-two years old when he became king, and he reigned in Jerusalem eight years. 18He walked in the ways of the kings of Israel, as the house of Ahab had done, for he married a daughter of Ahab. He did evil in the eyes of the LORD. 19Nevertheless, for the sake of his servant David, the LORD was not willing to destroy Judah. He had promised to maintain a lamp for David and his descendants forever.

20In the time of Jehoram, Edom rebelled against Judah and set up its own king. 21So Jehoram went to Zair with all his chariots. The Edomites surrounded him and his chariot commanders, but he rose up and broke through by night; his army, however, fled back home. 22To this day Edom has been in rebellion against Judah. Libnah revolted at the same time.

23 As for the other events of Jehoram's reign, and all he did, are they not written in the book of the annals of the kings of Judah? 24 Jehoram rested with his fathers and was buried with them in the City of David. And Ahaziah his son succeeded him as king.

Although Jehoshaphat "did what was right in the sight of the Lord" (1 Kings 22:43), he made several mistakes in judgment. His worst mistakes were standing at the side of King Ahab on the battlefield and arranging the marriage of his son Jehoram to Ahab's daughter Athaliah. That alliance now had disastrous consequences.

God warns us not to make similar mistakes. In Romans 16:17 Paul writes, "Watch out for those who cause divisions and put obstacles in your way that are contrary to the teaching you have learned. Keep away from them." In 2 Corinthians 6:14 and 17 he writes, "Do not be yoked together with unbelievers. . . . Come out from them and be separate." When faithful Christians cooperate (in religious matters) with unbelievers and with others who reject God's word, trouble will follow. Following God's warnings will not make us popular; ignoring God's warnings will be disastrous.

Jehoram is not the first king who began to walk in the ways of a heathen spouse. His father-in-law, King Ahab, had done the same thing. Many others have done the same thing in our own day.

Verse 19 deserves our special attention. The people of Judah now were committing the same sins that were common in Israel. Although Judah also deserved God's judgment, a gracious God spared this kingdom because he had promised to send the Savior into the world through the family of King David.

The work of King Jehoram is described in more detail in 2 Chronicles 21. Years of work done by God-fearing parents like King Jehoshaphat can be undone quickly by unbelieving children. The rebellion of Edom was part of God's judgment against Jehoram. The unbelieving king finally died of a painful, incurable disease of the bowels.

Ahaziah King of Judah

25In the twelfth year of Joram son of Ahab king of Israel, Ahaziah son of Jehoram king of Judah began to reign. 26Ahaziah was twenty-two years old when he became king, and he reigned in Jerusalem one year. His mother's name was Athaliah, a granddaughter of Omri king of Israel. 27He walked in the ways of the house of Ahab and did evil in the eyes of the LORD, as the house of Ahab had done, for he was related by marriage to Ahab's family.

28Ahaziah went with Joram son of Ahab to war against Hazael king of Aram at Ramoth Gilead. The Arameans wounded Joram; 29so King Joram returned to Jezreel to recover from the wounds the Arameans had inflicted on him at Ramoth in his battle with Hazael king of Aram.

Then Ahaziah son of Jehoram king of Judah went down to Jezreel to see Joram son of Ahab, because he had been wounded.

According to 2 Chronicles 22:1, Judah's new king, Ahaziah, was the youngest and the only surviving son of Jehoram. He was named after his uncle, the wicked king of Israel, who had the same name. We are not surprised to learn that Ahaziah lived in the same sins.

Back in 1 Kings 22 we saw how King Ahab had been mortally wounded in an unsuccessful attempt to capture Ramoth Gilead from Aram. Apparently Joram was more successful than his father, for we now see Israel defending this city. And apparently both Israel and Judah continued to view Ramoth, one of the six cities of refuge, as important to the nation. Therefore Ahaziah of Judah helped his Uncle Joram (the king of Israel) defend Ramoth against the Arameans.

Chapter 9 shows us that this story also has a tragic ending. When Ahaziah visited his wounded uncle in Jezreel, they both were killed at the hands of Jehu.

When Elijah had fled to Horeb (Sinai), God had commissioned him to anoint Jehu king of Israel (1 Kings 19:16). For some unknown reason Elijah did not carry out that assignment personally. But now, twenty years later, the time had come. God would avenge the blood of Naboth and the blood of the prophets shed by Ahab and Jezebel.

Jehu's Reforms in Israel (9:1—10:36)

Jehu Anointed King of Israel

9 **The prophet Elisha summoned a man from the company of the prophets and said to him, "Tuck your cloak into your belt, take this flask of oil with you and go to Ramoth Gilead. ²When you get there, look for Jehu son of Jehoshaphat, the son of Nimshi. Go to him, get him away from his companions and take him into an inner room. ³Then take the flask and pour the oil on his head and declare, 'This is what the LORD says: I anoint you king over Israel.' Then open the door and run; don't delay!"**

⁴So the young man, the prophet, went to Ramoth Gilead. ⁵When he arrived, he found the army officers sitting together. "I have a message for you, commander," he said.

"For which of us?" asked Jehu.

⁶Jehu got up and went into the house. Then the prophet poured the oil on Jehu's head and declared, "This is what the LORD, the God of Israel, says: 'I anoint you king over the LORD's people Israel. ⁷You are to destroy the house of Ahab your master, and I will avenge the blood of my servants the prophets and the blood of all the LORD's servants shed by Jezebel. ⁸The whole house of Ahab will perish. I will cut off from Ahab every last male in Israel—slave or free. ⁹I will make the house of Ahab like the house of Jeroboam son of Nebat and like the house of Baasha son of Ahijah. ¹⁰As for Jezebel, dogs will devour her on the plot of

ground at Jezreel, and no one will bury her.' " Then he opened the door and ran.

¹¹ When Jehu went out to his fellow officers, one of them asked him, "Is everything all right? Why did this madman come to you?"

"You know the man and the sort of things he says," Jehu replied.

¹²"That's not true!" they said. "Tell us."

Jehu said, "Here is what he told me: 'This is what the LORD says: I anoint you king over Israel.' "

¹³ They hurried and took their cloaks and spread them under him on the bare steps. Then they blew the trumpet and shouted, "Jehu is king!"

While Joram, king of Israel, was recovering from his wounds back in Jezreel, Jehu, the commander of Israel's army, remained on the battlefield at Ramoth Gilead. As Jehu was consulting with his officers, Elisha's servant, one of the seminary students, announced to Jehu the bloody task which God had assigned to him.

The last verses of this section give us an insight into Jehu's character. His first response to a question is often evasive and less than the whole truth. When his men asked Jehu to explain why the young prophet had visited him, he at first avoided the question. The aroma of the anointing oil, however, revealed that there was more to the story.

Just as Jehu was anointed by God's messenger to become king over God's people, so the Lord Jesus was anointed with the Holy Spirit to be King over God's believers. Just as God commissioned Jehu to take vengeance on his enemies, so God commissioned Jesus, our Captain, to do battle against Satan and to crush his head in the dust. Jesus, like Jehu, won a decisive victory.

Jehu Kills Joram and Ahaziah

¹⁴ So Jehu son of Jehoshaphat, the son of Nimshi, conspired against Joram. (Now Joram and all Israel had been defending

Ramoth Gilead against Hazael king of Aram, [15]but King Joram had returned to Jezreel to recover from the wounds the Arameans had inflicted on him in the battle with Hazael king of Aram.) Jehu said, "If this is the way you feel, don't let anyone slip out of the city to go and tell the news in Jezreel." [16]Then he got into his chariot and rode to Jezreel, because Joram was resting there and Ahaziah king of Judah had gone down to see him.

[17]When the lookout standing on the tower in Jezreel saw Jehu's troops approaching, he called out, "I see some troops coming."

"Get a horseman," Joram ordered. "Send him to meet them and ask, 'Do you come in peace?' "

[18]The horseman rode off to meet Jehu and said, "This is what the king says: 'Do you come in peace?' "

"What do you have to do with peace?" Jehu replied. "Fall in behind me."

The lookout reported, "The messenger has reached them, but he isn't coming back."

[19]So the king sent out a second horseman. When he came to them he said, "This is what the king says: 'Do you come in peace?' "

Jehu replied, "What do you have to do with peace? Fall in behind me."

[20]The lookout reported, "He has reached them, but he isn't coming back either. The driving is like that of Jehu son of Nimshi—he drives like a madman."

Jehu made plans immediately to carry out his assignment. Again he cloaked his plans with secrecy. He hoped to take the royal family by surprise.

Jehu was a forceful, energetic man. He and his men left Ramoth and headed for Jezreel, some fifty miles to the west, site of the king's summer palace. When they crossed the Jordan River, they were about halfway there. Then they traveled through the Valley of Jezreel to the City of Jezreel, a city built high above the valley on one of its slopes. The watchman in the tower spied Jehu and his men when they were still many miles away.

Soon the watchman could even recognize the impetuous leader of the horsemen. It was Jehu. The commander-in-chief had returned from the battlefield.

[21]"Hitch up my chariot," Joram ordered. And when it was hitched up, Joram king of Israel and Ahaziah king of Judah rode out, each in his own chariot, to meet Jehu. They met him at the plot of ground that had belonged to Naboth the Jezreelite. [22]When Joram saw Jehu he asked, "Have you come in peace, Jehu?"

"How can there be peace," Jehu replied, "as long as all the idolatry and witchcraft of your mother Jezebel abound?"

[23]Joram turned about and fled, calling out to Ahaziah, "Treachery, Ahaziah!"

[24]Then Jehu drew his bow and shot Joram between the shoulders. The arrow pierced his heart and he slumped down in his chariot. [25]Jehu said to Bidkar, his chariot officer, "Pick him up and throw him on the field that belonged to Naboth the Jezreelite. Remember how you and I were riding together in chariots behind Ahab his father when the LORD made this prophecy about him: [26]'Yesterday I saw the blood of Naboth and the blood of his sons, declares the LORD, and I will surely make you pay for it on this plot of ground, declares the LORD.' Now then, pick him up and throw him on that plot, in accordance with the word of the LORD."

[27]When Ahaziah king of Judah saw what had happened, he fled up the road to Beth Haggan. Jehu chased him, shouting, "Kill him too!" They wounded him in his chariot on the way up to Gur near Ibleam, but he escaped to Megiddo and died there. [28]His servants took him by chariot to Jerusalem and buried him with his fathers in his tomb in the City of David. [29](In the eleventh year of Joram son of Ahab, Ahaziah had become king of Judah.)

Here Jehu was speaking and acting as God's avenger. There could be no peace as long as the people lived in the idolatry and witchcraft fostered by the queen mother. Sin arouses God's just anger. No unbeliever can expect to live in peace.

Jehu personally shot the arrow which killed Joram, the son of Ahab. As Jehu's charioteer threw the body of the dead king out onto the field that had once belonged to Naboth, Jehu recalled the words of Elijah to King Ahab which he had overheard many years earlier: "In the place where dogs licked up Naboth's blood, dogs will lick up your blood—yes, yours!' " (1 Kings 21:19).

Because Ahaziah, the king of Judah, was a grandson of King Ahab, he also suffered God's vengeance. He was shot as he fled toward the garden house and died at nearby Megiddo.

But the severest judgment was reserved for Jezebel.

Jezebel Killed

30Then Jehu went to Jezreel. When Jezebel heard about it, she painted her eyes, arranged her hair and looked out of a window. 31As Jehu entered the gate, she asked, "Have you come in peace, Zimri, you murderer of your master?"

32He looked up at the window and called out, "Who is on my side? Who?" Two or three eunuchs looked down at him. 33"Throw her down!" Jehu said. So they threw her down, and some of her blood spattered the wall and the horses as they trampled her underfoot.

34Jehu went in and ate and drank, "Take care of that cursed woman," he said, "and bury her, for she was a king's daughter." 35But when they went out to bury her, they found nothing except her skull, her feet and her hands. 36They went back and told Jehu, who said, "This is the word of the LORD that he spoke through his servant Elijah the Tishbite: On the plot of ground at Jezreel dogs will devour Jezebel's flesh. 37Jezebel's body will be like refuse on the ground in the plot at Jezreel, so that no one will be able to say, "This is Jezebel.' "

Instead of putting on sackcloth and ashes, Jezebel put on eye shadow and adorned her hair. Although her son and

The Death of Jezebel (2 Kings 9:33)

grandson had just suffered the vengeance of a just God, she showed no signs of repentance. Looking down from a window, she called Jehu a "Zimri," that is an assassin (1 Kings 16:10).

When Jehu finished eating dinner, he ordered his men to show respect for Jezebel's royal descent by giving her a decent burial. Scavenger dogs, however, made their work impossible and unnecessary. When Jehu heard the facts, he again recalled the word Elijah had spoken many years earlier: "Dogs will devour Jezebel by the wall of Jezreel" (1 Kings 21:23).

The name "Jezebel" has become synonymous with wickedness and idolatry. In his letter to the church at Thyatira Jesus mentions a woman whom he calls "Jezebel." If she refused to repent of her false teaching and her idolatry, God would inflict on her a punishment like the one we read about here. God would "cast her on a bed of suffering" and "strike her children dead" (Revelation 2:20-23).

Modern Jezebels still offer us peace without repentance. They say to us, "Do not let your conscience bother you. Do not let the minister scare you with his talk about sin and judgment." But those words do not lead to peace. " 'There is no peace,' says my God, 'for the wicked' " (Isaiah 57:21).

But Jesus came into the world to obtain real peace. He battled Satan in the wilderness and when he cast demons out of those who had been possessed. He won the final victory over Satan when he paid for sin on Calvary's cross. Now, "since we have been justified through faith, we have peace with God through our Lord Jesus Christ" (Romans 5:1).

Now that the members of the royal family in Jezreel were dead, Jehu was ready to move against Ahab's other sons in the capital city of Samaria.

Ahab's Family Killed

10 Now there were in Samaria seventy sons of the house of Ahab. So Jehu wrote letters and sent them to Samaria: to the officials of Jezreel, to the elders and to the guardians of Ahab's children. He said, ²"As soon as this letter reaches you, since your master's sons are with you and you have chariots and horses, a fortified city and weapons, ³choose the best and most worthy of your master's sons and set him on his father's throne. Then fight for your master's house."

⁴But they were terrified and said, "If two kings could not resist him, how can we?"

⁵So the palace administrator, the city governor, the elders and the guardians sent this message to Jehu: "We are your servants and we will do anything you say. We will not appoint anyone as king; you do whatever you think best."

⁶Then Jehu wrote them a second letter, saying, "If you are on my side and will obey me, take the heads of your master's sons and come to me in Jezreel by this time tomorrow."

Now the royal princes, seventy of them, were with the leading men of the city, who were rearing them. ⁷When the letter arrived, these men took the princes and slaughtered all seventy of them. They put their heads in baskets and sent them to Jehu in Jezreel. ⁸When the messenger arrived, he told Jehu, "They have brought the heads of the princes."

Then Jehu ordered, "Put them in two piles at the entrance of the city gate until morning."

⁹The next morning Jehu went out. He stood before all the people and said, "You are innocent. It was I who conspired against my master and killed him, but who killed all these? ¹⁰Know then, that not a word the LORD has spoken against the house of Ahab will fail. The LORD has done what he promised through his servant Elijah." ¹¹So Jehu killed everyone in Jezreel who remained of the house of Ahab, as well as all his chief men, his close friends and his priests, leaving him no survivor.

¹²Jehu then set out and went toward Samaria. At Beth Eked of the Shepherds, ¹³he met some relatives of Ahaziah king of Judah and asked, "Who are you?"

They said, "We are relatives of Ahaziah, and we have come down to greet the families of the king and of the queen mother."

¹⁴"Take them alive!" he ordered. So they took them alive and slaughtered them by the well of Beth Eked—forty-two men. He left no survivor.

¹⁵After he left there, he came upon Jehonadab son of Recab, who was on his way to meet him. Jehu greeted him and said, "Are you in accord with me, as I am with you?"

"I am," Jehonadab answered.

"If so," said Jehu, "give me your hand." So he did, and Jehu helped him up into the chariot. ¹⁶Jehu said, "Come with me and see my zeal for the LORD." Then he had him ride along in his chariot.

¹⁷When Jehu came to Samaria, he killed all who were left there of Ahab's family; he destroyed them, according to the word of the LORD spoken to Elijah.

Sarcasm was another facet of Jehu's personality. In a letter addressed to the guardians of Ahab's children Jehu suggested that they choose one of the seventy sons, make him king and send that new king against Jehu on the battlefield. When the guardians wisely declined that offer, Jehu sent another letter. In it he asked them to demonstrate their complete submission to him by killing Ahab's sons and delivering their heads to him in baskets. The guardians complied with that bloody request, perhaps because they feared for their own lives. Jehu, according to the custom of the day, publicly displayed the heads at the gates of Jezreel.

Why did Jehu claim to know nothing about the deaths of these men? Apparently this was just another part of his secret mode of operation. The deaths of these men, in whatever way they occurred, fulfilled the prophecy of the Lord that the house of Ahab was doomed to perish. Jehu even went beyond the call of duty by putting to death men who were not related to the king, including Ahab's friends and advisers.

As he approached Samaria, Jehu met some other relatives of King Ahab. He had carried out his work so quickly that Ahab's relatives had not yet heard about the massacres.

Since these visitors were also part of Ahab's family, Jehu ordered his men to slay them also.

God has nowhere given us an assignment like the one he gave Jehu—to take vengeance on his enemies. But God has given us the assignment to proclaim the gospel to every creature. We pray that God would give us Jehu's eagerness to carry out our assignment.

The work God assigned to Jehu was more than a political revolution. It was also to lead to a religious reformation. As he continued toward Samaria, Jehu met Jehonadab. This upright man was from the family of the Recabites. Although they were not Israelites, they were zealous worshipers of the God of Israel. Later Jeremiah pointed to them as an example for God's wayward people (Jeremiah 35:1-19). As Jehu and Jehonadab rode together to Samaria, the new king told his friend how he planned to destroy the worshipers of Baal with one blow.

Ministers of Baal Killed

[18]Then Jehu brought all the people together and said to them, "Ahab served Baal a little; Jehu will serve him much. [19]Now summon all the prophets of Baal, all his ministers and all his priests. See that no one is missing, because I am going to hold a great sacrifice to Baal. Anyone who fails to come will no longer live." But Jehu was acting deceptively in order to destroy the ministers of Baal.

[20]Jehu said, "Call an assembly in honor of Baal." So they proclaimed it. [21]Then he sent word throughout Israel, and all the ministers of Baal came; not one stayed away. They crowded into the temple of Baal until it was full from one end to the other. [22]And Jehu said to the keeper of the wardrobe, "Bring robes for all the ministers of Baal." So he brought out robes for them.

[23]Then Jehu and Jehonadab son of Recab went into the temple of Baal. Jehu said to the ministers of Baal, "Look around and see that no servants of the LORD are here with you—only ministers of

Baal." ²⁴So they went in to make sacrifices and burnt offerings. Now Jehu had posted eighty men outside with this warning: "If one of you lets any of the men I am placing in your hands escape, it will be your life for his life."

²⁵As soon as Jehu had finished making the burnt offering, he ordered the guards and officers: "Go in and kill them; let no one escape." So they cut them down with the sword. The guards and the officers threw the bodies out and then entered the inner shrine of the temple of Baal. ²⁶They brought the sacred stone out of the temple of Baal and burned it. ²⁷They demolished the sacred stone of Baal and tore down the temple of Baal, and people have used it for a latrine to this day.

King Jehu continued his work with his usual zeal, deception, and brutality. He invited all the servants of Baal to come to the temple of Baal built in Samaria by King Ahab. At the appointed time the temple was filled to capacity. The garments Jehu issue to the ministers of Baal would make it easy to identify them in the slaughter that would follow.

The place that had once been sacred to Baal was now, fittingly, rezoned for use as a public toilet.

Finally the house of Ahab and the idolatry he introduced were eradicated. All others who oppose God can expect a similar fate at the hands of God or one of God's agents.

God has not anointed us through a prophet, but he has personally called us out of darkness into the light. God has not asked us to slay idolaters, but he does want us to drown our old Adam by daily contrition and repentance. Jesus died in order to make us a people "eager to do what is good" (Titus 2:14). We must not copy Jehu's methods, but we can imitate his zeal and decisiveness.

²⁸So Jehu destroyed Baal worship in Israel. ²⁹However, he did not turn away from the sins of Jeroboam son of Nebat, which he had caused Israel to commit—the worship of the golden calves at Bethel and Dan.

The Dead Bodies Thrown Outside the Temple (2 Kings 10:25)

³⁰The LORD said to Jehu, "Because you have done well in accomplishing what is right in my eyes and have done to the house of Ahab all I had in mind to do, your descendants will sit on the throne of Israel to the fourth generation." ³¹Yet Jehu was not careful to keep the law of the LORD, the God of Israel, with all his heart. He did not turn away from the sins of Jeroboam, which he had caused Israel to commit.

³²In those days the LORD began to reduce the size of Israel. Hazael overpowered the Israelites throughout their territory ³³east of the Jordan in all the land of Gilead (the region of Gad, Reuben and Manasseh), from Aroer by the Arnon Gorge through Gilead to Bashan.

³⁴As for the other events of Jehu's reign, all he did, and all his achievements, are they not written in the book of the annals of the kings of Israel?

³⁵Jehu rested with his father and was buried in Samaria. And Jehoahaz his son succeeded him as king. ³⁶The time that Jehu reigned over Israel in Samaria was twenty-eight years.

Like many before him and after him Jehu *began* to serve God. But he did not *continue* to be a faithful servant of the Lord. Because of his disobedience Israel's enemies grew powerful. Aram, Israel's enemy for many years, soon took over Israelite territory east of the Jordan River. That included, no doubt, the city of Ramoth Gilead, a city which is never again mentioned in the history of Israel.

Many confirmands today make the same mistake. They begin to serve God enthusiastically but then fall away. They deal successfully with the "big" sins of society but are later ensnared by the "smaller" sins in their personal lives.

God's faithful people continue to rejoice in the robe of righteousness won for them by the blood of their Savior. The robes worn by the ministers of Baal marked them for destruction. The robes of righteousness worn by those who believe in Christ render them acceptable in God's courtroom.

Now our writer shifts our attention back to Jerusalem and the Southern Kingdom.

Reforms in Judah (11:1-12:21)

Athaliah and Joash

11 When Athaliah the mother of Ahaziah saw that her son was dead, she proceeded to destroy the whole royal family. ²But Jehosheba, the daughter of King Jehoram and sister of Ahaziah, took Joash son of Ahaziah and stole him away from among the royal princes, who were about to be murdered. She put him and his nurse in a bedroom to hide him from Athaliah; so he was not killed. ³He remained hidden with his nurse at the temple of the LORD for six years while Athaliah ruled the land.

⁴In the seventh year Jehoiada sent for the commanders of units of a hundred, the Carites and the guards and had them brought to him at the temple of the LORD. He made a covenant with them and put them under oath at the temple of the LORD. Then he showed them the king's son. ⁵He commanded them saying, "This is what you are to do: You who are in the three companies that are going on duty on the Sabbath—a third of you guarding the royal palace, ⁶a third at the Sur Gate, and a third at the gate behind the guard, who take turns guarding the temple—⁷and you who are in the other two companies that normally go off Sabbath duty are all to guard the temple for the king. ⁸Station yourselves around the king, each man with his weapon in his hand. Anyone who approaches your ranks must be put to death. Stay close to the king wherever he goes."

⁹The commanders of units of a hundred did just as Jehoiada the priest ordered. Each one took his men—those who were going on duty on the Sabbath and those who were going off duty—and came to Jehoiada the priest. ¹⁰Then he gave the commanders the spears and shields that had belonged to King David and that were in the temple of the LORD. ¹¹The guards, each with his weapon in his hand, stationed themselves around the king—near the altar and the temple, from the south side to the north side of the temple.

225

Abraham insisted that his son Isaac marry a God-fearing woman. When a husband and wife share a common faith in the Lord, they not only encourage and strengthen each other, but they also have a basis for solving the problems of life.

When a Christian marries a heathen, the results are often quite different. King Jehoshaphat had unfortunately arranged a marriage between his son Jehoram and Athaliah, daughter of Ahab and Jezebel. Athaliah showed no regret when her son Ahaziah was killed by Jehu. Instead she saw his death as her opportunity to seize power for herself. Ahaziah had no brothers who could claim the throne. If Athaliah could kill Ahaziah's children (her own grandchildren!), the throne would be hers.

The following chart of names may be helpful:

Kingdom of Judah	*Kingdom of Israel*
King Jehoshaphat	King Ahab and Queen Jezebel
King Jehoram ......marries ...	Athaliah, daughter of Ahab and Jezebel
King Ahaziah, son of Jehoram and Athaliah, killed by Jehu up at Jezreel	
Jehosheba, daughter of Jehoram, sister of Ahaziah, wife of Jehoiada the high priest	
King Joash, son of Ahaziah, escaped the plot of Athaliah.	

If a woman like Athaliah is accustomed to offer babies as sacrifices to Baal, it is easy to take the next step, that is, to kill older children. Similar things can be said about abortion. When people tolerate the killing of unborn children, they will soon tolerate the killing of infants who are not born "normal" and older people who are no longer considered useful.

Since King Ahaziah was perhaps twenty-three years old when he died (2 Kings 8:26), we can assume that the children Athaliah killed were quite young. But she missed one—thanks to the quick thinking of Jehosheba. Jehosheba hid her one-year-old nephew Joash in the temple. Here he was safe. The temple was a building that the queen mother did not visit.

When Joash was seven years old, the God-fearing high priest Jehoiada made arrangements for a public coronation. He confided his secret plans to the temple guards. He gave them extra weapons and ordered them to protect the new king. The coronation would take place on a Sabbath day when there would be a double guard at the temple. The Carites were a particular class of guards. The Hebrew indicates that they were perhaps the executioners.

The pillar mentioned in verse 14 was evidently a platform where the kings stood on special occasions (2 Kings 23:3).

12Jehoiada brought out the king's son and put the crown on him; he presented him with a copy of the covenant and proclaimed him king. They anointed him, and the people clapped their hands and shouted, "Long live the king!"

13When Athaliah heard the noise made by the guards and the people, she went to the people at the temple of the LORD. 14She looked and there was the king, standing by the pillar, as the custom was. The officers and trumpeters were beside the king, and all the people of the land were rejoicing and blowing trumpets. Then Athaliah tore her robes and called out, "Treason! Treason!"

¹⁵Jehoiada the priest ordered the commanders of units of a hundred, who were in charge of the troops: "Bring her out between the ranks and put to the sword anyone who follows her." For the priest had said, "She must not be put to death in the temple of the LORD." ¹⁶So they seized her as she reached the place where the horses enter the palace grounds, and there she was put to death.

¹⁷Jehoiada then made a covenant between the LORD and the king and people that they would be the LORD's people. He also made a covenant between the king and the people. ¹⁸All the people of the land went to the temple of Baal and tore it down. They smashed the altars and idols to pieces and killed Mattan the priest of Baal in front of the altars.

Then Jehoiada the priest posted guards at the temple of the LORD. ¹⁹He took with him the commanders of hundreds, the Carites, the guards and all the people of the land, and together they brought the king down from the temple of the LORD and went into the palace, entering by way of the gate of the guards. The king then took his place on the royal throne, ²⁰and all the people of the land rejoiced. And the city was quiet, because Athaliah had been slain with the sword at the palace.

²¹Joash was seven years old when he began to reign.

When Athaliah rushed next door to see what was happening, she understood the situation immediately. The guards overtook her and killed her at the palace gate near the stables.

The death of Athaliah and the coronation of King Joash meant a new beginning for the people of Judah. When Joash was crowned, a copy of the five books of Moses was immediately placed into his hands. This is significant. In Deuteronomy 17:18 Moses told the people that when a king began to rule, he should make a copy of the law for himself. That book of the law was to be his daily meditation and guide for service. By means of a covenant the people, who for many years had been ruled by godless kings and queens, rededicated themselves to the Lord.

Under Athaliah's rule the holy city of Jerusalem had become the home of a temple for Baal. Mattan evidently had come from Samaria and was the first resident heathen high priest. Now, at least for a time, Baal worship was eliminated from both the Northern and Southern Kingdoms (10:27).

This bloody story is an important chapter in the history of God's promise. Here Athaliah, or we should say, Satan, almost succeeded in destroying God's plan to send a Savior. God had promised that one of King David's descendants would be *the* Anointed One, the Messiah. For many generations God had guarded that promise. One descendant after another sat on the king's throne in Jerusalem. Here that bloodline of descent was almost broken.

Just as God did not permit the baby Jesus to die when Herod ordered the death of the babies in Bethlehem, so God did not permit baby Joash to be slain with the others. No one can stop God from fulfilling his promises.

When *the* Anointed One finally came into the world, he also had to deal with a wicked enemy who had stolen power and authority over God's people. That enemy is Satan. He became a prince and a ruler when he convinced our first parents to disobey their Creator and instead to follow him. By nature Satan was also our prince and ruler. But Jesus stripped that enemy of his power when he paid for our sins. Satan was deposed as the ruler of our hearts when we were brought to faith in the Savior.

We read the word "rejoice" only once in 2 Kings. That is in this chapter. Because the old ruler has been deposed, because Jesus rules as King at the right hand of God and in our hearts, we, like the people of Jerusalem, have reason to rejoice.

We show our dedication to the Lord, not by tearing down false temples, but by drowning the old Adam and by crucifying our sinful flesh with all its desires.

The new king's dedication to the Lord was, unfortunately, short-lived.

Joash Repairs the Temple

12 In the seventh year of Jehu, Joash became king, and he reigned in Jerusalem forty years. His mother's name was Zibiah; she was from Beersheba. ²Joash did what was right in the eyes of the LORD all the years Jehoiada the priest instructed him. ³The high places, however, were not removed; the people continued to offer sacrifices and burn incense there.

⁴Joash said to the priests, "Collect all the money that is brought as sacred offerings to the temple of the LORD—the money collected in the census, the money received from personal vows and the money brought voluntarily to the temple. ⁵Let every priest receive the money from one of the treasurers, and let it be used to repair whatever damage is found in the temple."

⁶But by the twenty-third year of King Joash the priests still had not repaired the temple. ⁷Therefore King Joash summoned Jehoiada the priest and the other priests and asked them, "Why aren't you repairing the damage done to the temple? Take no more money from your treasurers, but hand it over for repairing the temple." ⁸The priests agreed that they would not collect any more money from the people and that they would not repair the temple themselves.

⁹Jehoiada the priest took a chest and bored a hole in its lid. He placed it beside the altar, on the right side as one enters the temple of the LORD. The priests who guarded the entrance put into the chest all the money that was brought to the temple of the LORD. ¹⁰Whenever they saw that there was a large amount of money in the chest, the royal secretary and the high priest came, counted the money that had been brought into the temple of the LORD and put it into bags. ¹¹When the amount had been determined, they

gave the money to the men appointed to supervise the work on the temple. With it they paid those who worked on the temple of the LORD—the carpenters and builders, [12]the masons and stonecutters. They purchased timber and dressed stone for the repair of the temple of the LORD, and met all the other expenses of restoring the temple.

[13]The money brought into the temple was not spent for making silver basins, wick trimmers, sprinkling bowls, trumpets or any other articles of gold or silver for the temple of the LORD; [14]it was paid to the workmen, who used it to repair the temple. [15]They did not require an accounting from those to whom they gave the money to pay the workers, because they acted with complete honesty. [16]The money from the guilt offerings and sin offerings was not brought into the temple of the LORD; it belonged to the priests.

If Joash "did right in the sight of the Lord," why did he not remove all of the heathen altars on the high places? Outsiders could look at our congregations today and ask similar questions: Why are some of the people not in church to worship? Why are some of the people involved in fornication? Why are some of the people spending their money on sinful pleasures? We will not find a perfect church or congregation in a sinful world.

Because Joash was a believer in the Lord and because the temple had been his nursery and sanctuary for six years and perhaps because he wanted to bring the worshipers back to the house of the Lord, Joash took the lead in repairing the temple, a building that was now 140 years old.

The king asked the priests to gather money for the repair project from three sources. Some would come from the census. At the time of a census every person over twenty was to contribute a half shekel to the temple treasury (Exodus 30:12). Other revenue would come from the payment of vows (Leviticus 27:1-8). The rest would come from free-will offerings.

That plan, however, did not work. Perhaps the people were not prompt in bringing their offerings. Perhaps the priests neglected to inform the people about their obligations and about the work that needed to be done. Perhaps the people did not trust those who were to handle the money. At any rate, after Joash had ruled twenty-three years, no repairs had been started, and an alternate plan was devised.

According to the new plan, responsibilities would be taken from the priests and given to others (verse 8). Worshipers would drop coins for this special "building fund" into a wooden chest. Soon the box was full of coins and the repairs could begin.

Church buildings today also need constant repairs. Who is going to pay for the upkeep? Certainly not the heathen. It is people like Joash and others who have been blessed through God's word and sacrament in their house of worship, people who love to worship the Lord.

Methods for raising the funds vary from time to time and from place to place. It often happens, as it did here, that special collections are successful to the degree that lay people are involved in them.

Unfortunately the man who proved to be unfaithful in this matter was King Joash himself.

[17]About this time Hazael king of Aram went up and attacked Gath and captured it. Then he turned to attack Jerusalem. [18]But Joash king of Judah took all the sacred objects dedicated by his fathers—Jehoshaphat, Jehoram and Ahaziah, the kings of Judah—and the gifts he himself had dedicated and all the gold found in the treasuries of the temple of the LORD and of the royal palace, and he sent them to Hazael king of Aram, who then withdrew from Jerusalem.

[19]As for the other events of the reign of Joash, and all he did, are they not written in the book of annals of the kings of Judah? [20]His

officials conspired against him and assassinated him at Beth Millo, on the road down to Silla. ²¹The officials who murdered him were Jozabad son of Shimeath and Jehozabad son of Shomer. He died and was buried with his fathers in the City of David. and Amaziah his son succeeded him as king.

According to 2 Chronicles 24:15 Jehoiada, the faithful high priest, died at the age of 130. Now that this stalwart voice was silent, King Joash listened to the other officials in Jerusalem. They persuaded him to abandon the Lord and worship idols. God sent prophets to call Joash to repentance, but the king would not listen. Joash even put to death one of those prophets. The man was Zechariah, the son of Jehoiada!

Because King Joash rejected the Lord, the Lord finally rejected Joash. Hazael, the Aramean king, who according to Elisha's prophecy would be a scourge to Israel, came down from Damascus and captured Gath, one of the old Philistine cities west of Jerusalem. 2 Chronicles 24 gives us the details. As Hazael and his army were returning home, they defeated a large army of Judean soldiers. When Joash realized that he could not be victorious on the battlefield, he offered to pay tribute to Hazael. How did he obtain tribute money? By raiding the temple. He gave the gold and silver once dedicated to the Lord to the heathen king of Aram.

Because of his unfaithfulness Joash died a shameful death. Those who assassinated him were executed later (2 Kings 14:5).

In chapter 10 we saw how Jehu destroyed Baal worship in Israel. Unfortunately he did not continue to serve the Lord with his whole heart. Because he did not fully turn from idolatry, God permitted Hazael and the Arameans to take portions of the land away from Israel.

Things did not improve during the reign of Jehu's son, Jehoahaz.

Other Weak Kings (13:1-16:20)

Jehoahaz King of Israel

13 In the twenty-third year of Joash son of Ahaziah king of Judah, Jehoahaz son of Jehu became king of Israel in Samaria, and he reigned seventeen years. ³He did evil in the eyes of the LORD by following the sins of Jeroboam son of Nebat, which he had caused Israel to commit, and he did not turn away from them. ³So the LORD's anger burned against Israel, and for a long time he kept them under the power of Hazael king of Aram and Ben-Hadad his son.

⁴Then Jehoahaz sought the LORD's favor, and the LORD listened to him, for he saw how severely the king of Aram was oppressing Israel. ⁵The LORD provided a deliverer for Israel, and they escaped from the power of Aram. So the Israelites lived in their own homes as they had before. ⁶But they did not turn away from the sins of the house of Jeroboam, which he had caused Israel to commit; they continued in them. Also, the Asherah pole remained standing in Samaria.

⁷Nothing had been left of the army of Jehoahaz except fifty horsemen, ten chariots and ten thousand foot soldiers, for the king of Aram had destroyed the rest and made them like the dust at threshing time.

⁸As for the other events of the reign of Jehoahaz, all he did and his achievements, are they not written in the book of annals of the kings of Israel? ⁹Jehoahaz rested with his fathers and was buried in Samaria. And Jehoash his son succeeded him as king.

"Jehoahaz" means "the Lord Jehovah is my Holder, or Sustainer." Unfortunately Jehoahaz did not live up to that name. That is not unusual. Today also there are children who do not live up to the expectations of their parents who gave them fine, Christian names at the time of their birth.

What is even more disappointing is to see churches that do not live up to their names: "Lutheran" churches that no longer cling to the teachings of the Bible as Luther did, "evangelical" churches who have distorted and even destroyed the gospel.

When God's people were unfaithful after the death of Joshua (that is, during the time of the judges), God permitted a heathen people to lord it over his own people. Something similar happened here with Jehoahaz.

When God's people repented during the time of the judges, God sent a judge, a deliverer. God made a similar promise here. That unnamed deliverer is probably the king's son, Jehoash, whom we read about in the next section. Others see the deliverer as Jeroboam II, whom we will read about in the next chapter (see especially 2 Kings 14:27).

Jehoash King of Israel

¹⁰In the thirty-seventh year of Joash king of Judah, Jehoash son of Jehoahaz became king of Israel in Samaria, and he reigned sixteen years. ¹¹He did evil in the eyes of the LORD and did not turn away from any of the sins of Jeroboam son of Nebat, which he had caused Israel to commit; he continued in them.

¹²As for the other events of the reign of Jehoash, all he did and his achievements, including his war against Amaziah king of Judah, are they not written in the book of the annals of the kings of Israel? ¹³Jehoash rested with his fathers, and Jeroboam succeeded him on the throne. Jehoash was buried in Samaria with the kings of Israel.

The name Jehoash (or, Joash) means "given by Jehovah." Even though this man also had a fine-sounding name, even though Jehoash had some respect for God's word, he also worshiped the golden calves. Those calf-shrines had now been at Bethel and Dan for 125 years. This idolatry had become so entrenched that getting rid of it would not be easy.

These four verses give us a thumbnail sketch of King Jehoash. In the rest of chapter 13 and in the first half of chapter 14 the inspired writer tells us of two particular incidents.

¹⁴Now Elisha was suffering from the illness from which he died. Jehoash king of Israel went down to see him and wept over him. "My father! My father!" he cried. "The chariots and horsemen of Israel!"

¹⁵Elisha said, "Get a bow and some arrows," and he did so. ¹⁶"Take the bow in your hands," he said to the king of Israel. When he had taken it, Elisha put his hands on the king's hands.

¹⁷"Open the east window," he said, and he opened it. "Shoot!" Elisha said, and he shot. "The LORD's arrow of victory, the arrow of victory over Aram!" Elisha declared. "You will completely destroy the Arameans at Aphek."

¹⁸Then he said, "Take the arrows," and the king took them. Elisha told him, "Strike the ground." He struck it three times and stopped. ¹⁹The man of God was angry with him and said, "You should have struck the ground five or six times; then you would have defeated Aram and completely destroyed it. But now you will defeat it only three times."

Elisha was probably in his eighties. For more than fifty of those years he had been God's spokesman to the people of Israel. He had taught the people. He had trained other men in the schools of the prophets. He had performed a dozen miracles. But now this man of God was on his deathbed.

Back in 2 Kings 6:31 we saw a former king of Israel threatening to kill Elisha. The present king had a different attitude. With the greeting, "My father! The chariots and horsemen of Israel!" Jehoash acknowledged Elisha as his spiritual father and as the protector of Israel. He quoted words which Elisha himself had spoken when God took Elijah to heaven in the fiery chariot (2 Kings 2:12).

Because King Jehoash humbled himself before God and before God's spokesman, the Lord promised to give the king one more blessing through his dying prophet: victory over Aram.

When Elisha directed the king to shoot an arrow out the east window toward Aram, Jehoash gave an enthusiastic response. Israel would defeat Aram at Aphek, a place east of the Sea of Galilee.

But when the king learned the meaning of Elisha's sign language, when he learned that God would require some work and some effort, even a battle against Aram, King Jehoash became timid. His enthusiasm was gone. He struck the ground only three times with the arrows and then stopped. In this way Jehoash rejected the complete victory God wanted to give him.

When God's people today give a half-hearted response to God's promises, they are making the same mistake. God has promised to bless the preaching of his mighty word, but at times we are afraid to speak up and afraid to send missionaries. God has given us the tools to win a victory over our old man and over sin itself, but at times we make only halfhearted efforts to drown the old Adam. God has promised to hear and answer every prayer, but at times our prayer becomes a halfhearted whimper instead of a bold storming of the gates of heaven. We meekly tap the ground three times instead of striking it five or six times. God has promised to raise us from the dead and give us eternal life, but at times we mope through life as though we had no God.

Perhaps we, like Jehoash, do not possess God's blessings because we have been too timid to ask for them. Our lack of enthusiasm is never pleasing to God.

20Elisha died and was buried.

Now Moabite raiders used to enter the country every spring. 21Once while some Israelites were burying a man, suddenly they saw a band of raiders; so they threw the man's body into Elisha's tomb. When the body touched Elisha's bones, the man came to life and stood up on his feet.

22Hazael king of Aram oppressed Israel throughout the reign of Jehoahaz. 23But the LORD was gracious to them and had compassion and showed concern for them because of his covenant with Abraham, Isaac and Jacob. To this day he has been unwilling to destroy them or banish them from his presence.

24Hazael king of Aram died, and Ben-Hadad his son succeeded him as king. 25Then Jehoash son of Jehoahaz recaptured from Ben-Hadad son of Hazael the towns he had taken in battle from his father Jehoahaz. Three times Jehoash defeated him, and so he recovered the Israelite towns.

For the past nineteen chapters, that is, ever since 1 Kings 17, Elijah and Elisha had been working among God's people. Elisha continued to be a blessing to God's people even after his death. He continued to show the people that the Lord, Israel's faithful covenant God, is the almighty God, the God of life and death. If the Israelites would serve that God, then they would not have to be afraid. The Lord would give them victory over Aram on the northeast, over Moab on the southeast, and even over death itself.

God's prophets and apostles, even though they died many years ago, continue to be a blessing to God's people today. As often as we hear or read the words of those prophets, God continues to speak to us. Those words are spirit and they are life. Through those written words he has created spiritual life in our hearts. Finally that same God will also raise our dead bodies from the grave and, for Jesus' sake, give us eternal life in heaven.

Verse 23 deserves our special attention. The people of Israel had spurned God's word and had worshiped idols for many generations. There was no earthly reason for God to spare the nation of Israel from destruction. But God did spare them—for the sake of Abraham, Isaac, and Jacob. For the sake of one believer God is willing to show mercy to a thousand generations (Exodus 20:6).

Jehoash defeated Hazael's son, Ben-Hadad III, just as the Lord had promised.

The reign of Amaziah ran a course similar to that of his father, King Joash. It had a good beginning but an unfortunate ending.

Amaziah King of Judah

14 **In the second year of Jehoash son of Jehoahaz king of Israel, Amaziah son of Joash king of Judah began to reign. ²He was twenty-five years old when he became king, and he reigned in Jerusalem twenty-nine years. His mother's name was Jehoaddin; she was from Jerusalem. ³He did what was right in the eyes of the LORD, but not as his father David had done. In everything he followed the example of his father Joash. ⁴The high places, however, were not removed; the people continued to offer sacrifices and burn incense there.**

⁵After the kingdom was firmly in his grasp, he executed the officials who had murdered his father the king. ⁶Yet he did not put the sons of the assassins to death, in accordance with what is written in the Book of the Law of Moses where the LORD commanded: "Fathers shall not be put to death for their children, nor children put to death for their fathers; each is to die for his own sins."

⁷He was the one who defeated ten thousand Edomites in the Valley of Salt and captured Sela in battle, calling it Joktheel, the name it has to this day.

By executing his father's assassins and sparing the innocent children, Amaziah followed the law of the Lord (Deuteronomy 24:16) rather than Oriental custom.

But trouble began for Amaziah when he planned an expedition against Edom (2 Chronicles 25). In order to conduct this campaign, Amaziah not only enlisted the men of Judah but also hired 100,000 soldiers from the northern kingdom of Israel. He paid them 100 talents of silver for their help. Through an unidentfied prophet, however, God told Amaziah to dismiss his hired soldiers. Since these mercenaries would now miss out on the profitable looting that ordinarily followed a victorious campaign, they returned home in anger. On the way they looted the cities of Judah and killed 3,000 people.

God gave Amaziah victory against Edom even without the hired soldiers. The Jewish king defeated the Edomites in the Valley of Salt south of the Dead Sea and captured the city of Sela.

⁸Then Amaziah sent messengers to Jehoash son of Jehoahaz, the son of Jehu, king of Israel, with the challenge: "Come, meet me face to face."

⁹But Jehoash king of Israel replied to Amaziah king of Judah: "A thistle in Lebanon sent a message to a cedar in Lebanon, 'Give your daughter to my son in marriage.' Then a wild beast in Lebanon came along and trampled the thistle underfoot. ¹⁰You have indeed defeated Edom and now you are arrogant. Glory in your victory, but stay at home! Why ask for trouble and cause your own downfall and that of Judah also?"

¹¹Amaziah, however, would not listen, so Jehoash king of Israel attacked. He and Amaziah king of Judah faced each other at Beth Shemesh in Judah. ¹²Judah was routed by Israel, and every man fled to his home. ¹³Jehoash king of Israel captured Amaziah king of Judah, the son of Joash, the son of Ahaziah, at Beth Shemesh. Then Jehoash went to Jerusalem and broke down

the wall of Jerusalem from the Ephraim Gate to. the Corner Gate—a section about six hundred feet long. [14]He took all the gold and silver and all the articles found in the temple of the LORD and in the treasuries of the royal palace. He also took hostages and returned to Samaria.

[15]As for the other events of the reign of Jehoash, what he did and his achievements, including his war against Amaziah king of Judah, are they not written in the book of the annals of the kings of Israel? [16]Jehoash rested with his fathers and was buried in Samaria with the kings of Israel. And Jeroboam his son succeeded him as king.

In order to get even with Israel for the rowdy actions of the hired soldiers, Amaziah foolishly challenged the king of Israel to a battle. But this time he would not be successful. Ever since his victory against Edom, Amaziah had been serving the powerless gods of Edom which he had captured. Because of that idolatry he forfeited the continued blessing of the Lord (2 Chronicles 25:14-16).

The proud king of Judah refused to listen to the parable spoken by the king of Israel. Jehoash defeated and captured Amaziah at Beth Shemesh west of Jerusalem. Because he held Amaziah as his prisoner, Jehoash could enter Jerusalem without a struggle. By destroying a section of Jerusalem's wall, Jehoash made the holy city defenseless against attacks from Samaria and other enemies from the north, and by taking Jewish hostages back to Samaria, Jehoash ensured the good behavior of the king in Jerusalem.

"Pride goes before destruction" (Proverbs 16:18). In spiritual matters also the person who relies on his own strength instead of on the Lord will not be victorious against his enemies.

[17]Amaziah son of Joash king of Judah lived for fifteen years after the death of Jehoash son of Jehoahaz king of Israel. [18]As for

the other events of Amaziah's reign, are they not written in the book of the annals of the kings of Judah?

¹⁹They conspired against him in Jerusalem, and he fled to Lachish, but they sent men after him to Lachish and killed him there. ²⁰He was brought back by horse and was buried in Jerusalem with his fathers, in the City of David.

²¹Then all the people of Judah took Azariah, who was sixteen years old, and made him king in place of his father Amaziah. ²²He was the one who rebuilt Elath and restored it to Judah after Amaziah rested with his fathers.

The second half of Amaziah's reign was not as glorious as the first. For unknown reasons he, like his father Joash, was assassinated. Lachish was an important fortress city near the Philistine border. It is not unusual for God to use rebels and even assassins to get rid of proud tyrants.

Jeroboam II King of Israel

²³In the fifteenth year of Amaziah son of Joash king of Judah, Jeroboam son of Jehoash king of Israel became king in Samaria, and he reigned forty-one years. ²⁴He did evil in the eyes of the LORD and did not turn away from any of the sins of Jeroboam son of Nebat, which he had caused Israel to commit. ²⁵He was the one who restored the boundaries of Israel from Lebo Hamath to the Sea of the Arabah, in accordance with the word of the LORD, the God of Israel, spoken through his servant Jonah son of Amittai, the prophet from Gath Hepher.

²⁶The LORD had seen how bitterly everyone in Israel, whether slave or free, was suffering; there was no one to help them. ²⁷And since the LORD had not said he would blot out the name of Israel from under heaven, he saved them by the hand of Jeroboam son of Jehoash.

²⁸As for the other events of Jeroboam's reign, all he did, and his military achievements, including how he recovered for Israel both Damascus and Hamath, which had belonged to Yaudi, are they

not written in the book of the annals of the kings of Israel? ²⁹Jeroboam rested with his fathers, the kings of Israel. And Zechariah his son succeeded him as king.

This passage introduces the second of Israel's kings to bear the name Jeroboam. To avoid confusing this king with the king who introduced calf-worship into Israel (1 Kings 12:25-32), the king whose reign is described here is usually referred to as Jeroboam II.

In spite of Jeroboam's idolatry the Lord had pity on Israel. God permitted him to have a long and flourishing reign. The wars begun by his father Jehoash were brought to a successful conclusion. He was victorious over Aram (2 Kings 13:4,5), and recaptured their chief cities Damascus and Hamath. The boundaries of Israel once again stretched from Lebanon in the north to the Dead Sea on the south. He reconquered Ammon and Moab (Amos 1:13; 2:1-3) and restored that territory east of the Jordan River to the Israelite tribes who had lived there (2 Kings 13:5). All of this land had been under King David's rule many generations earlier.

But all of this was merely an outward restoration. The prophets Hosea, Amos, and Jonah lived at the time of King Jeroboam. They paint a sorry picture of religious and moral conditions in Israel. Bethel continued to be the "king's sanctuary" (Amos 7:13). Drunkenness, licentiousness, and oppression were the order of the day (Amos 2:6-8). Idolatry was mingled with the worship of the Lord (Hosea 4:13; 13:1-6).

Amos, the shepherd from Tekoa, came to Israel to prophesy against it. But Amaziah, the high priest at Bethel, resented Amos's prophecies of doom and reported them to the king. The heathen priest told Amos, "Get out, you seer!

Go back to the land of Judah. Earn your bread there and do your prophesying there. Don't prophesy anymore at Bethel" (Amos 7:12,13).

Because of that hardened impenitence Amos began to foretell the captivity of Israel at the hands of a heathen nation from the north. Amos also foretold the severest judgment of all, a famine of God's word in Israel (Amos 8:11,12).

It was during this time of hardened impenitence that God removed the prophet Jonah from the land of Israel and sent him to Assyria, the nation that would ultimately destroy Israel. Ironically, the people of Ninevah repented when they heard Jonah's preaching.

Today also a church's outward size and statistical successes are often not true indications of its real worth.

For reasons unknown to us the Holy Spirit saw fit, in chapter 15, to describe several kings of Israel and Judah by means of only a thumbnail sketch.

Azariah King of Judah

15 **In the twenty-seventh year of Jeroboam king of Israel, Azariah son of Amaziah king of Judah began to reign. [2]He was sixteen years old when he became king, and he reigned in Jerusalem fifty-two years. His mother's name was Jecoliah; she was from Jerusalem. [3]He did what was right in the eyes of the LORD, just as his father Amaziah had done. [4]The high places, however, were not removed; the people continued to offer sacrifices and burn incense there.**

[5]The LORD afflicted the king with leprosy until the day he died, and he lived in a separate house. Jotham the king's son had charge of the palace and governed the people of the land.

[6]As for the other events of Azariah's reign, and all he did, are they not written in the book of the annals of the kings of Judah? [7]Azariah rested with his fathers and was buried near them in the City of David. And Jotham his son succeeded him as king.

Azariah is perhaps better known by the name Uzziah (verse 32). Although Uzziah was involved in military campaigns against the Philistines and in rebuilding Jerusalem (2 Chronicles 26), our writer mentions only that he recaptured the port of Elath on the Gulf of Aqaba far south of the Dead Sea (2 Kings 14:22). 2 Chronicles 26 also tells us that leprosy broke out on Uzziah's forehead when he attempted to take over the work of the priests by burning incense in the temple.

It has been the custom of our writer to state the age of the king and to tell us how many years he ruled. In certain cases the reign may have included a coregency with the king's father. That seems to be the case here.

Zechariah King of Israel

8In the thirty-eighth year of Azariah king of Judah, Zechariah son of Jeroboam became king of Israel in Samaria, and he reigned six months. 9He did evil in the eyes of the LORD, as his fathers had done. He did not turn away from the sins of Jeroboam son of Nebat, which he had caused Israel to commit.

10Shallum son of Jabesh conspired against Zechariah. He attacked him in front of the people, assassinated him and succeeded him as king. 11The other events of Zechariah's reign are written in the book of the annals of the kings of Israel. 12So the word of the LORD spoken to Jehu was fulfilled: "Your descendants will sit on the throne of Israel to the fourth generation."

God had chosen Jehu to destroy the house of Ahab and to rid the Northern Kingdom of Baal worship. Because he had done that work well, God promised him that his family would rule over the Kingdom of Israel for four generations of descendants (2 Kings 10:30). The brief, wicked reign of Zechariah was a fulfillment of that promise.

Shallum King of Israel

[13]Shallum son of Jabesh became king in the thirty-ninth year of Uzziah king of Judah, and he reigned in Samaria one month. [14]Then Menahem son of Gadi went from Tirzah up to Samaria. He attacked Shallum son of Jabesh in Samaria, assassinated him and succeeded him as king.

[15]The other events of Shallum's reign, and the conspiracy he led, are written in the book of the annals of the kings of Israel.

[16]At that time Menahem, starting out from Tirzah, attacked Tiphsah and everyone in the city and its vicinity, because they refused to open their gates. He sacked Tiphsah and ripped open all the pregnant women.

Those who rebel against authority "will bring judgment on themselves" (Romans 13:2). Shallum the assassin was in turn assassinated by a man more vicious than himself.

Tirzah, eight miles east of Samaria and famous for its beauty (Song of Songs 6:4), had been the capital city of the first four kings of Israel (1 Kings 14:17).

Tiphsah, the city that refused to cooperate with Menahem, is probably another city in that area rather than a city by the same name up at the Euphrates River. The brutal treatment accorded the people of Tiphsah was no doubt intended as a warning example to the entire area. It is significant that now a king of Israel practiced the brutality which had been mentioned previously only in connection with heathen kings (2 Kings 8:12).

Menahem King of Israel

[17]In the thirty-ninth year of Azariah king of Judah, Menahem son of Gadi became king of Israel, and he reigned in Samaria ten years. [18]He did evil in the eyes of the LORD. During his entire reign he did not turn away from the sins of Jeroboam son of Nebat, which he had caused Israel to commit.

¹⁹Then **Pul king of Assyria invaded the land, and Menahem gave him a thousand talents of silver to gain his support and strengthen his own hold on the kingdom.** ²⁰**Menahem exacted this money from Israel. Every wealthy man had to contribute fifty shekels of silver to be given to the king of Assyria. So the king of Assyria withdrew and stayed in the land no longer.**

²¹**As for the other events of Menahem's reign, and all he did, are they not written in the book of the annals of the kings of Israel?** ²²**Menahem rested with his fathers. And Pekahiah his son succeeded him as king.**

Many suppose that Menahem was one of Zechariah's generals and that he decided to seize power for himself after his king had been assassinated.

The most significant event of Menahem's reign is the appearance of the Assyrians and their King Pul, better known as Tiglath-Pileser (1 Chronicles 5:26). King Pul was converted from an enemy to a friend through a timely and handsome gift. The NIV footnote suggests that a thousand talents amounts to thirty-seven tons of silver. Menahem did not have a temple to strip. Therefore he had to raise the bribe money by taxing the wealthy.

Pekahiah King of Israel

²³**In the fiftieth year of Azariah king of Judah, Pekahiah son of Menahem became king of Israel in Samaria, and he reigned two years.** ²⁴**Pekahiah did evil in the eyes of the LORD. He did not turn away from the sins of Jeroboam son of Nebat, which he had caused Israel to commit.** ²⁵**One of his chief officers, Pekah son of Remaliah, conspired against him. Taking fifty men of Gilead with him, he assassinated Pekahiah, along with Argob and Arieh, in the citadel of the royal palace at Samaria. So Pekah killed Pekahiah and succeeded him as king.**

²⁶**The other events of Pekahiah's reign, and all he did, are written in the book of the annals of the kings of Israel.**

The reign of Pekahiah was no better than that of his predecessors. The man who assassinated him may have been one of his bodyguards.

Argob and Arieh were, it seems, two of Pekahiah's princes who were also put to death.

Pekah King of Israel

27In the fifty-second year of Azariah king of Judah, Pekah son of Remaliah became king of Israel in Samaria, and he reigned twenty years. 28He did evil in the eyes of the LORD. He did not turn away from the sins of Jeroboam son of Nebat, which he had caused Israel to commit.

29In the time of Pekah king of Israel, Tiglath-Pileser king of Assyria came and took Ijon, Abel Beth Maacah, Janoah, Kedesh and Hazor. He took Gilead and Galilee, including all the land of Naphtali, and deported the people to Assyria. 30Then Hoshea son of Elah conspired against Pekah son of Remaliah. He attacked and assassinated him, and then succeeded him as king in the twentieth year of Jotham son of Uzziah.

31As for the other events of Pekah's reign, and all he did, are they not written in the book of the annals of the kings of Israel?

The previous two kings of Israel had paid a heavy tribute to Assyria. The nation which Pekah now ruled was in a weakened condition.

King Pekah, however, was an ambitious man. He made an alliance with Aram, Israel's former enemy. Together they intended to capture Jerusalem (verse 37) and gain its wealth for themselves. Because King Jotham of Judah was faithful to God, the Lord did not permit the alliance to succeed during Jotham's lifetime (2 Chronicles 27:6).

When Jotham died and Ahaz became the new king of Judah, the allies continued their struggle against Jerusalem. Although they never did capture Jerusalem, they did take the port of Elath from Judah (2 Kings 16:5,6), captured thousands of prisoners, and took a great deal of plunder. According to 2 Chronicles 28:5-15 the prisoners and the plunder were later returned to Judah.

Pekah's ambitions came to an end when Ahaz, king of Judah, hired the king of Assyria to protect him (2 Kings 16:7-9). Tiglath-Pileser stripped Pekah of the northern part of his kingdom and all lands east of the Jordan. This included Naphtali as well as Gilead, the territory east of the Jordan formerly occupied by Reuben, Gad, and the half tribe of Manasseh (1 Chronicles 5:26). According to custom the inhabitants were resettled in other parts of the Assyrian empire. This would dilute any feelings of nationalism that might still exist among conquered people. Pekah's life came to a violent end when he was assassinated by Hoshea, who succeeded him on the throne. The fact that four of Israel's last six kings met death by assassination is an indication of how chaotic the last years of Israel's history were. Time was running out for Israel.

Jotham King of Judah

³²In the second year of Pekah son of Remaliah king of Israel, Jotham son of Uzziah king of Judah began to reign. ³³He was twenty-five years old when he became king, and he reigned in Jerusalem sixteen years. His mother's name was Jerusha daughter of Zadok. ³⁴He did what was right in the eyes of the LORD, just as his father Uzziah had done. ³⁵The high places, however, were not removed; the people continued to offer sacrifices and burn incense there. Jotham rebuilt the Upper Gate of the temple of the LORD.

³⁶As for the other events of Jotham's reign, and what he did, are they not written in the book of the annals of the kings of Judah? ³⁷(In those days the LORD began to send Rezin king of Aram and Pekah son of Remaliah against Judah.) ³⁸Jotham rested with his

fathers and was buried with them in the City of David, the city of
his father. And Ahaz his son succeeded him as king.

God rewarded the faithfulness of Jotham with a prosper-
ous reign. He not only rebuilt the principal gate of the
temple, but he fortified the city of Jerusalem and erected
castles and towers for defense in the wilderness areas of
Judah (2 Chronicles 27).

God protected him against the attacks of Israel and
Aram. Jotham regained control over Ammon, and they
again paid Judah a sizeable tribute (2 Chronicles 27).

More than half of chapter 16 describes the religious activity of King Ahaz. Unfortunately Ahaz was an idolater, and
his religious activity was an abomination.

Ahaz King of Judah

16 In the seventeenth year of Pekah son of Remaliah, Ahaz
son of Jotham king of Judah began to reign. ²Ahaz was
twenty years old when he became king, and he reigned in Jerusalem sixteen years. Unlike David his father, he did not do what was
right in the eyes of the LORD his God. ³He walked in the ways of
the kings of Israel and even sacrificed his son in the fire, following
the detestable ways of the nations the LORD had driven out before
the Israelites. ⁴He offered sacrifices and burned incense at the
high places, on the hilltops and under every spreading tree.

⁵Then Rezin king of Aram and Pekah son of Remaliah king of
Israel marched up to fight against Jerusalem and besieged Ahaz,
but they could not overpower him. ⁶At that time, Rezin king of
Aram recovered Elath for Aram by driving out the men of Judah.
Edomites then moved into Elath and have lived there to this day.

⁷Ahaz sent messengers to say to Tiglath-Pileser king of Assyria,
"I am your servant and vassal. Come up and save me out of the
hand of the king of Aram and of the king of Israel, who are
attacking me." ⁸And Ahaz took the silver and gold found in the
temple of the LORD and in the treasuries of the royal palace and

sent it as a gift to the king of Assyria. ⁹The king of Assyria complied by attacking Damascus and capturing it. He deported its inhabitants to Kir and put Rezin to death.

Ahaz had a father and grandfather who "did what was right in the eyes of the Lord" (2 Kings 15:3,34), but Ahaz worshiped idols. He even offered his sons as sacrifices to Molech and Milcom. According to 2 Chronicles 28:3 this happened more than once. Apparently he dabbled in astrology and set up the horses and chariots "dedicated to the sun" and the altars "on the roof near the upper room of Ahaz" (2 Kings 23:11,12). The stairway used as a sundial may also have been an instrument he used in his astrology (2 Kings 20:11).

Therefore God himself stepped in with judgment. The alliance of Israel and Aram (about which chapter 15 informed us) was a constant threat to Ahaz's power.

But even under these circumstances God showed his grace. When Ahaz the gross idolater stood helpless before the enemies threatening him from the north, the prophet Isaiah came to him and announced, "It will not take place!" (Isaiah 7:7). The kings of Israel and Aram would not enter Jerusalem. Isaiah pleaded with Ahaz to trust the Lord's promise. He even invited Ahaz to ask for a sign from God. But when Ahaz, in a mock show of piety and humility, refused to ask for a sign, Isaiah became angry. He declared, "The Lord himself will give you a sign: The virgin will be with child and will give birth to a son, and will call him Immanuel" (Isaiah 7:14). At this unusual moment God again reminded the world of that virgin-born Savior who would come into the world through the family of Ahaz. That Savior is Immanuel, "God with us."

But Ahaz still would not budge. He was determined to trust man, not God, for his salvation. The Hebrew word translated "save" in verse 7 is related to the name "Jesus," which means "Savior." The king of Assyria literally became a "Jesus" for King Ahaz. The messenger of Ahaz knelt at the feet of Tiglath-Pileser, pleading for his help. The money presented to the Assyrian king came from the temple of the Lord, the God whom Ahaz otherwise abhorred.

The story of Ahaz is repeated again and again in our own day. It is not unusual to see faithful grandparents worshiping the Lord God and unfaithful grandchildren who worship the pleasures this world has to offer. Tiglath-Pileser had earlier accepted a bribe from Israel but later turned against them. Here he accepted tribute from Judah, but a generation later he surrounded Jerusalem with his army and threatened to destroy the city. Those who trust in false gods today are often destroyed by the very gods they rely on. The gods of money, pleasure, and materialism demand our attention while we have good health, but they are powerless and forsake us when we are beset with troubles and when death comes near our door.

It is likely that verse 2 offers us an example of a coregency. The writer apparently means to tell us that Ahaz "became king at the age of 20, when his father was still living; and after his father died, he ruled alone as king for another 16 years." If we understood the words as saying that Ahaz died at the age of 36, then we would have Ahaz becoming the father of Hezekiah when he was only 11 years old (see 2 Kings 18:2).

¹⁰Then King Ahaz went to Damascus to meet Tiglath-Pileser king of Assyria. He saw an altar in Damascus and sent to Uriah the priest a sketch of the altar, with detailed plans for its construction. ¹¹So Uriah the priest built an altar in accordance with all the plans that King Ahaz had sent from Damascus and finished it before King Ahaz returned. ¹²When the king came back from

Damascus and saw the altar, he approached it and presented offerings on it. [13]He offered up his burnt offering and grain offering, poured out his drink offering, and sprinkled the blood of his fellowship offerings on the altar. [14]The bronze altar that stood before the LORD he brought from the front of the temple—from between the new altar and the temple of the LORD—and put it on the north side of the new altar.

[15]King Ahaz then gave these orders to Uriah the priest: "On the large new altar, offer the morning burnt offering and the evening grain offering, the king's burnt offering and his grain offering, and the burnt offering of all the people of the land, and their grain offering and their drink offering. Sprinkle on the altar all the blood of the burnt offerings and sacrifices. But I will use the bronze altar for seeking guidance." [16]And Uriah the priest did just as King Ahaz had ordered.

[17]King Ahaz took away the side panels and removed the basins from the movable stands. He removed the Sea from the bronze bulls that supported it and set it on a stone base. [18]He took away the Sabbath canopy that had been built at the temple and removed the royal entryway outside the temple of the LORD, in deference to the king of Assyria.

[19]As for the other events of the reign of Ahaz, and what he did, are they not written in the book of the annals of the kings of Judah? [20]Ahaz rested with his fathers and was buried with them in the City of David. And Hezekiah his son succeeded him as king.

The Assyrian King Tiglath-Pileser was happy to offer help to King Ahaz in his struggle against Israel and Aram. Not only did he receive a sizeable sum of money stolen from the Lord's temple, but he furthered his own political plans.

After Tiglath-Pileser's victory King Ahaz went up to Damascus to extend his thanks. There a particular heathen altar caught his attention. Even though the changes suggested by Ahaz conflicted with God's instructions for building his altar, Uriah the high priest gave his full cooperation.

The Sabbath canopy was apparently some covering used by the priests on the Sabbath when more of them were working at the temple.

The royal entryway to the temple was the beautiful staircase that had overwhelmed even the Queen of Sheba (1 Kings 10:5 KJV).

The stands on which the basins were set (1 Kings 7:28,29) and the twelve bronze bulls on which the Sea had rested (1 Kings 7:25) were also removed from the temple area lest the king of Assyria see the wealth and demand more and more tribute.

King Ahaz died without a hint of repentance. Like the rich man in Jesus' parable, he received his "good things" here on earth and then perished eternally (Luke 16:25). Because of his wickedness Ahaz was buried in Jerusalem but not in the tombs of the kings (2 Chronicles 28:27).

Our Lord is "slow to anger" (Psalm 103:8). But now God's patience had come to an end. Hoshea was the last king to rule over Israel. Even though he was not the worst of those nineteen kings, he and the people continued to live in idolatry, and the Lord was "very angry with Israel" (verse 18).

Israel Falls to Assyria (17:1-41)

Hoshea Last King of Israel

17 In the twelfth year of Ahaz king of Judah, Hoshea son of Elah became king of Israel in Samaria, and he reigned nine years. ²He did evil in the eyes of the LORD, but not like the kings of Israel who preceded him.

³Shalmaneser king of Assyria came up to attack Hoshea, who had been Shalmaneser's vassal and had paid him tribute. ⁴But the king of Assyria discovered that Hoshea was a traitor, for he had sent envoys to So king of Egypt, and he no longer paid tribute to the king of Assyria, as he had done year by year. Therefore

Shalmaneser seized him and put him in prison. ⁵The king of Assyria invaded the entire land, marched against Samaria and laid siege to it for three years. ⁶In the ninth year of Hoshea, the king of Assyria captured Samaria and deported the Israelites to Assyria. He settled them in Halah, in Gozan on the Habor River and in the towns of the Medes.

In 2 Kings 15:30 we heard that Hoshea became king in the twentieth year of Jotham. Here we are told that it was in the twelfth year of Ahaz. Evidently the two dates are identical and there was a time when both Jotham and Ahaz were counted as kings of Judah.

Shalmaneser V was the son of Tiglath-Pileser III, the Assyrian king about whom we read in the previous chapter. Assyria's power over Israel had now become so complete that Shalmaneser considered the king of Israel as his vassal.

Our writer takes time to review the sins of Israel and its kings. We can take a moment to do the same.

King Hoshea "did evil in the sight of the Lord." Perhaps Hoshea and his friends thought the assassination of the previous king had been justified, but God did not share that opinion. Perhaps Hoshea and his advisors thought it was wise to rely on So, the king of Egypt, instead of on the God who had made a covenant of grace with Israel, but God viewed that mistake as a great evil. Perhaps some would say that Hoshea's heathen religion was better than no religion at all, but God did not agree.

Sometimes people today ask, "Who are you to try to force your moral standards on other people? Who are you to judge the man and woman who are living together without being married?" Finally it makes no difference what I think or what the church thinks or what Hoshea thinks. The important question is, "What does the Lord think? What has he said?" He is our Creator and he will be the judge.

Since God's word clearly labels these actions as sinful, we will do the same.

King So is perhaps Pharaoh Sosenk IV, the last Libyan ruler of Egypt.

Now the hour had come for Israel's judgment. In 722 B.C. Shalmaneser (or perhaps it was his successor, Sargon II) captured Samaria and led the rest of the Israelites into captivity. He resettled them in districts of northern Mesopotamia.

From that moment the Kingdom of Israel became "the ten lost tribes." First they were lost spiritually. Then they became lost physically. They intermarried with others and ceased to be a political entity. Those who teach that the American Indians are descended from those lost tribes of Israel have no evidence to support their claims.

In a simple way our writer describes the ending of a major chapter of Old Testament history. All nineteen of the kings that ruled over Israel had rejected the King. Now, finally, the kings and their people were rejected by the King.

Israel Exiled Because of Sin

⁷All this took place because the Israelites had sinned against the LORD their God, who had brought them up out of Egypt from under the power of Pharaoh king of Egypt. They worshiped other gods ⁸and followed the practices of the nations the LORD had driven out before them, as well as the practices that the kings of Israel had introduced. ⁹The Israelites secretly did things against the LORD their God that were not right. From watchtower to fortified city they built themselves high places in all their towns. ¹⁰They set up sacred stones and Asherah poles on every high hill and under every spreading tree. ¹¹At every high place they burned incense, as the nations whom the LORD had driven out before them had done. They did wicked things that provoked the LORD to anger. ¹²They worshiped idols, though the LORD had said,

"You shall not do this." ¹³The LORD warned Israel and Judah through all his prophets and seers: "Turn from your evil ways. Observe my commands and decrees, in accordance with the entire Law that I commanded your fathers to obey and that I delivered to you through my servants the prophets."

¹⁴But they would not listen and were as stiff-necked as their fathers, who did not trust in the LORD their God. ¹⁵They rejected his decrees and the covenant he had made with their fathers and the warnings he had given them. They followed worthless idols and themselves became worthless. They imitated the nations around them although the LORD had ordered them, "Do not do as they do," and they did the things the LORD had forbidden them to do.

¹⁶They forsook all the commands of the LORD their God and made for themselves two idols cast in the shape of calves, and an Asherah pole. They bowed down to all the starry hosts, and they worshiped Baal. ¹⁷They sacrificed their sons and daughters in the fire. They practiced divination and sorcery and sold themselves to do evil in the eyes of the LORD, provoking him to anger.

¹⁸So the LORD was very angry with Israel and removed them from his presence. Only the tribe of Judah was left, ¹⁹and even Judah did not keep the commands of the LORD their God. They followed the practices Israel had introduced. ²⁰Therefore the LORD rejected all the people of Israel; he afflicted them and gave them into the hands of plunderers, until he thrust them from his presence.

²¹When he tore Israel away from the house of David, they made Jeroboam son of Nebat their king. Jeroboam enticed Israel away from following the LORD and caused them to commit a great sin. ²²The Israelites persisted in all the sins of Jeroboam and did not turn away from them ²³until the LORD removed them from his presence, as he had warned through all his servants the prophets. So the people of Israel were taken from their homeland into exile in Assyria, and they are still there.

It is not an accident that one nation becomes strong while another suffers under God's judgment. God permitted Israel to be conquered and led off into captivity by Assyria because of Israel's continued impenitence.

God's writer presents here a catalog of ways in which Israel had committed idolatry:

• They worshiped the Asherah poles, that is, posts on which they had carved the symbol of a female fertility goddess. This was the goddess who supposedly caused the crops to grow out of the ground and who was worshiped not only by burning incense but also through a kind of sacred fornication.

• They worshiped the golden calves which Jeroboam had set up at Bethel and at Dan many years earlier.

• They worshiped the starry hosts, that is, the sun, moon and stars.

• They worshiped Baal, the bloodthirsty god whom Jezebel had brought with her from Phoenicia.

• They burned their sons and daughters in the fire as offerings to Molech.

• They practiced witchcraft and superstition.

The Israelites were not ignorant of God's will. Through Moses God had specifically told the people not to worship the gods and goddesses of their heathen neighbors (see Leviticus 18:3; Deuteronomy 4:19; 18:10). God threatened the severest penalties for those who practiced such abominations. In his first commandment God had said, "You shall not make for yourself an idol in the form of anything in heaven above or on the earth beneath or in the waters below. You shall not bow down to them or worship them" (Exodus 20:4,5). But those were the gods Israel chose to worship!

The people deliberately followed "worthless idols." Literally they worshiped "nothings and good-for-nothings." Baal and Asherah are useless here and they will be good for nothing on judgment day as well.

By practicing idolatry, they rejected the only God who can save. They rejected the God who delivered them from bondage to Pharaoh in Egypt and who had sworn to deliver them from bondage to sin, death, and Satan through the Messiah.

Although over the centuries the people "sold themselves to do evil in the eyes of the Lord," God continued to show his mercy to Israel. He sent prophets who urged the people: "Repent! Turn from your evil ways!" Hosea, for example, was a prophet who lived at the time of King Hoshea. Hosea compared the Israelite people to an unfaithful wife who has left her husband to follow other lovers (Hosea 9:1). Hosea graphically described how the Assyrians would invade the land and how "their little ones will be dashed to the ground, their pregnant women ripped open" (Hosea 13:16). But the Israelites refused to listen. They stiffened their necks. Like stubborn animals, they refused to pull the plow.

In our country also many choose to worship golden calves —if not the calf, then at least the gold. Moneymaking has become a top priority. Sons and daughters are no longer sacrificed to idols by fire, but each year millions of babies are sacrificed on the altars of pleasure and convenience through abortion. Many have fooled themselves into thinking that we need not do foreign mission work since the heathen already have a religion of their own. They forget that any god who is not the Father, the Son, and the Holy Ghost is a "nothing and a good-for-nothing." Many turn their backs on *God's* "commands and decrees," thinking that it is of no importance to hear God's word.

If the books of Kings teach us one thing, it's that the Lord, the Savior God, controls history. If people in our nation continue to reject God's word and continue to worship false gods, they can expect the same judgment that struck down Israel. Our daily prayer ought to be: "Lord, lead many to repentance and faith!"

Samaria Resettled

²⁴The king of Assyria brought people from Babylon, Cuthah, Avva, Hamath and Sepharvaim and settled them in the towns of Samaria to replace the Israelites. They took over Samaria and lived in its towns. ²⁵When they first lived there, they did not worship the LORD; so he sent lions among them and they killed some of the people. ²⁶It was reported to the king of Assyria: "The people you deported and resettled in the towns of Samaria do not know what the god of that country requires. He has sent lions among them, which are killing them off, because the people do not know what he requires."

²⁷Then the king of Assyria gave this order: "Have one of the priests you took captive from Samaria go back to live there and teach the people what the god of the land requires." ²⁸So one of the priests who had been exiled from Samaria came to live in Bethel and taught them how to worship the LORD.

When the Assyrians conquered any territory, they resettled the people in a different area. In this way they hoped to destroy any spirit of nationalism and reduce the chances of rebellion.

The Assyrians removed the ten tribes of Irsael. Now Esarhaddon (Ezra 4:2) moved foreigners from cities in Aram, Assyria, and Babylonia into the land once occupied by God's chosen people. Gentiles again lived on the land God had given to the descendants of Abraham, the land once ruled by David, the land on which Jesus would walk seven hundred years later.

The heathenism of the new settlers did not please God any more than the idolatry of the former inhabitants. The Lord therefore sent lions among the people, just as at the time of Moses he had once sent poisonous snakes among his own people. The people got the point. They knew that the Lord was not pleased with their actions.

The heathen believed that there are many gods and that each rules a certain area of the world. Instead of crying out for mercy to the Lord, a God whom they did not know, instead of going to Jerusalem to ask for instructions from Isaiah or one of God's other prophets, they went to the king of Assyria. They requested that he send a priest to them who would teach them "what the god of the land requires."

But the priest sent by the king was not a faithful spokesman for the Lord. Instead of directing the people to the temple in Jerusalem, he apparently instructed them to serve the Lord by worshiping the golden calves set up by Jeroboam at Bethel and at Dan. Instead of teaching the people to celebrate the festivals commanded by God, he directed them to observe the feasts instituted by King Jeroboam.

The end result was a horrendous mixture of truth and error.

29Nevertheless, each national group made its own gods in the several towns where they settled, and set them up in the shrines the people of Samaria had made at the high places. 30The men from Babylon made Succoth Benoth, the men from Cuthah made Nergal, and the men from Hamath made Ashima; 31the Avvites made Nibhaz and Tartak, and the Sepharvites burned their children in the fire as sacrifices to Adrammelech and Anammelech, the gods of Sepharvaim. 32They worshiped the LORD, but they also appointed all sorts of their own people to officiate for them as priests in the shrines at the high places. 33They worshiped the LORD, but they also served their own gods in accordance with the customs of the nations from which they had been brought.

34To this day they persist in their former practices. They neither worship the LORD nor adhere to the decrees and ordinances, the laws and commands that the LORD gave the descendants of Jacob, whom he named Israel. 35When the LORD made a covenant with the Israelites, he commanded them: "Do not worship any other gods or bow down to them, serve them or sacrifice to them. 36But

261

the LORD, who brought you up out of Egypt with mighty power and outstretched arm, is the one you must worship. To him you shall bow down and to him offer sacrifices. [37]You must always be careful to keep the decrees and ordinances, the laws and commands he wrote for you. Do not worship other gods. [38]Do not forget the covenant I have made with you, and do not worship other gods. [39]Rather, worship the LORD your God; it is he who will deliver you from the hand of all your enemies."

[40]They would not listen, however, but persisted in their former practices. [41]Even while these people were worshiping the LORD, they were serving their idols. To this day their children and grandchildren continue to do as their fathers did.

The new residents of Samaria knew the name of the Lord, but they did not worship him according to the laws he gave at Mount Sinai. "They feared the LORD, and served other gods" (verse 33 KJV). They respected the power of the Lord who had sent lions among them, but with their hearts they served their former gods.

The old Jewish rabbis report that Succoth Benoth was worshiped in the form of a hen; Nergal in the form of a rooster; Ashima in the form of a goat; Nibhaz and Tartak in the form of a dog and a donkey respectively. The brutal sacrificing of children continued in the land.

This religious mixture was not acceptable to God. In his conversation with the Samaritan woman many years later Jesus said, "You Samaritans worship what you do not know; we worship what we do know, for salvation is from the Jews" (John 4:22). If people are lukewarm, if people outwardly worship a Lord whose name they learned in their youth but refuse to serve with their hearts and lives, the Lord will spit them out of his mouth (Revelation 3:16).

The Lord refuses to share his glory with anyone, for he is the only Deliverer. He rescued his people from bondage in

Egypt (verse 36) and he "will deliver you from the hand of all your enemies" (verse 39). The time was coming when the Messiah would rescue the people from sin, death, and Satan.

Satan was trying his best to destroy the nation from which the Messiah would come. The Assyrians had already removed Israel from its land. Now they wanted to do the same to Judah, the remnant of the chosen people that remained.

But God was faithful to his promises. At this critical time he gave Judah a king whose trust in God was unlike that of any king before or after him.

PART II

THE **KING** REJECTS JUDAH
2 KINGS 18:1-25:30

The Rule of Hezekiah

Hezekiah King of Judah

18 In the third year of Hoshea son of Elah king of Israel, Hezekiah son of Ahaz king of Judah began to reign. ²He was twenty-five years old when he became king, and he reigned in Jerusalem twenty-nine years. His mother's name was Abijah daughter of Zechariah. ³He did what was right in the eyes of the LORD, just as his father David had done. ⁴He removed the high places, smashed the sacred stones and cut down the Asherah poles. He broke into pieces the bronze snake Moses had made, for up to that time the Israelites had been burning incense to it. (It was called Nehushtan.)

⁵Hezekiah trusted in the LORD, the God of Israel. There was no one like him among all the kings of Judah, either before him or after him. ⁶He held fast to the LORD and did not cease to follow him; he kept the commands the LORD had given Moses. ⁷And the LORD was with him; he was successful in whatever he undertook. He rebelled against the king of Assyria and did not serve him. ⁸From watchtower to fortified city, he defeated the Philistines, as far as Gaza and its territory.

Hezekiah "trusted" in the Lord. The gods of the heathen had a reputation for changing their minds. But the words of the Lord are sure. When Hezekiah rested his heart on those words, he would not be disappointed.

Hezekiah "held fast" to the Lord. We read that same word in Genesis 2:24 where the Lord instituted marriage. Just as a man and woman are inseparable in the marriage bond, so Hezekiah and the Lord were inseparable.

Hezekiah's father did nothing to give his son proper training. Ahaz was an idolater, as we heard in chapter 16:2-4. Perhaps it was through the prayers and efforts of a faithful mother and grandfather (whose names are mentioned here) that the young king grew up to be a God-fearing man. If our guess is correct, Hezekiah would be very much like Timothy, who was reared by a God-fearing mother and grandmother.

Hezekiah showed his faithfulness by removing those things which his father held sacred. He destroyed the "high places," where temple prostitution was practiced. The "sacred stones" were gross representations of the male organ, symbolizing the male element in the fertility cult ritual. These Hezekiah destroyed.

He cut down the Asherah, that wood post which symbolized the female element in the fertility cult, which had been so popular in the Northern Kingdom (2 Kings 17:10).

Seven hundred years earlier God had told Moses to make a brass serpent and promised that whoever looked at it in faith would not die from his snake bite. The Israelites took that brass serpent along with them and were now actually using it superstitiously as a relic. Since there was no longer any good reason to preserve that serpent, Hezekiah destroyed it.

The mistake made by the Israelites is similar to the mistake made by a particular Christian denomination today. This group mistakenly teaches that the bread in the Sacrament of the Altar is actually changed into the body of Christ. The people are then encouraged to adore the communion bread, an idolatrous practice which the Bible nowhere commands.

In more recent times God sent his church another reformer who in many ways was like Hezekiah. That man was Martin Luther. Like Hezekiah, he was faithful to God's word above all else. Luther boldly attacked the idolatry and superstition that God's word rejects. Just as God gave success to King Hezekiah, so God protected Luther from physical danger and caused the work of the Reformation to prosper.

⁹**In King Hezekiah's fourth year, which was the seventh year of Hoshea son of Elah king of Israel, Shalmaneser king of Assyria marched against Samaria and laid siege to it.** ¹⁰**At the end of three years the Assyrians took it. So Samaria was captured in Hezekiah's sixth year, which was the ninth year of Hoshea king of Israel.** ¹¹**The king of Assyria deported Israel to Assyria and settled them in Halah, in Gozan on the Habor River and in towns of the Medes.** ¹²**This happened because they had not obeyed the LORD their God, but had violated his covenant—all that Moses the servant of the LORD commanded. They neither listened to the commands nor carried them out.**

¹³**In the fourteenth year of King Hezekiah's reign, Sennacherib king of Assyria attacked all the fortified cities of Judah and captured them.** ¹⁴**So Hezekiah king of Judah sent this message to the king of Assyria at Lachish: "I have done wrong. Withdraw from me, and I will pay whatever you demand of me." The king of Assyria exacted from Hezekiah king of Judah three hundred talents of silver and thirty talents of gold.** ¹⁵**So Hezekiah gave him all the silver that was found in the temple of the LORD and in the treasuries of the royal palace.**

¹⁶**At this time Hezekiah king of Judah stripped off the gold with which he had covered the doors and doorposts of the temple of the LORD, and gave it to the king of Assyria.**

A chapter earlier the writer told us how Samaria was captured and how the ten northern tribes were carried into captivity because of their continued impenitence. By repeating those facts here the writer shows us how the piety of King Hezekiah stood in sharp contrast to the attitude of others and how God protects all who trust in his mercy.

Ten years after Samaria fell, the mighty Assyrian armies invaded Palestine again. Sennacherib easily captured the fortified cities around Jerusalem. He was now encamped at Lachish, an imposing fortress some twenty miles southwest of Jerusalem. Humanly speaking, nothing would stop him from capturing Jerusalem and Egypt as well.

Hezekiah had purified the temple and had celebrated a Passover greater than any other since the time of Solomon (2 Chronicles 30:26). But when he saw the mighty forces of Assyria, even Hezekiah succumbed to a moment of weakness. Instead of trusting God to protect him, Hezekiah offered to pay Sennacherib whatever tribute money he might demand. The Assyrian king was not timid. The NIV footnote suggests that the tribute amounted to eleven tons of silver and one ton of gold.

Once again the king and the people found it convenient to steal precious metals from the Lord's temple in order to buy off the king of Assyria. We can only wonder how often that same sinful strategy is employed today, how often people take money that should have gone into the Lord's treasury and use it for their personal pleasure.

Unfortunately "the great king, the king of Assyria," as he proudly referred to himself, was not a man of his word. After receiving payment from Hezekiah, Sennacherib continued his plan to capture the holy city.

Sennacherib Threatens Jerusalem

17The king of Assyria sent his supreme commander, his chief officer and his field commander with a large army, from Lachish to King Hezekiah at Jerusalem. They came up to Jerusalem and stopped at the aqueduct of the Upper Pool, on the road to the Washerman's Field. 18They called for the king; and Eliakim son of Hilkiah the palace administrator, Shebna the secretary, and Joah son of Asaph the recorder went out to them.

¹⁹The field commander said to them, "Tell Hezekiah:

" 'This is what the great king, the king of Assyria, says: On what are you basing this confidence of yours? ²⁰You say you have strategy and military strength—but you speak only empty words. On whom are you depending, that you rebel against me? ²¹Look now, you are depending on Egypt, that splintered reed of a staff, which pierces a man's hand and wounds him if he leans on it! Such is Pharaoh king of Egypt to all who depend on him. ²²And if you say to me, "We are depending on the LORD our God"—isn't he the one whose high places and altars Hezekiah removed, saying to Judah and Jerusalem, "You must worship before this altar in Jerusalem"?

²³" 'Come now, make a bargain with my master, the king of Assyria: I will give you two thousand horses—if you can put riders on them! ²⁴How can you repulse one officer of the least of my master's officials, even though you are depending on Egypt for chariots and horsemen? ²⁵Furthermore, have I come to attack and destroy this place without word from the LORD? The LORD himself told me to march against this country and destroy it.' "

Before attacking Jerusalem, Sennacherib sent three high ranking officials to Hezekiah to offer terms of surrender. They approached the city of Jerusalem from the west and stood near the Upper Pool, a site which cannot be identified with certainty.

The words of the Assyrian messenger were another display of arrogance and blasphemy. As far as the Assyrians could see, no one had the power to free God's people from their predicament:

1. It would be foolish to trust in Egypt for military help. Relying on the king of Egypt would be like leaning on a splintered reed.

2. It appeared to the Assyrians that it would be just as foolish to rely on the Lord, Israel's Savior-God. The hea-

then Assyrians figured that God wanted many altars and that he must have become very angry when Hezekiah destroyed the heathen altars around Jerusalem.

3. In his arrogance the messenger suggested that Hezekiah could not supply horsemen even if Assyria provided the horses and that Israel's entire army was no match for even a squadron of Assyrian soldiers. Since God had already given unfaithful Israel over into the hands of Assyria, the messenger claimed that Judah and Jerusalem would now fall for the same reason.

[26]Then Eliakim son of Hilkiah, and Shebna and Joah said to the field commander, "Please speak to your servants in Aramaic, since we understand it. Don't speak to us in Hebrew in the hearing of the people on the wall."

[27]But the commander replied, "Was it only to your master and you that my master sent me to say these things, and not to the men sitting on the wall—who, like you, will have to eat their own filth and drink their own urine?"

[28]Then the commander stood and called out in Hebrew: "Hear the word of the great king, the king of Assyria! [29]This is what the king says: Do not let Hezekiah deceive you. He cannot deliver you from my hand. [30]Do not let Hezekiah persuade you to trust in the LORD when he says, 'The LORD will surely deliver us; this city will not be given into the hand of the king of Assyria.'

[31]"Do not listen to Hezekiah. This is what the king of Assyria says: Make peace with me and come out to me. Then everyone of you will eat from his own vine and fig tree and drink water from his own cistern, [32]until I come and take you to a land like your own, a land of grain and new wine, a land of bread and vineyards, a land of olive trees and honey. Choose life and not death!

"Do not listen to Hezekiah, for he is misleading you when he says, 'The LORD will deliver us.' [33]Has the god of any nation ever delivered his land from the hand of the king of Assyria? [34]Where are the gods of Hamath and Arpad? Where are the gods of Sepharvaim, Hena and Ivvah? Have they rescued Samaria from my hand? ³⁵Who of all the gods of these countries has been able to save his land from me? How then can the Lord deliver Jerusalem from my hand?"

³⁶But the people remained silent and said nothing in reply, because the king had commanded, "Do not answer him."

³⁷Then Eliakim son of Hilkiah the palace administrator, Shebna the secretary and Joah son of Asaph the recorder went to Hezekiah, with their clothes torn, and told him what the field commander had said.

In Psalm 50:15 God says, "Call upon me in the day of trouble; *I will deliver you*." The Assyrian messenger, like the devil himself back in Genesis 3, first questioned God's word and then boldly contradicted it. He insisted on speaking in the Jewish language so that the ordinary soldiers on the walls could understand his blasphemous words.

Blasphemy is a kind of cursing, a sin against the second commandment. Certain movies and advertisements in our day are guilty of that. They proclaim lies, deliberately distorting God's word, his good name; or they use Bible stories in a humorous or disrespectful way to sell their products.

Just as the devil promised happiness to Adam and Eve if they would disobey God's command, so the Assyrian messenger offered the people all sorts of blessings if they would forget God's promises. The messenger promised them peace and happiness if they would surrender to Assyria. Each resident of Jerusalem would live a quiet, domestic life beneath his own fig tree. Next he promised them what amounts to a heaven on earth. The king of Assyria would resettle them later in a different land, a rich land like God's description of Canaan (Deuteronomy 8:7-9). There they would live and not die.

But the "blessings" offered by Satan are not genuine, as our first parents soon learned. People who think that politicians today can create heaven on earth still have much to learn.

The Assyrian field commander could boast of one more thing. It was that the gods of the defeated nations and cities were powerless against Assyria. Of the cities that he mentions, Hamath would have a special significance for the people of Jerusalem, for this city, in the northernmost part of the promised land, had at one time been controlled by David and Solomon (2 Samuel 8:9,10; 2 Chronicles 8:4).

In fact it is not the Lord who is powerless but the gods of the Assyrians. Every idol will leave its worshipers helpless in a time of trouble.

Jerusalem's Deliverance Foretold

19 **When King Hezekiah heard this, he tore his clothes and put on sackcloth and went into the temple of the LORD. ²He sent Eliakim the palace administrator, Shebna the secretary and the leading priests, all wearing sackcloth, to the prophet Isaiah son of Amoz. ³They told him, "This is what Hezekiah says: This day is a day of distress and rebuke and disgrace, as when children come to the point of birth and there is no strength to deliver them. ⁴It may be that the LORD your God will hear all the words of the field commander, whom his master, the king of Assyria, has sent to ridicule the living God, and that he will rebuke him for the words the LORD your God has heard. Therefore pray for the remnant that still survives."**

⁵When King Hezekiah's officials came to Isaiah, ⁶Isaiah said to them, "Tell your master, 'This is what the LORD says: Do not be afraid of what you have heard—those words with which the underlings of the king of Assyria have blasphemed me. ⁷Listen! I am going to put such a spirit in him that when he hears a certain report, he will return to his own country, and there I will have him cut down with the sword.' "

King Hezekiah expressed his grief by tearing his clothes. By putting on sackcloth he expressed his sorrow over the sins of his own people.

But Hezekiah did not despair. This king, whose faith was unlike that of any other king (2 Kings 18:5), took the matter to the Lord. He not only came to the temple; he also sent messengers to Isaiah the prophet, who was now an old man, and asked him to intercede on behalf of God's people. With the powerful Assyrian army at their gates, God's people were like a woman in labor who suddenly loses her strength and is unable to give birth. Now that the ten northern tribes had been carried away into captivity, now that even the walled cities of Judah had fallen, God's people in Jerusalem were but a small remnant.

Jesus has told us, "Everyone who exalts himself will be humbled, and he who humbles himself will be exalted" (Luke 18:14). That is what happened here. God heard Hezekiah's humble prayer of faith and promised that the arrogant Assyrian would be struck down.

Hezekiah is a good example for us. God's people today also face problems and difficulties that nearly overwhelm us. But when we call out to God, when we seek comfort, strength and direction from God's prophets, we will never be disappointed. With the poet we sing, "Preserve, O Lord, thine honor, the bold blasphemer smite" (TLH 264:2).

8When the field commander heard that the king of Assyria had left Lachish, he withdrew and found the king fighting against Libnah.

9Now Sennacherib received a report that Tirhakah, the Cushite king ⌊of Egypt⌋ , was marching out to fight against him. So he again sent messengers to Hezekiah with this word: 10"Say to Hezekiah king of Judah: Do not let the god you depend on deceive you when he says, 'Jerusalem will not be handed over to the king of Assyria.' 11Surely you have heard what the kings of Assyria have done to all the countries, destroying them completely. And will you be delivered? 12Did the gods of the nations that were destroyed by my forefathers deliver them: the gods of Go-

zan, **Haran, Rezeph** and the people of **Eden** who were in **Tel Assar?** [13]**Where is the king of the city of Sepharvaim, or of Hena or Ivvah?"**

When the Assyrian field commander returned to his king, he found that the Assyrian armies had moved from Lachish, a city twenty miles southwest of Jerusalem, to Libnah, another Judean city some twenty miles west of Jerusalem, where trouble had evidently broken out. At the same time Sennacherib heard a report that Tirhakah, the king of Egypt, was preparing to fight against him farther south. Because Sennacherib had to meet this new threat, he didn't have time for a long siege of Jerusalem. He wanted to have the city of Jerusalem firmly under his control as soon as possible, so Sennacherib sent messengers to Hezekiah with another threat. He hoped that Hezekiah would surrender immediately and peacefully. The letter contained blasphemous boasts like the ones spoken earlier.

Hezekiah's Prayer

[14]**Hezekiah received the letter from the messengers and read it. Then he went up to the temple of the LORD and spread it out before the LORD. [15]And Hezekiah prayed to the LORD: "O LORD, God of Israel, enthroned between the cherubim, you alone are God over all the kingdoms of the earth. You have made heaven and earth. [16]Give ear, O LORD, and hear; open your eyes, O LORD, and see; listen to the words Sennacherib has sent to insult the living God.**

[17]**"It is true, O LORD, that the Assyrian kings have laid waste these nations and their lands. [18]They have thrown their gods into the fire and destroyed them, for they were not gods but only wood and stone, fashioned by men's hands. [19]Now, O LORD our God, deliver us from his hand, so that all kingdoms on earth may know that you alone, O LORD, are God."**

When Solomon dedicated the temple, he asked that it would be a place where God's people could come when they were troubled by their enemies (1 Kings 8:33). May God give us more leaders in the church, in the home, and in the state who intercede for their people with a mighty prayer of faith. Isaiah himself wrote, "Before they call I will answer; while they are still speaking I will hear" (Isaiah 65:24).

Hezekiah's prayer reminds us of the prayer spoken by Elijah on Mount Carmel (1 Kings 18). Both men asked for a response from heaven to show that the Lord alone is God.

Isaiah Prophesies Sennacherib's Fall

²⁰Then Isaiah son of Amoz sent a message to Hezekiah: "This is what the LORD, the God of Israel, says: I have heard your prayer concerning Sennacherib king of Assyria. ²¹This is the word that the LORD has spoken against him:

" 'The Virgin Daughter of Zion
  despises you and mocks you.
The Daughter of Jerusalem
  tosses her head as you flee.
²²Who is it you have insulted and
    blasphemed?
  Against whom have you raised your
      voice
  and lifted your eyes in pride?
  Against the Holy One of Israel!
²³By your messengers
  you have heaped insults on the Lord.
And you have said,
  "With my many chariots
I have ascended the heights of the
    mountains,
  the utmost heights of Lebanon.
I have cut down its tallest cedars,
  the choicest of its pines.

275

> I have reached its remotest parts,
> the finest of its forests.
> ²⁴I have dug wells in foreign lands
> and drunk the water there.
> With the soles of my feet
> I have dried up all the streams of
> Egypt."

Hezekiah did not have to wait long. The answer to Hezekiah's prayer is really God's message to Sennacherib.

We might paraphrase God's words this way: "Sennacherib, the Virgin Daughter of Jerusalem, who still lives in the home of her father (her heavenly Father), despises you and will laugh at you behind your back as you flee! You thought that you could mock God. Let me tell you that 'the One enthroned in heaven laughs; the Lord scoffs' at you!" (cf. Psalm 2:4).

"Sennacherib," God is saying, "when you arrogantly insulted the people of Jerusalem, you were blaspheming *me*, 'the Holy One of Israel'! Therefore you must reckon not with the armies of Hezekiah but with the hosts of God almighty."

"Sennacherib, you say, 'I have driven my chariots to the tops of the highest mountains; I have cut down the best cedar trees; I have made my camp in the remotest part of the forest; I have dug wells in foreign lands; I have even dried up the waters of Egypt with the sole of my foot.' That is blasphemy. By those words you claim to be equal with me, the God who made those things and who dried up the Red Sea and the Jordan River for his people."

Instead of bending his knees in repentance, the Assyrian king had boasted of his mighty deeds. The attitude of Sennacherib and the attitude of the Pharisee in the temple are one and the same.

²⁵ " 'Have you not heard?
>> Long ago I ordained it.
> In days of old I planned it;
>> now I have brought it to pass,
> that you have turned fortified cities
>> into piles of stone.
²⁶ Their people, drained of power,
>> are dismayed and put to shame.
> They are like plants in the field,
>> like tender green shoots,
> like grass sprouting on the roof,
>> scorched before it grows up.
²⁷ " 'But I know where you stay
>> and when you come and go
>> and how you rage against me.
²⁸ Because you rage against me
>> and your insolence has reached my ears,
> I will put my hook in your nose
>> and my bit in your mouth,
> and I will make you return
>> by the way you came.'
²⁹ "This will be the sign for you, O Hezekiah:
> "This year you will eat what grows
>> by itself,
>> and the second year what springs
>> from that.
> But in the third year sow and reap,
>> plant vineyards and eat their fruit.
³⁰ Once more a remnant of the house of
>> Judah
>> will take root below and bear fruit
>> above.
³¹ For out of Jerusalem will come a remnant,
>> and out of Mount Zion a band of
>> survivors.

The zeal of the LORD Almighty will accomplish this.

³²"Therefore this is what the LORD says concerning the king of Assyria:

> "He will not enter this city
> or shoot an arrow here.
> He will not come before it with shield
> or build a siege ramp against it.
> ³³By the way that he came he will return;
> he will not enter this city,
> declares the LORD.
> ³⁴I will defend this city and save it,
> for my sake and for the sake of
> David my servant."

God's answer to Hezekiah's prayer continues as an address to the proud Assyrian king. God is saying in effect, "Sennacherib, do you think that it was by *your* power that you captured so many cities and nations? You are wrong! Those cities were turned into heaps of ruins, those civilizations were withered like grass because *I* was permitting you to carry out *my* judgment on them.

"Sennacherib, do you think that *you* controlled the past and that *you* control the future? Wrong again! I know all about you—when you go out, when you come in, and even when you sit down. Your arrogance has come to the attention even of heaven. Now I am going to put a stop to it. I will put my hook in your nose, just as you would put a ring in the nose of an unruly bull. I am going to put my bridle in your lips, just as someone might treat a wild horse. And I am going to lead you back the way on which you came. You will not wage war against Jerusalem. You will not set foot in it. For I will defend this city—perhaps not for the sake of the people who live there now, but for my own sake, because here is the place where I have chosen to record my name; and for David's sake, that king whom I chose to be an ancestor of the Messiah."

This prophecy would certainly be fulfilled. "The zeal of the LORD Almighty will accomplish this." Israel's Lord is a zealous, jealous God, "punishing the children for the sin of the fathers to the third and fourth generation" of those who hate him (Exodus 20:5).

Soon the land of Judah, now occupied by invading Assyrian armies, would again be tilled by Jewish farmers and would produce its crops. A remnant of God's faithful people would "take root downward and bear fruit upward" (KJV).

35That night the angel of the LORD went out and put to death a hundred and eighty-five thousand men in the Assyrian camp. When the people got up the next morning—there were all the dead bodies! 36So Sennacherib king of Assyria broke camp and withdrew. He returned to Nineveh and stayed there.

37One day, while he was worshiping in the temple of his god Nisroch, his sons Adrammelech and Sharezer cut him down with the sword, and they escaped to the land of Ararat. And Esarhaddon his son succeeded him as king.

In Psalm 70 David prayed, "Make haste, O God, to deliver me; make haste to help me, O LORD" (KJV). When the time is right for God to send help, that help comes quickly. So it happened here. That very night the Angel of the Lord, a title used in the Old Testament to indicate the Son of God himself, destroyed 185,000 in the camp of the Assyrians. The Jewish historian Josephus tells us that this happened as the result of a plague. When the few surviving Assyrian soldiers awoke the next morning, they viewed a scene of utter devastation. Sennacherib had to withdraw to Nineveh, his capital city, some 750 miles to the north and east.

But even this dramatic judgment of God did not soften the heathen king's stony heart. He continued to worship his false god, Nisroch. There, in the heathen temple, Sennacherib was killed by two of his sons, as Isaiah foretold in verse 7. Sennacherib's god was unable even in his own temple to answer the prayer of his royal devotee. Hezekiah's God, on the other hand, had answered his prayer for deliverance. A third son, Esarhaddon, succeeded Sennacherib as king.

The pride of Sennacherib is like the pride of the devil himself. Just as the Assyrian king dared to insult God and God's people, so Satan dared to lie to our first parents when they still possessed God's image, and dared to confront the holy Son of God in the wilderness. Satan and his modern army of unbelieving "Sennacheribs" dare to insult God and his people today by twisting and contradicting God's word.

But just as the Angel of the Lord won a victory over the boastful king of Assyria, so the Lord Jesus has won a victory over the devil, the "slanderer," by his atoning death and his victorious resurrection. By faith in Christ that victory is ours. With God at our side we can join God's Old Testament people in taunting our enemies and singing,

> Satan, I defy thee;
> Death, I now decry thee;
> Fear, I bid thee cease. (TLH 347:3)

The Assyrian army had posed a threat to all the people of Jerusalem. That threat had been removed, but now a new danger confronted King Hezekiah. Personal troubles entered his life. The mighty God, who had spared the whole nation, now showed his personal love to a particular individual.

Hezekiah's Illness

20 **In those days Hezekiah became ill and was at the point of death. The prophet Isaiah son of Amoz went to him and said, "This is what the LORD says: Put your house in order, because you are going to die; you will not recover."**

²Hezekiah turned his face to the wall and prayed to the LORD, ³"Remember, O LORD, how I have walked before you faithfully and with wholehearted devotion and have done what is good in your eyes." And Hezekiah wept bitterly.

⁴Before Isaiah had left the middle court, the word of the LORD came to him: ⁵"Go back and tell Hezekiah, the leader of my people, 'This is what the LORD, the God of your father David, says: I have heard your prayer and seen your tears; I will heal you. On the third day from now you will go up to the temple of the LORD. ⁶I will add fifteen years to your life. And I will deliver you and this city from the hand of the king of Assyria. I will defend this city for my sake and for the sake of my servant David.' "

⁷Then Isaiah said, "Prepare a poultice of figs." They did so and applied it to the boil, and he recovered.

King Hezekiah was afflicted with a boil—apparently an ulcer, which was a symptom of a fatal infection. The same Hebrew word is used in Exodus 9:9-11, where we are told that "festering boils" broke out on the skin of the Egyptians.

We do not expect God to tell us which sickness will prove to be fatal for us. But the very fact that sickness comes into our life is a constant reminder that the perfectness of Eden is gone. We now live in a sinful world. We also are going to die. We are in need of a Savior. It is high time for us to put our own house in order.

A lawyer can help us put our affairs in order for the probate court. But when we die, we will stand in the courtroom of God. Our lifetime is a time of grace, a time to seek the Lord, a time to put our spiritual house in order. By faith in God's Son we are counted righteous in that courtroom.

God invites us to call on him "in the day of trouble" (Psalm 50:15), to pray, "deliver us from evil." In his time of trouble Hezekiah also turned to the Lord. His prayer was not a boastful recital of the good things he had done like the prayer of the Pharisee in the temple. Hezekiah does not point to his track record as the reason he deserved a reward but as evidence that his faith is living. Hezekiah "trusted in the LORD, the God of Israel" (2 Kings 18:5), and he showed that faith by his behavior. According to Isaiah 38:19 Hezekiah wanted a longer life here on earth that he might bring forth more fruits of faith, that he might continue to praise God in the temple and might have a longer time to give his children Christian training. Hezekiah was also fearful that without proper royal leadership the work of reformation he had begun might collapse.

The Savior has redeemed us for a similar purpose. Our Lord wants us to be "eager to do what is good" (Titus 2:14). Each new day that the Lord adds to our life is an opportunity for that kind of service.

Motivated by mercy and faithfulness, God answered the king's prayer immediately. The Lord, who delivers his church from mighty enemies, is able also to deliver individual Christians from deadly sickness.

8Hezekiah had asked Isaiah, "What will be the sign that the LORD will heal me and that I will go up to the temple of the LORD on the third day from now?"

9Isaiah answered, "This is the LORD's sign to you that the LORD will do what he has promised: Shall the shadow go forward ten steps, or shall it go back ten steps?"

20"It is a simple matter for the shadow to go forward ten steps," said Hezekiah. "Rather, have it go back ten steps."

11Then the prophet Isaiah called upon the LORD, and the LORD made the shadow go back the ten steps it had gone down on the stairway of Ahaz.

To see the sun move backward! That would be a real miracle. The almighty Creator, who put the sun, moon, and stars into the heavens, ordered the sun to stop and move back ten steps. Although many human beings do not listen to or obey the voice of their Creator, the sun obeyed its Maker.

This sundial may originally have been involved in the astrology practiced by King Ahaz, Hezekiah's father. Evidently the sundial was so constructed that the shadow of a pole fell on a series of elevated steps and was on the highest step at noon.

Our writer makes no attempt to provide a scientific explanation for what happened. Whether God caused the earth to rotate backwards or whether God caused the sun's light to be refracted is not stated. Nor does the writer intend to promote either a heliocentric or a geocentric concept of the universe. To underscore his promise to Hezekiah, God temporarily suspended the laws of nature.

The Bible mentions other times when God gave miraculous signs to demonstrate the truth of his words. Zechariah was not able to speak until John the Baptist was born (Luke 1:20). Gideon squeezed water out of the fleece, while the ground around it remained dry (Judges 6:38).

Perhaps it is significant that here God gave a sign involving the sun, that heavenly body which determines "seasons and days and years" (Genesis 1:14). In this way God is telling us, "*I* am the one who determines how long a day should be and how long a year should be. *I* am the one who determines how long your life will be. And your life, dear child, will not be a minute longer or shorter than *I* want it to be."

God's word came true. Hezekiah, who at this time was only 39 (2 Kings 18:2), lived another 15 years.

Envoys From Babylon

[12]At that time Merodach-Baladan son of Baladan king of Babylon sent Hezekiah letters and a gift, because he heard of Hezekiah's illness. [13]Hezekiah received the messengers and showed them all that was in his storehouses—the silver, the gold, the

spices and the fine oil—his armory and everything found among his treasures. There was nothing in his palace or in all his kingdom that Hezekiah did not show them. ¹⁴Then Isaiah the prophet went to King Hezekiah and asked, "What did those men say, and where did they come from?"

"From a distant land," Hezekiah replied. "They came from Babylon."

¹⁵The prophet asked, "What did they see in your palace?"

"They saw everything in my palace," Hezekiah said. "There is nothing among my treasures that I did not show them."

¹⁶Then Isaiah said to Hezekiah, "Hear the word of the LORD: ¹⁷The time will surely come when everything in your palace, and all that your fathers have stored up until this day, will be carried off to Babylon. Nothing will be left, says the LORD. ¹⁸And some of your descendants, your own flesh and blood, that will be born to you, will be taken away, and they will become eunuchs in the palace of the king of Babylon."

¹⁹"The word of the LORD you have spoken is good," Hezekiah replied. For he thought, "Will there not be peace and security in my lifetime?"

²⁰As for the other events of Hezekiah's reign, all his achievements and how he made the pool and the tunnel by which he brought water into the city, are they not written in the book of the annals of the kings of Judah? ²¹Hezekiah rested with his fathers. And Manasseh his son succeeded him as king.

It seems that Hezekiah could endure days of trouble better than days of good fortune. His heart was now filled with pride (2 Chronicles 32:25). With a boastful heart he welcomed the visitors from Babylon and showed them his power and wealth. The purpose of the visit was very likely not just to congratulate Hezekiah on his recovery from life-threatening illness. Babylon's king was interested in entering into friendly negotiations with a nation that had withstood Assyrian power, and he hoped to gain an ally in the struggle against Assyria. We can understand why he was interested in seeing Hezekiah's armory.

Isaiah issued a strong rebuke to Hezekiah and foretold how the citizens of Judah would be captured and carried into Babylon. In the book which bears his name Isaiah also foretold how God would deliver his people from their captivity and how the Messiah would finally come to deliver his people from their spiritual enemies.

Hezekiah evidently also forgot his promise to train his children in the fear of the Lord. Manasseh, who was born three years after Hezekiah was healed, grew up to be a heathen man who did not walk in the ways of his father. When Christian parents are busy seeking earthly wealth and power instead of heavenly riches, the children often do not receive the training they need.

In the summary of Hezekiah's reign special mention is made of an amazing engineering feat for which he was responsible. He constructed a tunnel 1700 feet long through solid rock to bring water from the Spring Gihon, which was outside of Jerusalem to the east, to the Pool of Siloam inside the city. This would provide the city with a good supply of water even in times of war. This tunnel was discovered about a century ago. An inscription on its wall told of its construction. (See 2 Chronicles 32:30; 2 Kings 20:20.)

By God's grace Hezekiah, like King David, repented of his sins and died as a believer in the Lord.

If we think the children of Christian parents will automatically worship the Lord, we are mistaken. Each new generation is separated from God's kingdom at birth. Each generation must learn and relearn the truths of the Scripture. Only after the new generation has learned to appreciate the grace of God will they desire to worship him.

King Manasseh had a God-fearing father. He grew up in the shadow of the temple. But despite all those advantages he did not follow the Lord. He deliberately brought back the idolatrous practices that his father had destroyed.

Wicked Reigns of Manasseh and Amon

Manasseh King of Judah 2,15·0⁷

21 Manasseh was twelve years old when he became king, and he reigned in Jerusalem fifty-five years. His mother's name was Hephzibah. ²He did evil in the eyes of the LORD, following the detestable practices of the nations the LORD had driven out before the Israelites. ³He rebuilt the high places his father Hezekiah had destroyed; he also erected altars to Baal and made an Asherah pole, as Ahab king of Israel had done. He bowed down to all the starry hosts and worshiped them. ⁴He built altars in the temple of the LORD, of which the LORD had said, "In Jerusalem I will put my Name."⁵In both courts of the temple of the LORD, he built altars to all the starry hosts. ⁶He sacrificed his own son in the fire, practiced sorcery and divination, and consulted mediums and spiritists. He did much evil in the eyes of the LORD, provoking him to anger.

⁷He took the carved Asherah pole he had made and put it in the temple, of which the LORD had said to David and to his son Solomon, "In this temple and in Jerusalem, which I have chosen out of all the tribes of Israel, I will put my Name forever. ⁸I will not again make the feet of the Israelites wander from the land I gave their forefathers, if only they will be careful to do everything I commanded them and will keep the whole Law that my servant Moses gave them." ⁹But the people did not listen. Manasseh led them astray, so that they did more evil than the nations the LORD had destroyed before the Israelites.

The high places were the old worship sites on the hilltops surrounding Jerusalem. Baal was the bloodthirsty god of the Phoenicians. Asherah was his sister-spouse. The Asherah pole was a post symbolizing the female principle in the fertility cult ritual. Understandably, her worship was associated with adultery and temple prostitution.

Persons guilty of gross idolatry are often inclined to make use of astrology and the occult. Manasseh was involved with all three.

The same three often go together today as well. The person who becomes involved in the occult, generally will not worship or continue to worship the Lord God actively. Satanism and astrology take God's place.

Even human life lost its value for Manasseh as he sacrificed his son to Molech in the Valley of Ben Hinnom.

Although God had promised earlier to declare his good and saving name at his temple in Jerusalem, now things had changed. King Manasseh had ousted the Lord from the temple. The people "would not listen." Although Manasseh was a "religious" man, God calls his actions "detestable."

Now God would act according to his wrath instead of his mercy. Because the sins of Manasseh were strikingly similar to the sins mentioned in chapter 20, God resolved to send on Judah a judgment like the one he sent against her sister kingdom of Israel.

10The Lord said through his servants the prophets: 11"Manasseh king of Judah has committed these detestable sins. He has done more evil than the Amorites who preceded him and has led Judah into sin with his idols. 12Therefore this is what the Lord, the God of Israel, says: I am going to bring such disaster on Jerusalem and Judah that the ears of everyone who hears of it will tingle. 13I will stretch out over Jerusalem the measuring line used against Samaria and the plumb line used against the house of Ahab. I will wipe out Jerusalem as one wipes a dish, wiping it and turning it upside down. 14I will forsake the remnant of my inheritance and hand them over to their enemies. They will be looted and plundered by all their foes, 15because they have done evil in my eyes and have provoked me to anger from the day their forefathers came out of Egypt until this day."

¹⁶Moreover, Manasseh also shed so much innocent blood that he filled Jerusalem from end to end—besides the sin that he had caused Judah to commit, so that they did evil in the eyes of the LORD.

¹⁷As for the other events of Manasseh's reign, and all he did, are they not written in the book of the annals of the kings of Judah? ¹⁸Manasseh rested with his fathers and was buried in his palace garden, the garden of Uzza. And Amon his son succeeded him as king.

Several factors intensified the guilt of King Manasseh:

1. The idolatrous practices listed in verses 1-9 had been specifically mentioned and forbidden in the books of Moses (Deuteronomy 18:9-11).

2. King Manasseh seduced others and persuaded them to follow his wicked example. Jesus said, "If anyone causes one of these little ones who believe in me to sin, it would be better for him to have a large millstone hung around his neck and to be drowned in the depths of the sea" (Matthew 18:6).

3. The king shed "much innocent blood." If anyone disagreed with the king or tried to correct him, that man was put to death. According to Jewish tradition the prophet Isaiah, who at this time would have been an old man, was also put to death by King Manasseh.

Therefore God would bring a shocking, almost unbelievable judgment on Jerusalem. People's ears would tingle when they heard it: God would deal with his people as he had once dealt with the people of Samaria (who had been carried away by the Assyrians) and with the house of Ahab (which had been completely destroyed). The measuring line (or level) portrays how Jerusalem and Judah would be leveled by her enemies.

In 2 Chronicles 33:11 we learn how King Manasseh was carried off to Babylon in bronze chains. When Jerusalem was finally destroyed, "the sins of Manasseh" are listed as one of the causes (2 Kings 24:3). Judah committed the same sins as Israel; she would rest under the same judgment (2 Kings 17:16-18).

2 Chronicles 33:12,13 tell us that in the last days of his life Manasseh repented. His prayer of repentance is one of the books of the Apocrypha. His repentance, however, does not mean that his life is a model for anyone. He is the only Judean king that is compared to Ahab (verse 3). His long, wicked reign of fifty-five years ranks him as perhaps the worst ruler in Jerusalem, worse even than the heathen whom the Lord drove out at the time of Joshua.

Sometimes people today say, "Pastor, do not worry about the ones who are 'sowing their wild oats.' They always come back." Sometimes, by God's grace, they do come back. Prayers of repentance, however, cannot undo a wasted life. God alone knows the harm that was caused to others by this king's bad example over the years.

Amon King of Judah

¹⁹Amon was twenty-two years old when he became king, and he reigned in Jerusalem two years. His mother's name was Meshulle-meth daughter of Haruz; she was from Jotbah. ²⁰He did evil in the eyes of the LORD, as his father Manasseh had done. ²¹He walked in all the ways of his father; he worshiped the idols his father had worshiped, and bowed down to them. ²²He forsook the LORD, the God of his fathers, and did not walk in the way of the LORD.

²³Amon's officials conspired against him and assassinated the king in his palace. ²⁴Then the people of the land killed all who had plotted against King Amon, and they made Josiah his son king in his place.

²⁵As for the other events of Amon's reign, and what he did, are they not written in the book of the annals of the kings of Judah? ²⁶He was buried in his grave in the garden of Uzza. And Josiah his son succeeded him as king.

The short reign of Amon marked a continuation of the idolatrous practices begun by his father. His assassination was a lawless act—and the villains received their just reward. But God caused even that sin to work for the good of his people. The next king, Josiah, would make the final attempts at reform before the fall of Jerusalem.

The nation of Judah was doomed to fall into the hands of Babylon, but before that would happen one king carried out a far-reaching reformation. That God-fearing king was Josiah.

Josiah's Reforms in Judah

The Book of the Law Found

22 **Josiah was eight years old when he became king, and he reigned in Jerusalem thirty-one years. His mother's name was Jedidah daughter of Adaiah; she was from Bozkath. ²He did what was right in the eyes of the LORD and walked in all the ways of his father David, not turning aside to the right or to the left.**

³In the eighteenth year of his reign, King Josiah sent the secretary, Shaphan son of Azaliah, the son of Meshullam, to the temple of the LORD. He said: ⁴"Go up to Hilkiah the high priest and have him get ready the money that has been brought into the temple of the LORD, which the doorkeepers have collected from the people. ⁵Have them entrust it to the men appointed to supervise the work on the temple. And have these men pay the workers who repair the temple of the LORD—⁶the carpenters, the builders and the masons. Also have them purchase timber and dressed stone to repair the temple. ⁷But they need not account for the money entrusted to them, because they are acting faithfully."

Josiah's father and grandfather were unbelievers. Like many fathers today, they did not carry out God's command to bring up their children in the fear of the Lord. Since idolatry was now rampant in Judah, we can assume that many other fathers were guilty of that same sin of neglect. Few spoke of God's word morning and evening as God had commanded (Deuteronomy 6:7).

The new king, however, was one of God's elect. Perhaps it was through the work of his mother Jedidah or his maternal grandfather Adaiah that Josiah learned to trust the true God and walk in the ways of King David. In this way Josiah rejected the example of his own father.

Unfortunately, in our day it is sometimes necessary for a child to make a choice between following the Lord and following his unbelieving parents. Then we need to remember the words of Jesus: "Anyone who loves his father or mother more than me is not worthy of me" (Matthew 10:37).

Josiah showed his faith by his actions. Apparently no repairs had been made in the temple since the days of King Joash two centuries earlier (2 Kings 12). Since buildings deteriorate, it was time for something to be done.

Other people shared Josiah's concerns. There was still a remnant of faithful people who brought offerings to the temple treasury, skilled laborers to do the work, and faithful overseers who would handle the money honestly.

⁸Hilkiah the high priest said to Shaphan the secretary, "I have found the Book of the Law in the temple of the LORD." He gave it to Shaphan, who read it. ⁹Then Shaphan the secretary went to the king and reported to him: "Your officials have paid out the money that was in the temple of the LORD and have entrusted it to the workers and supervisors at the temple." ¹⁰Then Shaphan the secretary informed the king, "Hilkiah the priest has given me a book." And Shaphan read from it in the presence of the king.

¹¹When the king heard the words of the Book of the Law, he tore his robes. ¹²He gave these orders to Hilkiah the priest, Ahikam son of Shaphan, Acbor son of Micaiah, Shaphan the secretary and Asaiah the king's attendant: ¹³"Go and inquire of the LORD for me and for the people and for all Judah about what is

written in this book that has been found. Great is the LORD's anger that burns against us because our fathers have not obeyed the words of this book; they have not acted in accordance with all that is written there concerning us."

Before he died, Moses instructed the Levites to place the Book of the Law next to the ark of the covenant (Deuteronomy 31:26). Although each king was to have his personal copy of the Law, the Bible had become a forgotten, unused book at Josiah's time.

The repair work in the temple, however, resulted in an unexpected discovery. Hilkiah the priest found either the original scroll written by Moses or a copy of that original in the temple.

Evidently the parts Shaphan read to the king included the detailed instructions regarding worship in the temple, regarding celebration of the Passover, and regarding destruction of the idols worshiped by the heathen. Evidently he also read parts in which God threatened to devastate the land and lead the people into captivity if they would not observe his will (Deuteronomy 29:23-28; 31:17,18).

At any rate King Josiah got the point. He realized that the idolatry of his fathers had earned God's wrath. He knew that even he personally was not giving full obedience to God's will. He expressed his profound grief and repentance by tearing his robes. Then he sent a delegation of five men to inquire from the Lord.

We meet one of these five men, Ahikam, in Jeremiah 26:24. He befriended God's prophet when the people wanted to put Jeremiah to death.

God's law continues to be a mirror to show us our thorough depravity in the sight of a holy God. The Apostle Paul wrote later that he would not have known lust, he would not have realized that God is offended by our sinful thoughts, were it not for the 9th and 10th commandments, where God says, "Do not covet" (Romans 7:7). When the Bible becomes a lost and unused book, people lose not only the sweet comfort of the gospel; they also fail to recognize the full extent of their sin and guilt.

By nature we do not like to rend our own garments in repentance. Our proud heart claims to be innocent. The world warns its own to beware of any preacher who sends you on a "guilt trip." But Josiah offers us a good example. God still wants people to come to him by rending their hearts, if not their garments (Joel 2:13). Only after people see their sin will they recognize their need for the Savior's forgiveness.

In Luther's day also the Bible had become a hidden treasure. It was a lost and unused book. But through Luther the truth was rediscovered. The Bible was put into the language of the people, and the gospel message of free salvation by faith in Christ was again proclaimed. Therefore we sing in one of our hymns,

> O God, our Lord,
> Thy holy Word
> Was long a hidden treasure
> Till to its place
> It was by grace
> Restored in fullest measure. (TLH 266:1)

14Hilkiah the priest, Ahikam, Acbor, Shaphan and Asaiah went to speak to the prophetess Huldah, who was the wife of Shallum son of Tikvah, the son of Harhas, keeper of the wardrobe. She lived in Jerusalem, in the Second District.

15She said to them, "This is what the LORD, the God of Israel, says: Tell the man who sent you to me, 16'This is what the LORD says: I am going to bring disaster on this place and its people, according to everything written in the book the king of Judah has read. 17Because they have forsaken me and burned incense to

other gods and provoked me to anger by all the idols their hands have made, my anger will burn against this place and will not be quenched.' ¹⁸Tell the king of Judah, who sent you to inquire of the LORD, 'This is what the LORD, the God of Israel, says concerning the words you heard: ¹⁹Because your heart was responsive and you humbled yourself before the LORD when you heard what I have spoken against this place and its people, that they would become accursed and laid waste, and because you tore your robes and wept in my presence, I have heard you, declares the LORD. ²⁰Therefore I will gather you to your fathers, and you will be buried in peace. Your eyes will not see all the disaster I am going to bring on this place.' "

So they took her answer back to the king.

Josiah's five trusted servants inquired of the Lord by visiting the prophetess Huldah.

Huldah had a twofold message for the king. First of all, Josiah was right. The idolatry and unfaithfulness of the people had aroused God's anger. The time would come when Jerusalem would be destroyed and the Jews would be delivered to the Babylonians.

Six hundred years later, on Palm Sunday, Jesus had a similar message for the Jews of Jerusalem. Because they had rejected the Messiah, Jerusalem would be destroyed by the Romans.

On the other hand, Huldah had a personal message of comfort and forgiveness for the king. God does not despise the humble and contrite heart (Psalm 51:17). Therefore God would postpone his judgment on Jerusalem, and Josiah would come to his grave in peace.

This does not mean that Josiah would escape all trouble. As a matter of fact, he was killed later in a battle at Megiddo (2 Kings 23:29). But Josiah would be "gathered to his fathers." Here is the only time we read this expression in 1 and

2 Kings. It means something more than the usual expression, he "slept with his fathers." Hezekiah was like faithful Abraham, who not only died but "was gathered to his people" (Genesis 25:8). He would some day eat bread in heaven with Abraham, Isaac, and Jacob. His sins were forgiven for the sake of that Savior who would be born from his family (Matthew 1:10,11).

God's apostles and prophets continue to have a message for all people. The unbelievers remain under God's judgment. For "the wrath of God is being revealed from heaven against all the godlessness and wickedness of men" (Romans 1:18). Those who repent of their sins rest under God's mercy. "If we confess our sins, he is faithful and just and will forgive us our sins and purify us from all unrighteousness" (1 John 1:9). God continues to postpone his judgment for the sake of his penitent people.

People sometimes point to Huldah in an effort to prove that the pastoral ministry should include women. The Scripture does not lead us to that conclusion. It is true that at a time when the men and the people in general had no use for God's word, the Lord did transmit messages to the people through a woman. This was not a one-time occurrence. Hagar (Genesis 16:8; 21:17,18) and the Virgin Mary (Luke 1:26-28) had the same experience, to say nothing of the daughters of Philip (Acts 21:9). In doing so, however, they did not upset the male headship principle which God ordained at the creation and which Paul explained more fully later on.

This is the only story in which Huldah is mentioned in the Bible. We have no indication that she did any pastoring or preaching in Jerusalem. Even Josiah learned the full truth of God's word through Shaphan's reading of the Bible and not through Huldah's message of forgiveness. Her work here was deliberately limited. It was intended for one man only, that is, King Josiah. Perhaps the five men in the delegation were also penitent sinners. But Huldah did not preach a word of forgiveness to them.

Today also the called ministers of God announce the forgiveness of sins only to those who declare their sincere repentance and express the desire to amend their sinful lives.

King Josiah had responded to God's word privately. As king, however, he had a bigger responsibility. He wanted all the people to hear that Book of the Covenant and wanted all of them to give an appropriate response to it.

Josiah Renews the Covenant

23 **Then the king called together all the elders of Judah and Jerusalem. ²He went up to the temple of the LORD with the men of Judah, the people of Jerusalem, the priests and the prophets—all the people from the least to the greatest. He read in their hearing all the words of the Book of the Covenant, which had been found in the temple of the LORD. ³The king stood by the pillar and renewed the covenant in the presence of the LORD—to follow the LORD and keep his commands, regulations and decrees with all his heart and all his soul, thus confirming the words of the covenant written in this book. Then all the people pledged themselves to the covenant.**

Josiah publicly announced his intention to keep the Lord's covenant and invited the people to do the same. In this way Josiah is a good example for every Christian pastor. A faithful pastor will apply God's word to his own heart and life before preaching it to the people. God's people will respond today as the people of Jerusalem responded, with repentance and faith.

The gathering in Jerusalem took place at the temple. The pillar mentioned here was evidently the place reserved for the king on solemn occasions. It is also the place where Joash stood when he was proclaimed king (2 Kings 11:14).

God's people continue to gather in their earthly temples to hear God's word. There we hear God's law, which demands perfect love and condemns us for even the smallest offense. There we hear the gospel of forgiveness. Our hearts, our feelings, are not always a reliable guide. They tell us something about our guilt, but they tell us nothing about God's forgiveness in the Savior.

Genuine repentance involves more than a change of heart. It involves actions, the kind that are described in the remainder of this chapter.

4The king ordered Hilkiah the high priest, the priests next in rank and the doorkeepers to remove from the temple of the LORD all the articles made for Baal and Asherah and all the starry hosts. He burned them outside Jerusalem in the fields of the Kidron Valley and took the ashes to Bethel. 5He did away with the pagan priests appointed by the kings of Judah to burn incense on the high places of the towns of Judah and on those around Jerusalem—those who burned incense to Baal, to the sun and moon, to the constellations and to all the starry hosts. 6He took the Asherah pole from the temple of the LORD to the Kidron Valley outside Jersualem and burned it there. He ground it to powder and scattered the dust over the graves of the common people. 7He also tore down the quarters of the male shrine prostitutes, which were in the temple of the LORD and where women did weaving for Asherah.

8Josiah brought all the priests from the towns of Judah and desecrated the high places, from Geba to Beersheba, where the priests had burned incense. He broke down the shrines at the gates—at the entrance to the Gate of Joshua, the city governor, which is on the left of the city gate. 9Although the priests of the high places did not serve at the altar of the LORD in Jerusalem, they ate unleavened bread with their fellow priests.

10He desecrated Topheth, which was in the Valley of Ben Hinnom, so no one could use it to sacrifice his son or daughter in the fire to Molech. 11He removed from the entrance to the temple

of the LORD the horses that the kings of Judah had dedicated to the sun. They were in the court near the room of an official named Nathan-Melech. Josiah then burned the chariots dedicated to the sun.

¹²He pulled down the altars the kings of Judah had erected on the roof near the upper room of Ahaz, and the altars Manasseh had built in the two courts of the temple of the LORD. He removed them from there, smashed them to pieces and threw the rubble into the Kidron Valley. ¹³The king also desecrated the high places that were east of Jersualem on the south of the Hill of Corruption—the ones Solomon king of Israel had built for Ashtoreth the vile goddess of the Sidonians, for Chemosh the vile god of Moab, and for Molech the detestable god of the people of Ammon. ¹⁴Josiah smashed the sacred stones and cut down the Asherah poles and covered the sites with human bones.

Nine hundred years earlier God had given the land of Canaan to his chosen people as their homeland. In this land the Son of God would live a perfect life as our substitute and would shed his holy, precious blood as a payment for our sins.

But God's own people had desecrated that land. When they were about to enter Canaan, God told his people to "break down their altars, smash their sacred stones, cut down their Asherah poles and burn their idols in the fire" (Deuteronomy 7:5). At first God's faithful people followed those directions. But since the days of Solomon it was the leaders of God's own people who had filled the land of Canaan with all sorts of idolatry. The Lord, speaking to Jeremiah, described it this way: "Have you seen what faithless Israel did? She went up on every high hill and under every green tree, and she was a harlot there" (Jeremiah 3:6 NASB).

Some of the idolatry went way back to the days of Solomon. The male shrine prostitutes mentioned in verse 7 were present at the time of Solomon's son, Rehoboam (1 Kings

14:24). More recent kings, notably Ahaz (2 Kings 16:15) and Manasseh (2 Kings 21:4-7) had brought idolatry into the temple itself.

The women were just as guilty as the men. Back in Exodus 35:25,26 Moses tells us how the women served God by making hangings for the tabernacle. Now the women are busy "weaving hangings (literally 'houses') for the Asherah" (verse 7 NASB). We can only guess what these little houses were used for.

The idolatrous practices had crept in gradually over the years. What one generation burned in the fire the next generation tolerated. What one generation tolerated the next generation worshiped. Slowly and quietly the people had turned their backs on the Lord.

Although our holy God had every reason to send an immediate judgment on the land and on the people, he sent one more king to conduct a real reformation. Josiah began that reformation at home, right in the temple. Vessels used in Baal worship and the wooden Asherah pole were burned, and the ashes were scattered on the graves of people who once had used them in worship (2 Chronicles 34:4). The building that housed the temple prostitutes was torn down. The pagan priests mentioned in verse 5 were "put to rest" (that is the literal translation), either by being put to death or by being retired from office.

Josiah's work with a sledge hammer continued outside Jerusalem. The pagan altars on the Judean hilltops were desecrated from Geba in extreme northern Judah to Beersheba in extreme southern Judah. Curiously, the priests who were involved in heathen worship were not allowed to sacrifice at the Lord's altar, but they were permitted to eat meals with the priests of the Lord.

The valley of Ben Hinnom, called Gehenna in the New Testament, is just south of Jerusalem. It was a deep ravine with steep, rocky walls. Some thought the entrance to that ravine looked like the entrance to hell itself. Here they had erected a monster idol called Molech. The statue was made of brass and was hollow. It had the form of a human body but the head of an ox. When a fire had been built beneath it and the statue had become red hot, little children were placed onto its outstretched arms. Even King Manasseh engaged in this barbarous practice (2 Kings 21:6).

Since the founders of Carthage were relatives of Queen Jezebel, we are not surprised to learn that the statue of Saturn among the Carthaginians was similar to the statue of Molech. Both Molech and Remphan (mentioned in Acts 7:43) represented the planet Saturn, to which the Ammonites and other neighbors of Israel offered human sacrifices.

In many cases Josiah scattered human bones on the places he desecrated. Since the Jew who touched the bones of the body of a dead man would become ceremonially unclean, no self-respecting Jew would want to go near those places again.

15Even the altar at Bethel, the high place made by Jeroboam son of Nebat, who had caused Israel to sin—even that altar and high place he demolished. He burned the high place and ground it to powder, and burned the Asherah pole also. 16Then Josiah looked around, and when he saw the tombs that were there on the hillside, he had the bones removed from them and burned on the altar to defile it, in accordance with the word of the LORD proclaimed by the man of God who foretold these things.

17The king asked, "What is that tombstone I see?"

The men of the city said, "It marks the tomb of the man of God who came from Judah and pronounced against the altar of Bethel the very things you have done to it."

18"Leave it alone," he said. "Don't let anyone disturb his bones." So they spared his bones and those of the prophet who had come from Samaria.

¹⁹Just as he had done at Bethel, Josiah removed and defiled all the shrines at the high places that the kings of Israel had built in the towns of Samaria that had provoked the LORD to anger. ²⁰Josiah slaughtered all the priests of those high places on the altars and burned human bones on them. Then he went back to Jerusalem.

Josiah's reformation even went beyond the borders of Judah to what had been the Kingdom of Israel. Bethel was one of the two cities where Jeroboam, the first king of Israel, had set up calf shrines.

Three hundred years earlier a man of God from Judah had spoken against that altar, saying, "A son named Josiah will be born to the house of David. On you he will sacrifice the priests of the high places who now make offerings here, and human bones will be burned on you" (1 Kings 13:2). Now, our inspired writer reminds us, that prophecy was fulfilled.

John the Baptist would have been pleased with Josiah's actions. John also urged the people to repent of their sins and to show their repentance by their works. God's people today can also find things in their lives that should be removed, a few things in their homes that should be burned to powder. We welcome our Savior into our hearts and homes by recognizing our need for his forgiveness and by casting away all that displeases him.

²¹The king gave this order to all the people: "Celebrate the Passover to the LORD your God, as it is written in this Book of the Covenant." ²²Not since the days of the judges who led Israel, nor throughout the days of the kings of Israel and the kings of Judah, had any such Passover been observed. ²³But in the eighteenth year of King Josiah, this Passover was celebrated to the LORD in Jerusalem.

²⁴Furthermore, Josiah got rid of the mediums and spiritists, the household gods, the idols and all the other detestable things seen

in Judah and Jerusalem. This he did to fulfill the requirements of the law written in the book that Hilkiah the priest had discovered in the temple of the LORD. ²⁵Neither before nor after Josiah was there a king like him who turned to the LORD as he did—with all his heart and with all his soul and with all his strength, in accordance with all the Law of Moses.

²⁶Nevertheless, the LORD did not turn away from the heat of his fierce anger, which burned against Judah because of all that Manasseh had done to provoke him to anger. ²⁷So the LORD said, "I will remove Judah also from my presence as I removed Israel, and I will reject Jerusalem, the city I chose, and this temple, about which I said, 'There shall my Name be.' "

²⁸As for the other events of Josiah's reign, and all he did, are they not written in the book of the annals of the kings of Judah?

²⁹While Josiah was king, Pharaoh Neco king of Egypt went up to the Euphrates River to help the king of Assyria. King Josiah marched out to meet him in battle, but Neco faced him and killed him at Megiddo. ³⁰Josiah's servants brought his body in a chariot from Megiddo to Jerusalem and buried him in his own tomb. And the people of the land took Jehoahaz son of Josiah and anointed him and made him king in place of his father.

Josiah's reformation consisted of more than just destroying the paraphernalia of false worship. It also had a positive side. Apparently the Passover had been virtually ignored for many years. That was unfortunate for two reasons. First of all, ignoring the festival God had commanded was a sin against God. Secondly, ignoring the Passover festival robbed the people of the gospel message, for the Passover lamb was a shadow reminding the people of *the* Lamb of God who would offer his blood on the altar of the cross as payment for all sin.

In the eighteenth year of his reign, the same year he rediscovered the Book of the Law in the temple, King Josiah encouraged the people to celebrate the Passover according to God's instructions. 2 Chronicles 35:7 tells us that Josiah personally donated thousands of sacrificial animals so that all of the people could join in the celebration. It was a Passover the likes of which had not been seen since the days of the prophet Samuel (2 Chronicles 35:18).

Since the Lamb of God is not willing to share our hearts with anyone or anything, Josiah removed five more things from Jerusalem and Judah. "Mediums" were women like the witch at Endor who attempted to foretell the future by contacting the spirits of the dead. "Spiritists" were men who engaged in the same activity. Many of the people thought that the "household gods" (teraphim) could also be helpful in determining the future. Even Rachel, the wife of Jacob, thought so highly of the teraphim that she stole them from her father when Jacob moved back to Canaan. The "idols" were literally logs or blocks of wood. The Hebrew word, interestingly enough, also means "dung pellets." The final word, "detestable things," sums up God's attitude toward the idolatry and witchcraft carried on in ancient Jerusalem.

In the last years of her existence Judah had no other king like King Josiah. His guide was not his own heart or the current whims of the people but the Law of Moses. His worship was sincere. His works of service were examples for others.

But even the zeal and dedication of Josiah could not undo the sins of his grandfather, King Manasseh. As we read the Book of Jeremiah, the prophet who began his work five years before the rediscovery of the Book of the Law (compare Jeremiah 25:3 and 2 Kings 22:3), it is clear that the reforms of Josiah did not have a real or permanent effect on the hearts of the people. Even though God had chosen to establish his name in Jerusalem, even though God met here with his people and here accepted the sacrifices of his people, the city of Jerusalem and the temple would be destroyed just as God had declared earlier.

The prophet Zephaniah also lived and wrote during the reign of King Josiah. Now would be a good time to read his short book in your Bible. He wrote repeatedly about "the day of the Lord," a day when, according to God's own words, "I will stretch out my hand against Judah and against all who live in Jerusalem" (Zephaniah 1:4).

Twenty years after the death of Josiah, Babylonian soldiers destroyed both the temple and the city.

Martin Luther, like King Josiah, also rediscovered the Bible. Josiah's reformation reminds us of the one carried on by Luther. Just as King Josiah's piety could not pay for the sins of his grandfather, so the works of Martin Luther could not satisfy the holiness of God. In one of his hymns Paul Speratus, a friend of Luther, wrote,

> It was a false, misleading dream,
> That God his Law had given
> That sinners could themselves redeem
> And by their works gain heaven. (TLH 377:3)

People today need to learn and relearn that same lesson.

Just as King Josiah rejected all that is false, so Martin Luther condemned all that is false. He rejected indulgences because the Bible says forgiveness of sins is available only as a free gift. He rejected the church's teaching about purgatory because the Bible says believers in Christ enter immediately into heaven. Today many are afraid to reject what is false. Some, unfortunately, do not know the difference between truth and error. Others are silent because they do not want to lose anyone's friendship. They do not realize that keeping silent could lose a friend for eternity.

King Josiah wanted the people to celebrate the Passover. Martin Luther wanted to hold *the* Passover Lamb, Jesus Christ, before the eyes of the people. He wanted even children to learn that Jesus "has redeemed me, a lost and condemned creature, purchased and won me from all sins, from death and from the power of the devil, not with gold or silver, but with his holy, precious blood and with his innocent suffering and death."

Today a gracious God has chosen to record his saving name at our churches. If God's people, however, no longer care to listen to his word or to worship him according to his name, then God may withdraw his blessing. History teaches us that no nation can count on having God's word as a permanent possession.

King Josiah's life ended tragically on the battlefield. When Pharaoh Neco (whom we know from secular history as the mighty Rameses II) went from Egypt to help the Assyrians against the rising power of Babylon, King Josiah stood in his way. Although Pharaoh Neco had no quarrel with Josiah at this time, their armies met at Megiddo. There Josiah was slain at the foot of Mount Carmel in the plain of Jezreel. (See the map on page 176.)

We read the name Megiddo again in Revelation 16:16. Armageddon (that is, "the hill of Megiddo") is the symbolic name of the place where the almighty God will win a final victory over all the kings of the earth who have opposed him.

Jehoahaz King of Judah

³¹Jehoahaz was twenty-three years old when he became king, and he reigned in Jerusalem three months. His mother's name was Hamutal daughter of Jeremiah; she was from Libnah. ³²He did evil in the eyes of the LORD, just as his fathers had done. ³³Pharaoh Neco put him in chains at Riblah in the land of Hamath so that he might not reign in Jerusalem, and he imposed on Judah a levy of a hundred talents of silver and a talent of gold. ³⁴Pharaoh Neco made Eliakim son of Josiah king in place of his father Josiah and changed Eliakim's name to Jehoiakim. But he took Jehoahaz and carried him off to Egypt, and there he died. ³⁵Je-

hoiakim paid Pharaoh Neco the silver and gold he demanded. In order to do so, he taxed the land and exacted the silver and gold from the people of the land according to their assessments.

Children do not always walk in the footsteps of God-fearing parents. The sons of Samuel were not worthy to succeed their father. David's son Absalom was a rebel. The sons of King Josiah possessed neither the faith nor the zeal of their pious father.

In tracing the history of Judah's last kings, the inspired account now begins to sound like a broken record. Jehoahaz "did evil in the eyes of the LORD, just as his fathers had done"(verse 33). Jehoiakim, another son of Josiah, "did evil in the eyes of the LORD, just as his fathers had done" (verse 37). Jehoiachin, a grandson of Josiah, "did evil in the eyes of the LORD, just as Jehoiakim had done" (2 Kings 24:9). The last king of Judah was Zedekiah, another son of good King Josiah. He also "did evil in the sight of the LORD, just as Jehoiakim had done" (2 Kings 24:19).

We see a similar pattern in families, nations, and churches today. Very seldom do things gradually get better from one generation to the next. They usually get progressively worse. Occasionally a gifted leader, an elect man of God, carries out drastic reforms to bring people back to God. Otherwise the corrupt human heart falls from one sin to the other. The Bible description of regression directly contradicts evolution's theory of progression. Therefore faithful pastors must continually call God's people to repentance.

Nine hundred years earlier God had told the Israelites through Moses that, if the people forsake him, then he would deliver them to their enemies (Deuteronomy 28:15-68). Now God's threat was about to be fulfilled. During the final days of the Old Testament the Kingdom of Judah would become a political football, subservient to its enemies.

After killing Josiah at Megiddo, Pharaoh Neco went up north to the Euphrates River to help the Assyrians fight against the Babylonians.

By changing Eliakim's name to Jehoiakim the Egyptian king showed that Jehoiakim was only a puppet ruler.

The period of Jehoiakim's reign saw an important shift in world power. Four years after Josiah's death at Megiddo Pharaoh Neco was involved in battle with the Babylonian army up north at the Euphrates River. Neco and the Assyrians were soundly defeated at the Battle of Carchemish in 605 B.C. A young Babylonian prince named Nebuchadnezzar, the man destined to become the next king, led the Babylonians to victory. For the next ninety years Israel's history would be intertwined with that of Babylon, now the dominant power in the ancient Near East.

Judah Falls to Babylon

Jehoiakim King of Judah

36Jehoiakim was twenty-five years old when he became king, and he reigned in Jerusalem eleven years. His mother's name was Zebidah daughter of Pedaiah; she was from Rumah. 37And he did evil in the eyes of the LORD, just as his fathers had done.

24 During Jehoiakim's reign, Nebuchadnezzar king of Babylon invaded the land, and Jehoiakim became his vassal for three years. But then he changed his mind and rebelled against Nebuchadnezzar. 2The LORD sent Babylonian, Aramean, Moabite and Ammonite raiders against him. He sent them to destroy Judah, in accordance with the word of the LORD proclaimed by his servants the prophets. 3Surely these things happened to Judah according to the LORD's command, in order to remove them from his presence because of the sins of Manasseh and all he had done, 4including the shedding of innocent blood. For he had filled Jerusalem with innocent blood, and the LORD was not willing to forgive.

⁵As for the other events of Jehoiakim's reign, and all he did, are they not written in the book of the annals of the kings of Judah? ⁶Jehoiakim rested with his fathers. And Jehoiachin his son succeeded him as king.

⁷The king of Egypt did not march out from his own country again, because the king of Babylon had taken all his territory, from the Wadi of Egypt to the Euphrates River.

After his victory at Carchemish Nebuchadnezzar marched south into the areas that had been controlled by Egypt. He also came to Jerusalem. King Jehoiakim wisely declined to fight against the Babylonians. It was at this time that Nebuchadnezzar took some young men from leading Jewish families as captives back to Babylon. These young men, including Daniel, Shadrach, Meshach, and Abednego, would be trained for service in the Babylonian government. Their story is related in the Book of Daniel.

Three years later Jehoiakim rebelled against the Babylonians. He was quickly defeated and was taken in chains to Babylon, together with items from the temple (2 Chronicles 36:5-8). Later he was permitted to return to Jerusalem.

God's people were powerless against their enemies.God himself was sending heathen nations to scourge his unfaithful people.

It is worth noting that the sins practiced in the last days of Jerusalem are common also now in the last days of the world. The "sins of Manasseh," according to 2 Kings 21:4-7, included Baal worship, witchcraft, and spiritism, sins which often provide the theme for today's movies and music. The shedding of innocent blood also continues today in America's abortion mills. When those who claim to be God's people will not respond to God's word but choose to live in impenitence, then God's judgment is near. "If the salt loses its saltiness, how can it be made salty again? It is no longer good for anything, except to be thrown out and trampled by men" (Matthew 5:13).

Some of the people of Judah still hoped to receive help from Egypt, their neighbor to the south. But that was not to be. Secular records tell us that in 588 B.C. Pharaoh Neco signed a peace treaty with Nebuchadnezzar. According to its terms Neco conceded all of Palestine, including Jerusalem, to Nebuchadnezzar. In return Nebuchadnezzar agreed to leave Egypt alone.

Neco had taxed the people of Judah but was powerless to help them against the Babylonians. When God's people trust in worldly powers to keep them safe, they will finally be disappointed.

Jehoiachin King of Judah

⁸Jehoiachin was eighteen years old when he became king, and he reigned in Jerusalem three months. His mother's name was Nehushta daughter of Elnathan; she was from Jerusalem. ⁹He did evil in the eyes of the LORD, just as his father had done.

¹⁰At that time the officers of Nebuchadnezzar king of Babylon advanced on Jerusalem and laid siege to it, ¹¹and Nebuchadnezzar himself came up to the city while his officers were besieging it. ¹²Jehoiachin king of Judah, his mother, his attendants, his nobles and his officials all surrendered to him.

In the eighth year of the reign of the king of Babylon, he took Jehoiachin prisoner. ¹³As the LORD had declared, Nebuchadnezzar removed all the treasures from the temple of the LORD and from the royal palace, and took away all the gold articles that Solomon king of Israel had made for the temple of the LORD. ¹⁴He carried into exile all Jerusalem: all the officers and fighting men, and all the craftsmen and artisans—a total of ten thousand. Only the poorest people of the land were left.

¹⁵Nebuchadnezzar took Jehoiachin captive to Babylon. He also took from Jerusalem to Babylon the king's mother, his wives, his officials and the leading men of the land. ¹⁶The king of

Babylon also deported to Babylon the entire force of seven thousand fighting men, strong and fit for war, and a thousand craftsmen and artisans. [17]He made Mattaniah, Jehoiachin's uncle, king in his place and changed his name to Zedekiah.

Jehoiachin, like his father Jehoiakim, was powerless against mighty Babylon. He had been on the throne for only three months when Nebuchadnezzar came to Jerusalem again and besieged the city. Jehoiachin wisely surrendered without a fight just as his father had done eight years earlier in 605 B.C.

This time Nebuchadnezzar carried off to Babylon Jehoiachin and his wives, the soldiers and craftsmen, and the vessels from the temple. We will read about those sacred vessels again in Daniel 5 when, sixty years later, Belshazzar and his guests used them as their drinking cups the night Babylon was conquered by the Medes and Persians. Since her best warriors and craftsmen had been carried away, it would now be difficult for Judah to wage war or even to make weapons for war.

Nebuchadnezzar also had the power to place the next man on the throne of Judah. His choice was Mattaniah, another son of Josiah, the full brother of Jehoahaz. Nebuchadnezzar changed his name to Zedekiah. When Zedekiah became king, he swore an oath in God's name to be loyal to Nebuchadnezzar (2 Chronicles 36:13).

Zedekiah King of Judah

[18]**Zedekiah was twenty-one years old when he became king, and he reigned in Jerusalem eleven years. His mother's name was Hamutal daughter of Jeremiah; she was from Libnah. [19]He did evil in the eyes of the LORD, just as Jehoiakim had done. [20]It was because of the LORD's anger that all this happened to Jerusalem and Judah, and in the end he thrust them from his presence.**

God's final judgment on Judah and Jerusalem would come during the reign of Zedekiah. This man "did not humble himself before Jeremiah the prophet, who spoke the word of the LORD" (2 Chronicles 36:12). Therefore God in his anger would "thrust them from his presence."

The Jeremiah mentioned in verse 18 is not Jeremiah the prophet.

Through Ezekiel God announced, "*I* will spread *my* net for him [Zedekiah], and he will be caught in *my* snare. *I* will bring him to Babylon and execute judgment upon him there because he was unfaithful to *me*" (Ezekiel 17:20). Judah and her king Zedekiah would fall to the Babylonians because God himself now willed it.

The Fall of Jerusalem

Now Zedekiah rebelled against the king of Babylon.

25 **So in the ninth year of Zedekiah's reign, on the tenth day of the tenth month, Nebuchadnezzar king of Babylon marched against Jerusalem with his whole army. He encamped outside the city and built siege works all around it. ²The city was kept under siege until the eleventh year of King Zedekiah. ³By the ninth day of the ⌊fourth⌋ month the famine in the city had become so severe that there was no food for the people to eat. ⁴Then the city wall was broken through, and the whole army fled at night through the gate between the two walls near the king's garden, though the Babylonians were surrounding the city. They fled toward the Arabah, ⁵but the Babylonian army pursued the king and overtook him in the plains of Jericho. All his soldiers were separated from him and scattered, ⁶and he was captured. He was taken to the king of Babylon at Riblah, where sentence was pronounced on him. ⁷They killed the sons of Zedekiah before his eyes. Then they put out his eyes, bound him with bronze shackles and took him to Babylon.**

 Humanly speaking, Zedekiah's reign as Nebuchadnezzar's puppet could have continued indefinitely. But he foolishly rebelled against Babylon.

Zedekiah Taken Captive to Babylon (2 Kings 25:7)

When the city of Jerusalem had been under siege for a year and a half, the people ran short of food and there was a great famine. Some even practiced cannibalism (Lamentations 4:10).

When King Zedekiah realized that the Babylonians would be victorious (as Jeremiah had foretold), and when he realized that many of his own people had already defected to the Babylonians, he decided to run for his life. He left Jerusalem at night, sneaked through the enemy lines and headed for the Jordan River, perhaps twenty-five miles away, hoping to cross over into Moab. But he did not escape. Babylonians soldiers overtook him on the plains of Jericho and brought him to Nebuchadnezzar at Riblah, some 200 miles to the north, where Nebuchadnezzar apparently had established his headquarters. Riblah is one of the cities God had mentioned as being at the northernmost boundary of the promised land (see Numbers 34:10,11). There Nebuchadnezzar spoke a horrible sentence of judgment on the disloyal king. The last thing Zedekiah was permitted to see was his sons being put to death, and then he was blinded.

8On the seventh day of the fifth month, in the nineteenth year of Nebuchadnezzar king of Babylon, Nebuzaradan commander of the imperial guard, an official of the king of Babylon, came to Jerusalem. 9He set fire to the temple of the LORD, the royal palace and all the houses of Jerusalem. Every important building he burned down. 10The whole Babylonian army, under the commander of the imperial guard, broke down the walls around Jerusalem. 11Nebuzaradan the commander of the guard carried into exile the people who remained in the city, along with the rest of the populace and those who had gone over to the king of Babylon. 12But the commander left behind some of the poorest people of the land to work the vineyards and fields.

Nebuchadnezzar permitted his generals to finish the job at Jerusalem. The fateful year was 586 B.C., an anchor date in Old Testament history. Under the direction of Nebuzaradan, captain of the guard, the temple, whose upper portions had been made of wood, was burned. The king's house and the other large, beautiful houses in Jerusalem suffered a similar fate.

Many of the people thought it could never happen. They viewed the temple in a superstitious way and thought God would never permit it or the city of Jerusalem to be destroyed by an enemy. When Jeremiah warned them, they answered by saying, "This is the temple of the LORD, the temple of the LORD, the temple of the LORD!" (Jeremiah 7:4). Since God's people had rejected their Lord, God now removed the temple, the visible symbol of his presence, from them.

Now the rest of the population was deported to Babylon as exiles. Only some of the poorest people were left behind to tend the fields and the vineyards lest the land revert to its wild state.

But God had not forgotten his promises about a Savior. Seventy years later when the Jews returned from their captivity, the city of Jerusalem and the temple were rebuilt. This was just as God promised. Although the new temple was not as beautiful as Solomon's, the city of Jesus' time was once again an impressive sight. In Matthew 24, however, Jesus announced that, after his saving work was completed, Jerusalem and the temple again would be destroyed. This time the Roman armies would not leave one stone on another. That destruction is a shadow of the end of the world, a reminder that the Savior will return for judgment and will destroy the world by fire on the last day.

¹³The Babylonians broke up the bronze pillars, the movable stands and the bronze Sea that were at the temple of the LORD and

they carried the bronze to Babylon. [14]They also took away the pots, shovels, wick trimmers, dishes and all the bronze articles used in the temple service. [15]The commander of the imperial guard took away the censers and sprinkling bowls—all that were made of pure gold or silver.

[16]The bronze from the two pillars, the Sea and the movable stands, which Solomon had made for the temple of the LORD, was more than could be weighed. [17]Each pillar was twenty-seven feet high. The bronze capital on top of one pillar was four and a half feet high and was decorated with a network and pomegranates of bronze all around. The other pillar, with its network, was similar.

[18]The commander of the guard took as prisoners Seraiah the chief priest, Zephaniah the priest next in rank and the three doorkeepers. [19]Of those still in the city, he took the officer in charge of the fighting men and five royal advisers. He also took the secretary who was chief officer in charge of conscripting the people of the land and sixty of his men who were found in the city. [20]Nebuzaradan the commander took them all and brought them to the king of Babylon at Riblah. [21]There at Riblah, in the land of Hamath, the king had them executed.

So Judah went into captivity, away from her land.

The Books of Kings have been called "the story of Solomon's temple." In the beginning of 1 Kings we read how that beautiful, expensive temple was put together and how God's glory filled that magnificent building. At the end of 2 Kings we are told how the building was destroyed, how the utensils were broken and carried away in pieces. The Books of Kings are the shameful history of man's unfaithfulness to a gracious God and of how God finally sends a judgment on people who have despised his blessings.

Let no one be fooled. If God's people today do not worship God in true repentance, then the blessings we enjoy will be taken away.

To complete the calamity, several dozen Judean leaders who were still in the city were murdered by Nebuchadnezzar, who was still camped at Riblah.

And so the seventy years of captivity in the land of Babylon began.

22Nebuchadnezzar king of Babylon appointed Gedaliah son of Ahikam, the son of Shaphan, to be over the people he had left behind in Judah. 23When all the army officers and their men heard that the king of Babylon had appointed Gedaliah as governnor, they came to Gedaliah at Mizpah—Ishmael son of Nethaniah, Johanan son of Kareah, Seraiah son of Tanhumeth the Netophathite, Jaazaniah the son of the Maacathite, and their men. 24Gedaliah took an oath to reassure them and their men. "Do not be afraid of the Babylonian officials," he said. "Settle down in the land and serve the king of Babylon, and it will go well with you."

25In the seventh month, however, Ishmael son of Nethaniah, the son of Elishama, who was of royal blood, came with ten men and assassinated Gedaliah and also the men of Judah and the Babylonians who were with him at Mizpah. 26At this, all the people from the least to the greatest, together with the army officers, fled to Egypt for fear of the Babylonians.

The prophet Jeremiah relates these events in greater detail in chapters 40-44 of his book. The similarity between the last section of 2 Kings and the last sections of Jeremiah leads us to suggest that Jeremiah also wrote 1 and 2 Kings.

Gedaliah's father, Ahikam, had befriended Jeremiah on a previous occasion (Jeremiah 26:24). The governor's advice to the remnant in Judah to make the best of a bad situation and Jeremiah's advice to the captives in Babylon to "seek the peace and prosperity of the city" (Jeremiah 29:7) breathe the same practical intent.

Unfortunately the men who were with Gedaliah refused to listen to his practical wisdom. They killed the new governor and, contrary to the advice of Jeremiah, fled to Egypt taking Jeremiah with them. In this small way the final curse announced by Moses in Deuteronomy 28:68 was fulfilled. A small group of unfaithful Israelites returned to the land of bondage which they had left 900 years earlier.

Jehoiachin Released

27In the thirty-seventh year of the exile of Jehoiachin king of Judah, in the year Evil-Merodach became king of Babylon, he released Jehoiachin from prison on the twenty-seventh day of the twelfth month. 28He spoke kindly to him and gave him a seat of honor higher than those of the other kings who were with him in Babylon. 29So Jehoiachin put aside his prison clothes and for the rest of his life ate regularly at the king's table. 30Day by day the king gave Jehoiachin a regular allowance as long as he lived.

1 and 2 Kings are the story of THE King (God) and the kings. Although the kings and the people of Israel and Judah rejected God, THE King did not totally reject his people or forget his promises. There is a glimmer of hope in the final paragraph of our book.

Although Zedekiah's sons and many of the other princes of Judah had been put to death, God would not permit his promise of a Savior to go unfulfilled. The line of descent which other inspired writers had traced from Adam through Noah, Shem, Abraham, Judah, and David would not be entirely cut off. God brought it about that Jehoiachin, the second last king of Judah, was released from prison in Babylon.

Jehoiachin is called Jeconiah in Matthew 1:11. Through that man the KING OF KINGS would finally be born into the world. That King would establish a heavenly kingdom by suffering and dying on a cross. That King invites all people to enter his kingdom now by repenting of their sins and putting their trust in him. On the final judgment day that King will say to his people, "Come, you who are blessed by my Father; take your inheritance, the kingdom prepared for you since the creation of the world" (Matthew 25:34).

May we also be counted among the faithful subjects of that King!

APPENDIX

THE KINGS OF JUDAH AND ISRAEL

JUDAH (South)

REHOBOAM, son of Solomon and Naamah, age 41, reigned 17 years (1 Kings 14:21)

ABIJAH, son of Rehoboam and Maacah, year 18 of Jeroboam, reigned 3 years (1 Kings 15:1,2)

ASA, son of Abijah, year 20 of Jeroboam, reigned 41 years (1 Kings 15:9,10)

ISRAEL (North)

JEROBOAM, son of Nebat reigned 22 years (1 Kings 14:20)

NADAB, son of Jeroboam, year 2 of Asa, reigned 2 years (1 Kings 15:25)

BAASHA*, son of Ahijah, age 24, year 3 of Asa, reigned 24 years (1 Kings 15:33)

ELAH, son of Baasha, year 26 of Asa, reigned 2 years (1 Kings 16:8)

ZIMRI*, year 27 of Asa, reigned 7 days (1 Kings 16:10,15)

OMRI*, year 31 of Asa, reigned 12 years (1 Kings 16:16,23)

AHAB, son of Omri, year 38 of Asa, reigned 22 years (1 Kings 16:29)

JEHOSHAPHAT, son of Asa and Azubah, age 35, year 4 of Ahab, reigned 25 years (1 Kings 22:41,42)

AHAZIAH, son of Ahab, year 17 of Jehoshaphat, reigned 2 years (1 Kings 22:51)

JORAM, son of Ahab, year 18 of Jehoshaphat and year 2 of Jehoram, reigned 12 years (2 Kings 3:1; 1:17)

JEHORAM, son of Jehoshaphat, age 32, year 5 of Joram, reigned 8 years (1 Kings 22:50; 2 Kings 8:16,17)

AHAZIAH, son of Jehoram and Athaliah, age 22, year 12 of Joram, reigned 1 year (2 Kings 8:25,26)

(ATHALIAH), reigned 6 years (2 Kings 11:3)

JOASH, son of Ahaziah and Zibiah, age 7, year 7 of Jehu, reigned 40 years (2 Kings 11:21; 12:1)

AMAZIAH, son of Joash and Jehoaddin, age 25, year 2 of Jehoash, reigned 29 years (lived 15 years after death of Jehoash) (2 Kings 14:1,17)

AZARIAH (UZZIAH), son of Amaziah and Jecoliah, age 16, year 27 of Jeroboam II, reigned 52 years (2 Kings 15:1)

JEHU*, son of Jehoshaphat, reigned 28 years (2 Kings 9:14; 10:36)

JEHOAHAZ, son of Jehu, year 23 of Joash, reigned 17 years (2 Kings 13:1)

JEHOASH, son of Jehoahaz, age 16, year 37 of Joash, reigned 16 years (2 Kings 13:10)

JEROBOAM II, son of Jehoash, year 15 of Amaziah, reigned 41 years (2 Kings 14:23)

ZECHARIAH, son of Jeroboam II, year 38 of Azariah, reigned 6 months (2 Kings 15:8)

SHALLUM*, son of Jabesh, year 39 of Uzziah, reigned 1 month (2 Kings 15:13)

MENAHEM*, son of Gadi, year 39 of Uzziah, reigned 10 years (2 Kings 15:17)

PEKAHIAH, son of Menahem, year 50 of Uzziah, reigned 2 years (2 Kings 15:23)

JOTHAM, son of Uzziah and Jerusha, age 25, year 2 of Pekah, reigned 16 years (2 Kings 15:32)

AHAZ, son of Jotham, age 20, year 17 of Pekah, reigned 16 years (2 Kings 16:1)

HEZEKIAH, son of Ahaz and Abijah, age 25, year 3 of Hoshea, reigned 29 years (2 Kings 18:1)

MANASSEH, son of Hezekiah and Hephzibah, age 12, reigned 55 years (2 Kings 21:1)

AMON, son of Manasseh and Meshullemeth, age 22, reigned 2 years (2 Kings 21:19)

JOSIAH, son of Amon and Jedidah, age 8, reigned 31 years (2 Kings 22:1)

JEHOAHAZ, son of Josiah and Hamutal, age 23, reigned 3 months (2 Kings 23:31)

ELIAKIM (JEHOIAKIM), son of Josiah and Zebidah, age 25, reigned 11 years (2 Kings 23:34,36)

JEHOIACHIN, son of Jehoiakim and Nehushta, age 18, reigned 3 months and 10 days (2 Kings 24:8; 2 Chronicles 36:9)

MATTANIAH (ZEDEKIAH), son of Josiah and Hamutal, age 21, reigned 11 years (2 Kings 24:18)

PEKAH*, son of Remaliah, year 52 of Uzziah, reigned 20 years (2 Kings 15:27)

HOSHEA*, son of Elah, year 20 of Jotham, year 12 of Ahaz, reigned 9 years (2 Kings 15:30; 17:1)

NOTE: An asterisk (*) indicates a new dynasty. Apparent inconsistencies in dates are due to coregencies and other irregularities.